## Praise for *Riding More w*

"What other maintenance manual observes, 'The biggest barriers to riding bikes are capitalism, classism, sexism, and racism'? If your bicycle lies somewhere between the Tour de France and the local landfill, this book is for you. Seasoned wrench and rider Sam Tracy combines decades of personal experience with input from dedicated community bike shops thriving on low-cost or no-cost repairs. Even as bicycle transportation remains undervalued, cycling generates a sense of freedom that is hard to replicate yet begs to be shared. Some maintenance required."
—Craig O'Hara, Bike Den, State College, Pennsylvania

## For *Bicycle! A Repair & Maintenance Manifesto* (PM Press, 2013)

"Tracy's second edition boasts five years' worth of additional hands-on experience since his first, gained during his bicycling pursuits around the globe. He writes in a humorous, unintimidating tone, e.g., saying of bike frame creaks, 'They exist to mock us.' Maintenance, repair, and selecting the right type of bike are all covered, and, from headsets to wheels and brakes to drive trains, the mechanics are discussed. Additional helpful chapters include 'Winter Riding,' 'Boxing Bikes,' and 'Scavenging, Rust, and Security.' From seasoned bike builders to novice bike riders, everyone will find something of value in this manifesto. VERDICT: A smart buy for any library serving a bike culture."
—*Library Journal*

"Keeping a bike running can be done with anyone with a little ambition and know-how. *Bicycle! A Repair & Maintenance Manifesto* is an educational manual from Sam Tracy, who advises readers on how to keep their bikes rolling for years to come, even when improvising on the go. With additional thoughts on those who want to build their own bikes, fighting rust, safety and security, and much more, *Bicycle!* is a fine addition to any collection focusing on practical bicycling wisdom."
—*Midwest Book Review*

"Sam isn't scared to tell you to use a hammer and duct tape when called for—this isn't the manual for those with plastic bikes and torque wrenches, this is more geared toward keeping your bike working in the real world, sometimes with scavenged parts, sometimes by forcing the issue to keep the wheels rolling. This book is more about low-cost and no-cost repairs than upgrades and weighing your bike. Make no mistake, Sam is an accomplished mechanic and his tech advice is spot on. An ideal book for novice mechanics put off by the tech jargon of other tech manuals, experienced wrenches will also find solid advice from his experience working in bicycle co-ops and in the less-than-ideal conditions of Mauritania."
—*Urban Velo*

"Sam Tracy, a bike mechanic and former bike messenger, also wrote *Roadside Bicycle Repair: A Pocket Manifesto* and *How to Rock and Roll: A City Rider's Repair Manual*. This third book in Tracy's bike-care trilogy has been updated to include low-cost and no-cost solutions he learned during his Peace Corps stint in Mauritania. It's geared toward people who are seriously into their bikes. Owning it is like having a bike mechanic to chat with while you undertake repairs yourself."
—*Carbusters*

"Lots of examples from the less sophisticated end of the spectrum of machines.... Equally, Sam's at home with lightweight carbon and has plenty to say about that."
—*Seven Day Cyclist*

# RIDING MORE WITH LESS
## A FUTURE FOR BIKE REPAIR

**Sam Tracy**

**PM**

*Riding More with Less: A Future for Bike Repair*
© 2024 Sam Tracy
This edition © 2024 PM Press

All rights reserved. No part of this book may be transmitted by any means without permission in writing from the publisher.

ISBN: 979-888-744-022-4 (paperback)
ISBN: 979-888-744-027-9 (ebook)
Library of Congress Control Number: 2023936671

Cover by John Yates / www.stealworks.com
Interior design by briandesign

10 9 8 7 6 5 4 3 2 1

PM Press
PO Box 23912
Oakland, CA 94623
www.pmpress.org

Printed in the USA.

*For Atticus, his cousins, and all their friends*

# CONTENTS

|  | Introduction | ix |
|---|---|---|
| I | Tools | 1 |
| II | Frames | 9 |
| III | Headsets | 17 |
| IV | Stems | 27 |
| V | Handlebars | 33 |
| VI | Wheels | 40 |
| VII | Tires and Inner Tubes | 54 |
| VIII | Hubs | 61 |
| IX | Saddles and Seatposts | 78 |
| X | Control Cables | 84 |
| XI | Brakes | 101 |
| XII | Drivetrains | 135 |
| XIII | Rust | 231 |
| XIV | A Future for Bike Repair | 241 |
|  | Acknowledgments | 231 |
|  | Image Credits | 250 |
|  | Index of Subjects | 251 |
|  | Index of Names | 255 |
|  | About the Author | 256 |

# INTRODUCTION

When your bicycle needs repair, it may be simplest to visit your friendly local bike shop for their service and expertise. They probably deserve our support—precious few strike it rich fixing bikes, and our business helps ensure their continuing presence—but there might be other options as well. Given the time and inclination, odds are good that you can learn to fix it yourself.

This book explores resourceful approaches to bike repair. As we'll see, just *how* things are made becomes a major factor here. Among the better-quality goods sold at our independent bike shops, the fetishization of "intellectual property" can sometimes present complications—while such an emphasis may have helped some small-scale inventors and creators along the way, the enduring effect on the actual practice of fixing bikes has been the construction of arbitrary barriers, each walling off contrived fiefdoms. Beyond various expedient formatting standards, our major bicycle and component manufacturers literally design some of their products *not* to work together. (The industry's endemic product recall patterns suggest the "innovation" fig leaf typically proffered as justification here merits greater scrutiny.)

At the opposite end of the spectrum, the budget bikes sold in big-box stores share far more in common with each other, but only in the negative sense: their sneeringly misanthropic "manufacturers" represent the worst possible failures in motivation and imagination. Yet budget bikes still dominate the market, because most people are still denied their due dignity, even as bicycle transportation remains undersold and undervalued.

Taken together, these circumstances demand a fundamental and thoroughgoing overhaul of our industry's priorities, as well as its productive capacities. In this respect, community bike shops may be ahead of their time—while no two are alike, they tend to be comfortable places where you can find good used bikes and parts, learn repair skills, and even fix your own bike. Best of all, community bike shops famously provide for truly welcoming and inclusive environments.

For purposes of this project, they also lend us some excellent points of reference. Creative mechanics at community bike shops the world over keep countless riders safely awheel over all manner of obstacles, to sometimes include a lack of funds, and there is much they can teach us. As a means to broaden our understanding, this volume thus includes technical insights, commentary, and survey data (both individual and collective) provided by staff at thirty-four community bike shops in four countries, as listed on page 248.

Finally, while I remain grateful for everything our friends have shared for purposes of this project, I am principally responsible for assembling this book, and any errors found herein are mine alone.

# 1
# TOOLS

**Bike repair stands** do two important things: they bring everything up where we can work on it more easily, and they lift the wheels off the ground. We can check our work on the brakes and drivetrain, and without kneeling or squatting.

Better stands have heavier bases—they won't tip over. Their clamps will be adjustable as well, accommodating frame tubes of varying sizes. Be careful when clamping high-end aluminum or carbon fiber frame tubes, which can be vulnerable to compression damage—grab the seatpost instead. And if the post is ovalized, or itself made of carbon, use a dummy post of the same size. Pull it out a bit if the clamp needs more room; mark the original height with electrical tape.

See page 9 for more on identifying different frame materials. Clamps can erase decals and stickers: wrap a clean rag around the jaws if either is precious.

If you are working on a regular steel frame—far and away the most common, for all of human history—go ahead and chomp down on the seat tube just beneath the top tube, with the clamp's adjustment mechanism facing into the frame's main triangle. Clamping on the frame instead of the post makes it easier to reposition the bike to better angles more suitable to different repair tasks—tilting the back end up near level to work on the front brakes, for example.

Park Tool and other manufacturers produce stands with removable clamps, which can be useful indeed when working on more substantial machines like tandems, adult trikes, or electric bikes. First, remove the clamp and chomp down to a midpoint on the frame before hoisting the package up into the stand. You might ask a comrade to assistance here, depending.

**Park Tool PCS-4 repair stand.**

No stand? Flip the bike upside down on a hard surface before applying significant torque to pedals, cranks, and bottom brackets. Alternately—for less strenuous adjustments on cables, brakes, or derailleurs—you might just hang the bike up. "A simple alternative to using a repair stand is two lengths of rope hanging from rafters or a tree branch," notes Jody Chandler at the Hub Bike Co-op in Minneapolis. "One rope comes down, goes under the saddle and back

TOOLS 3

**Park TS-2 truing stand.**

up to the rafter. The other does the same under the stem. If ½" webbing is used, it can be mated with toe straps to give easy height adjustability."

As with our repair stands, the better **wheel truing stands** are heavier—they'll hold a wheel without letting it shimmy around while you work, which makes truing (straightening) the wheel a lot easier. Mechanics often secure truing stands in bench vises or bolt them to wooden bases for just this reason.

For **hand tools**, a set of quality screwdrivers would be a great place to start—3 mm and 6 mm flat tip, alongside a #0 and a #2 Phillips—followed by set of metric box wrenches, 8 through 17 mm. A hammer will unfortunately earn its place on your bench, as will a rubber mallet, metal and woodworking files, box and needle-nose pliers, and a strong magnet. Our metal tools of course prefer dry, slightly oily environments.

The standard set for metric **Allen wrenches** includes 1.5, 2, 2.5, 3, 4, 5, 6, 8, and 10 mm keys, and among the bikes we'll find uses for all of these. The best Allen keys are known as ball drivers: the longer ends are beveled and drawn in, allowing us to make adjustments at angles, greatly simplifying our access to the various tight spots we'll encounter. They can also be spun more quickly, rolled across the fingertips basically, but only the Allen wrenches' short ends will deliver the torque required to truly secure bolts. Shorty's corners wear down in consequence, until the wrench eventually slips right off the bolt head—a problem the nearest bench-mounted grinder should be happy to fix. Just grind 'em flat again, filing off any resultant burrs. The bike shops' ubiquitous 2/2.5/3 mm and 4/5/6 mm Allen Y-wrenches both earn their keeps, as does the equally common 8/9/10 mm three-way socket.

With only a few exceptions—the "English" bottom brackets (BBs) foremost among them—the threading used on bikes is wonderfully, increasingly standardized. Almost every bolt head accepts a metric wrench and bears metric threading as well: M4, M5, or M6, most often. We may use 3, 4, 5, or 6 mm Allen keys to turn any of these, depending on where we find them. (Older Campagnolo crank bolts may require a 7 mm Allen key, but nobody else will.)

You should *never* require much force when starting a set of threads. It's always a good idea to make sure the two sets of threads are entirely parallel with each other, lest you face the tragic but all-too-common trauma of cross-threaded parts. Keep threaded fittings clean—clear out any rust or other debris with a rag before engaging them. And unless you're installing brakes, as we'll see, dab a smudge of grease across the threads' starting point before putting things together.

The modern spring-loaded adjustable wrenches are preferable to the old dial-up versions, in that they're far less likely to strip out our nuts and bolts. This said, the bigger crescent wrenches can deliver useful torque in certain larger applications, such as with threaded headsets. Some of the oldest threaded headsets feature adjustable nuts bearing only knurled surfaces, rather than wrench flats, and these will correspond best with a big pair of **Channellock pliers**. The dreaded **Vise-Grip pliers** are most useful for holding other tools—making extra-long Allen keys, for example.

**Side cutters** are best for cutting or trimming zip ties. They'll also cut brake cable housing, but a **cable housing cutter**, which you'll need to cut any linear-wrapped shifter housing, will give better results. Wound steel control cables will yield to these, or to **cable cutters**. Either may loosen with use—the jaws should be just loose enough to pivot freely.

The uniquely useful **fourth hand cable puller** directs its charge into a cable-sized alley, allowing us to hold the cable's position while tightening the binder bolt at the same time. These are key when working on caliper or cantilever brakes; we can also use them to help stretch out new cables. (There was also a "third hand" tool, which merely held the brake pads to arbitrarily fixed positions alongside the rim, but these are long obsolete.)

All but the oldest cable housing is lined with plastic. Cutting the housing compresses this. This doesn't always prevent new (uncut) cables from passing through, but the rest will get blocked or frayed. We reopen compressed housing segments with a cable-sized pick or awl. These are easy to find at hardware stores, but you can also just sharpen up a broken spoke on a bench grinder. Crimp a couple 90-degree bends to the far end and you get a kind of minicrank, which is easier to use.

We can also supplement the mighty fourth hand with a simple homemade extension, speaking of this lining—just snip off a thumb's worth of brake cable housing, capping each end with a housing cap. Racks, fenders, and the like can sometimes prevent us from cinching up the fourth hand directly against the brake as we'd like to; this surrogate extends that interaction back to a more convenient distance. In keeping with the theme, in my last book I proposed we call these "spare fingers."

Only older bikes will have any use for **spanners**, which hold the adjustable cups on the oldest bottom brackets while we finalize their adjustments. (We'll discuss the spanner specifics in due time, on pages 179–80). **Lockring tools** trace back to the same era, meaning to address various old-fashioned hub, headset, or track hub lockrings.

Neither the box nor the crescent wrenches will have anything to say to the conspicuously narrow lowermost wrench flats aboard old-style threaded headsets, which are far too narrow for them—we need the broad and flat **headset wrenches** instead. Possible sizes here are 30, 32, 35, 36, and 40 mm; 32 and 36 mm are far and away the most common. Also: check out the drive-side bottom bracket cup, just inside the chainrings. See any wrench flats? These will *almost* always be 36 mm. There is of course a specific tool for this as well, which grips the full circumference of the cup, but a 36 mm headset wrench might fill in as needed.

The pedals' wrench flats are sometimes just as narrow, but they also require a lot of torque for safe installation and removal, so you'll want an actual **pedal wrench** as well. These may have two sets of flats: we'll use the larger one (marked 15 mm) for most pedals and the slightly smaller one (9/16") for those found on various older, cheaper, or kids' bikes. (No flats? Look for a metric socket around back, cut into the axle's base. Your 6 or 8 mm Allen wrench should work.)

**Cone wrenches** are wispy little creatures; far too thin for use with the pedals. Their sizes range from 13 to 18 mm, with the odd sizes being most common. We use them to adjust our hubs. The **offset brake wrenches** are similar, but the wrench flats are offset 90 degrees, to better greet various older road bike caliper brakes. Sizes range from 10 to 14 mm, with an odd one meant for grasping the caliper springs as well.

Cranksets arrive in a few distinct formats—read from page 176 for more specifics. The originals, known as cottered cranks, were attached with steel cotter pins. We'll still see these on the road sometimes, but cottered cranks haven't been standard on new bikes in the North American market for more than fifty years. We rely on threaded **crank extractors** to remove the more modern ("cotterless") three-piece cranksets. A few standards have been used with these, as we'll see, of which only two remain common.

The crank threads and bolt head may be hidden beneath a dust cap. You'll want a 14 mm socket for the bolt—or, more rarely, 15 mm. More modern crank bolts marry the dust cap to a fitting for a 5, 6, 7, 8, or 10 mm Allen wrench. The 8 mm, mostly. Nicer three-piece cranksets use clever self-extracting bolts, obviating the need for the extractor, but the sad truth is that the wispy crank threads are too easily ruined—stripped cranks, as we'll see, can become a real problem. Use all due caution when pulling three-piece cranks, as described on page 181.

What are sold as "consumer" crank extractors feature long, flat handles. The shop versions skip the handles, offering sets of wrench flats instead. The central distinction among crank extractors, however, relates to the width of the bottom bracket spindles. We'll use a tool such as Park's blue-handled CCP-22 to remove cranks from the older and narrower square-tapered spindles. It will be another tool, such as Park's black-handled CCP-44, that addresses cranks on the newer and wider-splined pipe-style spindles like Octalink and ISIS Drive. Older versions of the CCP-22 extractor also feature a second, shorter and slightly wider stack of threads: these only correspond with older Stronglight cranks. Some older Campagnolo cranks require a proprietary extractor with left-handed threads.

A **crank backer** such as Park's CNW-2 will hold the backs of the chainring bolts as you tighten them. Nothing else really works here: small, and thus inexpensive, but crucial.

Excepting the bolt-on track cogs, the gears on rear wheels will either thread into place (freewheels) or slip down over free-spinning splined freehub bodies (cassettes). The internally geared hub sprockets look more like track cogs, but they function more as cassettes—see page 216 for more.

Freewheel removal requires an extraction tool, a funny-looking socket basically, of which there are several. Cassette removal enlists a chain whip, a cassette lockring tool—of which there are also a few—and either a vise, a second chain whip, or a big adjustable wrench. Tools used for freewheel and cassette removal are detailed beginning from pages 64 and 70, respectively.

To my experience, Park's CT-3 is our best **chain tool.** The CT-5 provides for essentially the same design advantages in a smaller and less expensive package. Cheap chain tools suck—they're poorly made, and they break. You'll also want a decent **floor pump** for tires, **tire levers** to fix flats—I'd recommend the mighty Quik Stik—and a patch kit.

We use **spoke wrenches** to true or build wheels. The wrong wrench either won't fit or will strip out smaller spoke nipples, so the sizing is key here. Park's red-handled SW-2 is most common; the black-handled SW-0 fits new or replacement spoke nipples; the green SW-1 is for some older bikes, in the US market at least. (A tiny fraction of high-end racing wheels eschew the spoke wrenches all the other wheels use. See their vendors for more info, if this is you.)

Other tools hold us accountable. A **tensiometer** can verify a given spoked wheel's health and strength; the **torque wrench** is like a lie detector for bolts. ("Are you *really* tight?") This last is most important with the pedals, cranks, and bottom brackets. Component manufacturers provide torque recommendations, and a torque wrench is our only way to check.

Finally, get yourself an **encouragement bar**—the down tube from a dead bike frame, for example. A long pipe wide enough to swallow a big wrench's handle, for use when you need extra leverage.

**Lubrication**? The ideal chain is just wet enough not to squeak, yet dry enough to avoid attracting excessive debris. On that basis I'd recommend using so-called gel lubricants like Rock "N" Roll, which suspend oil in an alcohol base—this evaporates, leaving the chain sublime. Whatever you do, try to use an **oil dropper** rather than a spray bottle. It's often easy enough to refill Tri-Flow and other oil dropper bottles—just grip the plastic tip with your pliers, pull it out, and fill. This will probably flatten the tip's tiny hole—rotate the pliers 90 degrees and squeeze to round it out again. Always wipe the chain down once you're done.

Working on bearings? Get a **grease gun**. These, too, are refillable—the home mechanic versions use tubes, which we roll up and clip as we go, just like with toothpaste. The shop versions are unscrewed and literally spoon-fed from tubs of grease. Either provides a precision useful for potentially messy work. And, given the way that open tubs of grease tend to attract all kinds of grit, grease guns can also help us avoid transferring such contaminants into our parts.

Directly opposite the lubricants we find the **thread-locking compounds**. The vibrations generated through riding conspire to loosen our bikes' various threaded fittings, and thread lockers introduce friction between them. The original approach to this was strictly mechanical—serrated or spring-loaded split washers, shoving threads together basically. The **nyloc nuts** are more modern—the nut accommodates a nylon ring, which holds the threads more predictably. We also see a broad range of liquid thread lockers, from blue Loctite's kind-of-tighter to red Loctite's not-going-anywhere, for example.

# II
# FRAMES

Given the opportunity, riding a decent frame can make a big difference. The ride will be more comfortable; the handling will be more consistent; the frame will probably last longer.

Better frames are often lighter. The welds or brazing at the joints will be cleaner and more even. The **frame tubing decals**—found on the seat tube or down tube, and perhaps a fork blade as well—provide us a useful shorthand here. Be sure to read the fine print: a frame decal only mentions "main tubes," for example, when confessing that its fork and rear triangle are made of lesser materials. "Butted" frame tubes are machined to be slightly thinner through their midsections, a treatment that makes them stronger and lighter both. Double-butted chromoly steel tubes provide a basic benchmark for quality; triple-butted is better and rarer. Either enlists steel's inherent resiliency to deliver a less jarring ride. Each tubing manufacturer uses their own numbering or naming protocol to describe their own projects, but they'll all mention butted tubes whenever they can, so this is the key word to look out for.

Frame tubes of any material may be joined with **lugs**, which are what we call the sleeved fittings joining one or more tubes together. Their presence is not necessarily determinative of frame quality—cheap and quality tubes alike will be designed to either join directly or through lugs.

Most bikes are made of steel. High-tensile ("Hi-Ten") steel is cheaper and weaker than chromium-molybdenum ("chromoly") steel. Both can be heavier than other frame materials, which include aluminum alloys, carbon composites, titanium, and even bamboo. Steel can also rust, which is why mechanics in coastal areas often recommend coating such frames' interior dimensions with Frame Saver treatment for protection.

Reynolds 853—Seamless Air-Hardened Heat-Treated Steel.

Carbon fiber might crack on impact, especially in the deep cold, and as a petroleum derivative it will also burn. The ride quality can be quite supple, however, prior to any such events. Aluminum is more rigid—a tendency that leads some to say the material is better used for bike parts rather than frames. This comes through in the design of alloy frames as well: manufacturers often pair suspension forks, carbon forks, and even carbon chainstays with aluminum frames, in part to take the edge off.

Titanium and bamboo each have their own advantages, but in our time both may be safely described as boutique frame materials. "There are so many great steel frames going to waste," says Jack Kelleher of the Clonakilty Bike Circus in Clonakilty, Ireland. "Bamboo appeals to the survivalist in us all, but why bother? The heart of a bike is steel, and that requires heavy industry. There won't be ball bearings or chains after the bomb. We'll ride donkeys."

We trust a frame or fork's **dropouts** to accept wheel axles of the appropriate dimensions, of which there have been only a few. The original dropouts were horizontal—elongated slits, basically—allowing our forebears to set up their wheels at varying distances from their pedaling axes. We still use this formula to set the chain tension on fixed gear, BMX, and other monocog bikes.

Horizontal dropouts can complicate wheel removal, however. Indexed drivetrains—where gear changes correspond with clicks—also work best when their axles sit at fixed points, rather than just somewhere along a horizontal spectrum. Reducing the distance between our pedaling and drive axes also allows for greater efficiency. Thus do modern multispeed bike frames incorporate vertical dropouts instead; the axle slips in from below. The semivertical dropouts are less common; they split the difference.

With multispeed bikes of any vintage, the rear derailleur will almost always attach to a small threaded fitting on the frame known as the **derailleur hanger**. These get bent all the time: the bike falls over, the derailleur takes the hit, the hanger gets bent. When you look at the derailleur from the rear, its pulleys would angle inward.

A bent hanger will torpedo your shifting, and possibly even throw your rear derailleur into the spokes, so straightening derailleur hangers becomes a very common repair. This is easy enough on steel frames—derailleur hanger alignment tools, such as Park's DAG-2.2, are literally designed for this. No alignment tool? Plug your Allen wrench's short end into the derailleur's mounting bolt, then grasp its long end with one hand and the derailleur body with the other, moving both simultaneously.

The hangers on aluminum frames, being more rigid, are less easily aligned. "If it's aluminum, I'm not going to bother with it," says Dave Falini of the Newark Bike Project in Newark, Delaware. The slowest, *most* even pressure *might* straighten a bent aluminum hanger rather than snapping it right off, but there are no guarantees. This is why more modern aluminum frames use **replaceable derailleur hangers**. These may be unbolted and replaced, once you pass through the suspiciously dark and confusing forest of replacement hangers: only a *precise* replacement among dozens of nearly identical pretenders will suffice. Look for your bike's brand, model, and perhaps even the model year. (Cheaper generic replicas are also sometimes available.)

Bike axles have long been standardized, to 9 × 1 mm front and 10 × 1 mm rear. Newer high-end mountain bikes substitute stout "thru axles" instead, as we'll see beginning on page 61. And while 100 mm remains the hub spacing standard up front—excepting the narrower folding-bike forks—the width out back may span 110 to 197 mm, with 130 and 135 mm being the current road and mountain bike standards respectively.

It's often useful to clarify which side you're talking about when discussing bike frames. That with the gearing is the **drive side**; its opposite is the **neutral side**. You may hear these terms often, discussing repair scenarios at bike shops.

Our frames' greatest remaining controversies arguably focus on the bottom bracket shell, and to a lesser extent the head tube. Historically, BB shells were typically threaded to one of three standards. The French (marked as 35 × 1 mm) is essentially obsolete; the Italian (36 × 24 mm) is a high-end road-racing thing, mostly on Italian bikes. ISO or English (1.37" × 24 threads per inch, or TPI) is the default, with shells mostly 68 mm or 73 mm in width. This was the norm for quite a long time, but in recent decades numerous manufacturers have introduced various proprietary BB shells, many of them threadless, wider, or broader than the old ISO standard.

ISO BBs still churn within the vast majority of bikes in the North American market, and their replacements tend to be relatively common and inexpensive, so all the recent BB noise still bypasses most of us. The press-fit BBs really spin in a whole world of their own, as we'll see beginning on page 199.

The BB shells associated with the one-piece cranks we find on kids' bikes, old beach cruisers, and mass-market bikes of a certain vintage are far wider than our ISO standard—they'd need to be, for us to pass the crank arm through. These threadless BB shells are intended for press-fit bearing cups designed to fit one-piece cranks. Retrofit kits allow us to replace everything with more modern parts, should the need arise. This is also where the **eccentric bottom brackets** come into our story—briefly, this is an adapter in which an ISO-threaded BB shell is cut off-centered into an American BB–sized block of aluminum, while a lateral slit and corresponding pinch bolts are added to the intended frame's American BB shell, and suddenly we can adjust chain tension simply by rotating the eccentric BB fore and aft in its shell. We see these on tandem bikes a lot, for managing the chain tension over on the (neutral) stoker chain side.

The rear hub spacing and the bottom bracket width intersect in the chainline, which describes how well the chain parallels the frame's centerline. Our multispeed derailleur systems redraw the chainline on a continual basis, shifting up and down the gears, but they're all designed to work within reasonable parameters. Our frames themselves will gesture toward their preferred solutions—wider BB shells line up best with wider rear hub spacing, in order to maintain a decent chainline.

Beyond the ubiquitous bent derailleur hangers, cross-threading might be the most common form of **frame damage**. While remedies are sometimes available for cross-threaded BBs, the same is not always true for the other threaded fittings we'll find on our various bikes. Both M5 (water bottle and fender mounts) and M6 (brakes) threads can often be repaired with metric taps, and the 10 mm threads we find inside rear derailleur hangers may be retapped as well—or even drilled out and replaced with new threaded inserts, given the space—but that's about it. *Always use cutting oil whenever cutting threads.*

Frame damage severe enough to compromise a frame's integrity can often be seen—bent fork legs or a dangerous new crimp just behind the head tube, for example, after riding into a fixed object. Hold a ruler against the bottom of the down tube; look for discrepancies. Crimps in the tubes become stress risers: places where the frame or fork is more likely to break with continued use. Strip anything such for parts and recycle it.

Sometimes we're luckier, and frames merely need to be straightened. Minor problems with **frame alignment** can often be corrected with shop tools—using Park's FFS-2 to straighten any slightly bent frame tubes, for example, then their FFG-2 set to align dropouts, and finally their FAG-2 (Frame Alignment Guide) to validate the results.

Any **creaks** heard while riding may or may not trace back to your frame. Creaks are born wherever metals or other materials may intersect—in the absence of lubrication, typically—and they tend to coincide with specific actions. You'll only hear a creak when pedaling hard, for example, or standing up over the handlebars to crank up a hill.

Creaks can also indicate cracks or other frame damage, however, so it's worth tracking them down. Go find a quiet place to ride—a peaceful street at night, or a big empty room somewhere—and do the thing that makes the creak, listening very carefully to determine where it comes from. Anything bolted to your handlebars can creak, from light mounts to the stem itself, as can headsets. Seats and seatposts are equally happy to creak. Loose crank bolts, pedal cages, and bottom brackets may also cause creaks down below. It's a process of elimination, and a lack of lubrication is usually the issue. Creaking metal parts typically respond well to a dab of grease; use carbon assembly paste or similar for carbon fiber.

○○○○

**Forks** are designed for use with specific frames, beginning from the wheel size. The **steerer tube**—the segment running through the frame's head tube—further differentiates the forks. The uppermost sections of the original forks' steerers were cut with threads, as we'll see in the chapter following, in anticipation of the original threaded headsets. The more modern threadless headsets erased these threads in favor of other methods, as we'll see, splitting the steerer tubes between threaded and threadless versions.

The original steerer tubes consolidated around the 1" (25.4 mm) width. The 1⅛" (28.6 mm) and 1¼" (31.8 mm) steerers both rode in on the 1980s mountain bike boom. Both the 1⅛"—and, to a lesser extent, the 1"—were later reformatted for use with threadless headsets.

Steerer tubes were traditionally a consistent width as they met the upper and lower bearing sets, but some newer high-end bikes begged to differ. Wider bearing sets fared better down below; sticking with the narrower ones up top shaved a few grams off the weight. Thus did we witness the rise of forks with **tapered steerer tubes**, a novel designation that rendered the antecedents as **straight steerer tubes**. Various manufacturers have since collaborated to present the Standard Headset Information System (SHIS), a shared naming pattern used to categorize and describe headsets in a broad range of potential configurations, and a topic we'll return to in the following chapter.

Fork legs are sized to fit (nominal) wheel sizes from 12" to 29". The great majority of bikes awheel today rely on front hubs with 9 mm axles, installed in dropouts spaced 100 mm apart. The fit should be snug; you may need to spread the fork just a bit to fit the hub in. Folding-bike forks set their drops 70 or 75 mm apart. Fat-bike forks space them up to 150 mm wide and might require the thicker thru axles as well.

Picture a line running straight down the middle of the steerer tube, with a second line coming off at 90 degrees to meet the front

**Fork with straight threaded steerer tube.**

axle: this is the **fork rake**, which describes the distance the fork's steerer tube trails the axle. (Modern straight-bladed forks still have rake; it's simply concentrated within the fork crown.) More fork rake can make the ride more supple; less rake makes the handling quicker. Either should reflect the inclinations already expressed in a frame's head tube angle: a proper touring bike may have more rake, matched to a 71-degree head tube; its zippy roadster cousin might go with less rake and 73 degrees.

Think your fork is bent? Take the wheel out and look at the fork from the side across both blades: their profiles should match perfectly.

No crimps; no bending slightly backward; none of that. Use frame tools such as those mentioned above to verify any suspect fork's integrity before using it.

Steel dropouts are aligned regularly, but straightening steel fork legs is more tenuous—bends create stress risers, which make the fork legs afflicted more vulnerable to sudden failure. "Forks are almost always a no-no once they've been bent. If there's any rippling on the frame, that won't fly either," says one community bike shop mechanic. Glen Mason of Melbourne's Community Bike Hub concurs: "We align rear ends of steel frames, but not forks. If they're damaged, I don't trust them anymore."

"The frame and fork alignment service is really only for older steel bikes," notes Jesse Cooper of the Bike Kitchen in Vancouver. "Nothing else, and only on rare occasions. Otherwise we see it as a stress riser and potential danger to the rider. Especially considering the age of the bike. Twenty years ago it wasn't much of an issue, but those extra decades sure do a number on the bike's material integrity."

Aluminum forks cannot be safely repaired. Various specialists offer carbon fiber repair services, which could potentially address damage to carbon fiber fork blades. You'd need to ask them.

When **replacing a fork**, we must account for the sizing and formatting details noted above, as well as the headset's **stack height**. For threaded steerers, this is the total height of the headset's exposed pieces: two bearing cups, a locknut, and any lockrings or spacers. Threadless steerer tube heights must also accommodate a threadless stem. A threaded fork's threads might be extended down the steerer tube with thread-cutting dies, if you can find a shop that still has them, but nowadays this is an uncommon repair. There'd probably be simpler things to do.

## III
# HEADSETS

**Headsets** are the bearing sets sandwiching our frames' head tubes. The best among them may serve for decades with only the occasional overhaul. Like every other component, however, they've been produced across a range of quality standards, and the cheaper ones run into more problems.

    The basic format is simple enough: two sets of loose bearings, caged bearings, or bearing cartridges rotate in plane together, each one riding the gap between **bearing races** beneath and **bearing cups** above. The lowermost bearing surface we call the **crown race**; we hammer it into place atop the fork crown. A bearing cup comes down over the upstairs bearings, which we adjust as required to maintain consistent steering.

    On bikes with functional front brakes, **loose headsets** are best noticed with the bike on the floor. Grip the frame's lower bearing cup and the fork's crown race between your fingers, squeeze the front brake, and gently rock the bike back and forth; the fork and frame should move as one, without rocking against each other. No front brake? Lift and drop the handlebars—a bike with a loose headset will rattle as it lands. (This test may indicate other problems as well, such as loose hubs; start with the headset.)

    Headsets rarely become too tight—absent an original misadjustment, at least—but this, too, becomes obvious enough. Set the bike up in the stand, angling the head tube such that the fork can be easily swayed back and forth: the bearings would feel as if they were ratcheting into position were the headset too tight. Ridden long or hard enough, the bearings in a maladjusted headset dig tiny burrows in the races, only reluctantly jumping from one to the next as we steer—a condition known as indexed steering. Time for a different headset, if so.

A headset that loosens repeatedly may need to be tightened more forcefully. While we don't want to crush the bearings, we'll always want to make sure the headset adjustment hardware becomes tight indeed. Bearing races missing a ball or two can also torpedo our adjustments, as can improperly installed bearing cups or races. We'll discuss headset bearings in the coming pages. Misaligned headsets can be reinstalled, as described on page 23. It's also possible, but less likely, that a buildup of paint or excess frame material may be leaving the bearing surfaces less than parallel. Your friendly local bike shop should have the metal-cutting dies needed to face the head tube in such cases. Even more rarely, truly hard riding may eventually flare out a head tube, causing the headset to loosen continually—if ever the bearing cups lose purchase on their own, it's time for a different frame.

**Threaded headsets** are the originals. We'll identify them by the wrench flats cut laterally across the upper bearing cup, as well as the **locknut** we'll look for above it. A tiny minority of old Mavic and Stronglight headsets may combine or conceal these features, but in more usual circumstances we countertighten this locknut against the upper threaded bearing cone to establish and confirm our adjustments. We should always see a thin **keyed washer** between the two: a metal stub protrudes inward from its interior, lining up with a long, narrow slit cut down the steerer tube's backside. (On older bikes, both features were sometimes replaced with corresponding flattened segments.) Any cable guides would also need to appear between the locknut and upper bearing cup, and these would need to be appropriately keyed as well.

The locknut flats will measure 30, 31, 32, 36, or 40 mm. The most common are 32 and 36 mm, for 1" and 1⅛" headsets respectively. The bearing cup will likely also bear 32 or 36 mm flats; 40 mm shows up occasionally on old mountain bikes. Any of these last will be too narrow for adjustable wrenches; you'll need a correspondingly thin headset wrench. The oldest 1" headsets may substitute lousy knurled collars for wrench flats on the upper bearing cup, for which we can only use Channellock pliers.

**Threadless headsets** move the bearing adjustment indoors: rather than relying on exterior wrench flats, the bearing adjustment happens within the steerer tube's interior. We use a hammer and a **crown race setter** to install an internally threaded **star nut** to a specified depth

HEADSETS

**Threaded headset.**

within a threadless steerer tube, then drop an M6 **preload bolt** through the **top cap**, a broad washer above the stem. Finally, the all-important **compression ring**, a slotted conical intermediary set just above the upper bearing cup, facilitates the initial bearing adjustment.

Dial down on the preload bolt to set the threadless headset's adjustment. Here as well, we're looking for the fine balance between too loose and too tight: the fork turns only on a level plane, and the bearings do not bind. We'll find a **pinch bolt** or two set laterally across the stem, usually behind (but sometimes in front of) the steerer tube—tightening these finalizes the threadless headset's bearing adjustment and also secures the stem to the steerer tube.

**Threadless headset.**

When it appears in front of the steerer tube, the pinch bolt's head may be hidden beneath a plastic cap. Be sure to loosen any other pinch bolts clamped around the steerer tube, such as those found on cable hangers, before adjusting a threadless headset's preload bolt. Weight-conscious preload bolts are sometimes made of aluminum, and they get away with it because we never really need much torque to set them—save your muscles for the stem's pinch bolts, which must become tight enough to keep it in place.

We align threadless stems by eye, with the assembled bike upright on the ground. First, clamp the front wheel between your feet, then get the stem's pinch bolt(s) halfway snug—enough to keep the stem from lolling around independently. Tighten them fully once the alignment is set.

Frames with **internal** or **zero stack headsets** effectively suck the lower cup and upper bearing race up into the headtube, dazzling passersby with an eye-catching streamlined effect. The **integrated headsets**, however, are the true zealots—these eschew the cups and races entirely in favor of skin-to-skin contact with their bearing cartridges themselves. Both zero stack and internal headsets are built around the threadless headset format described above.

Has the bike been sitting a few years? Steering feels a bit grainy or stiff? Did somebody maybe toss it in the pond? Best to undertake a **headset overhaul**. In addition to the headset tools noted above, you will want thin oil such as Tri-Flow, a rag or two, and a grease gun. This operation is best performed with the bike suspended in a repair stand, or by other means.

Remove the front wheel and bind fork to frame with a toe strap or a shoelace to keep it from suddenly falling out when you take the headset apart.

You will also want a plan for the handlebars, which in most cases will remain attached to the bike via one or more control cables. Bending the housing to extreme angles can create problems; avoid this by tying the bar to the frame's top tube while you work. Yet another use for toe straps.

Old 3-, 5-, and 6-speed bikes may yet have loose bearing headsets—in such cases, skip the toe strap and instead flip it upside down in the stand prior to disassembly—the bearings will (hopefully) stay in their bearing cups rather than scattering across the floor.

The descriptions in the paragraphs above outline the sequences we'll use to begin our headset overhauls. For threaded headsets, first remove the stem, using a 6 mm Allen key to loosen the bolt at the top. The stem should become loose—you may need to tap the bolt head down with a hammer to free its expander nut. A lack of any movement at all may indicate a seized stem; see page 235. This done, remove the headset's locknut, lockring, and upper threaded cup. For threadless headsets, loosen the stem pinch bolts, unthread the preload bolt, and remove the top cap. For both, also remove any spacers or cable hangers on the steerer tube.

Undo the toe strap and pull the fork out. You will now discover, if you didn't know already, what sorts of bearings you have in your headset. As noted, the oldest bikes may yet have **loose ball bearings**. Their number can vary between upper and lower cups—we'll generally hope to see between twenty-two and twenty-five, with the rule being that there should always remain enough space for one more. Bearings sized 5/32", 1/8", and 3/16" have all been used with loose bearing headsets.

**Caged bearings** are far more common among headsets: a thin metal retainer holds them in a tight circle. These retainers seem to wear just a bit over time and may eventually lose a bearing or two; be sure to fill in any gaps with appropriately sized replacements. **Needle bearings** use tiny rolling pins instead, held fast within resin cages. **Sealed-bearing cartridges** are just what they sound like: balls and grease are trapped within squared metal donuts, the walls of which take on their rotational responsibilities.

When overhauling headsets, we always want to check all the bearing surfaces for scarring or pitting—get in there with a rag and really scope things out. Any headset with less than perfect bearing surfaces should be replaced, as discussed below. Drop a bit of lightweight oil on a rag to rub out any old dried-up grease you may find around the bearing surfaces. The same oily rag should shine up loose ball bearings nicely, and the caged bearings as well in a pinch. When possible, it's better to soak caged bearings in citrus-based solvent or similar to remove the buildups of grease within the retainer rings, as described on page 225. Cartridge bearings are generally replaced as whole units when necessary. Note that there isn't really a standard size with these; take the code printed on their seals to a bike shop or bearing supply store, and they should be able to find what you need.

Once the bearings, cups, and races are clean and dry, grab your grease gun. For either loose or caged bearings, lay down a nice fat donut of grease in each bearing cup. The cartridge bearings are less needy; just smear on a thin coating across the cups and races prior to reassembly. Make sure your caged or cartridge bearings are oriented correctly in relation to their cups and races—only the bearings (or rotating surfaces, for cartridges) should contact the working surfaces inside the cups and races. It'd be pretty obvious if things were upside down—the bearings wouldn't roll correctly, and we'd also see a wider gap between bearing cup and race upon reassembly.

Be careful with the lower bearing seals, if you see them. It's all too easy to install these upside down or off-center on some older and cheaper headsets, such that they get pinched and destroyed. So get the bearings and their seal seated atop the crown race *before* reinstalling the fork. Then push the fork carefully into place from below, give it a spin to confirm everything's still cool, and hold it right like that while threading the upper bearing cup into place. You'll be pressing the fork into the lower bearing cup with one hand, until you reach an initial bearing adjustment upstairs.

Older and cheaper headsets sometimes lack any bearing seals, but we can make some. Clip a couple inch-wide rubber bands from a dead mountain bike inner tube and slide them up each end of the head tube prior to installing the fork. Put the headset back together as normal, then slide your new DIY headset seals over the upper and lower bearing cups. It's best to allow for a bit of overlap above and below, to better protect the bearings from the road grit that would ruin them. These will dampen the steering, but only as you spin the fork in the stand; the effect isn't strong enough to impact the steering when you're actually riding the bike.

Following the overhaul, the bearings will need to settle into their grease a bit—once the hardware is tightened to approximately the correct adjustment, take it out of the stand and lightly bounce the front wheel a couple times to help this happen. Doing so will likely cause the headset to loosen just a bit; readjust accordingly. Last thing is the final adjustment—countertightening the threaded headset's locknut and bearing cone or cinching down the threadless stem's pinch bolts.

If any bearing surfaces are damaged, you should **replace the headset**. Out with the old, firstly. Squeeze a splined **headset cup remover** into the head tube: it will expand to meet the inner edges of each headset cup in turn. Hammer on the tool's exposed end until they pop out.

The fork's crown race might be removed with nothing more than a hammer and punch, applied from the underside. Campagnolo and

**Crown race and crown race hammer.**

other manufacturers make forked punches specifically for this process, but we'll need access to the crown race's edges in order to make it happen. Crown races can be trickier to remove from wide-crowned suspension forks, the breadth of which denies us opportunities to pound the crown races from beneath. Various manufacturers offer **crown race removers** meant for just such situations; Stein Tool's may be the best of them.

Unless you're working with carbon fiber—in which case you'd want to substitute a carbon-safe substance, such as Finish Line's

Carbon Fiber Assembly Gel—prep the head tube's ends with a couple light smears of grease, both upstairs and downstairs. The **headset press** is a threaded rod with stepped fittings at each end, corresponding to our various head tube dimensions; turning the handle presses these evenly into the frame. The headset press succeeds by keeping the bearing surfaces perfectly parallel going in. Stop when both races are flush with the frame's head tube.

The **crown race hammer** is a stout section of steel tubing corresponding with aluminum fittings just wide enough to smash the crown race into place on the fork crown. The crown race's interior dimensions may become a factor here. Some budget bikes use a 27.0 mm Japanese Industrial Standard (JIS) inner diameter for 1" headset races, just wider than the more common 26.4 mm industry standard. If a crown race won't stay on—or won't fit at all, conversely—this may be why. Older shops may have the odd knurling tool you'd need to convince the 26.4 mm fork to embrace a 27.0 mm inner diameter race.

Here we must return to the **Standard Headset Information System (SHIS)**, the naming convention used to describe the different headsets we use for our various framesets. SHIS reads as a pair of alphanumeric strips separated by a vertical bar (|), with each strip further subdivided by a forward slash (/). The first strip describes the upper headset assembly; the second, the lower. The system facilitates some mixing and matching—of complete upper or lower headset assemblies, at least—so long as the replacement parts bear the same SHIS coding as the original.

Numerous manufacturers make the SHIS tables available in various posters and so on, and each should convey essentially the same information. Information captured in the SHIS code includes the headset type, steerer tube outer diameter, head tube size, and crown race size.

No headset tools? While I strongly recommend the replacement method described earlier, it is often possible to replace a headset regardless, but with less predictable results. Check out the crown race first: its lower edge might be attacked with a hammer and punch if we're lucky. (If not, you may want to stop right there—I have no home recipe for removing spent crown races from the wider crowns we find atop suspension forks.) The head tube's cup and race should surrender to a hammer and a longer punch, with patience. That same hammer ducks behind a block of wood when the time comes to tap the lower bearing cup and upper bearing race into the head tube; both are installed individually. This rougher approach also risks flaring out aluminum head tubes—any headset installed therein would lose its adjustment quickly—so this is only a possibility for old steel bikes. Nothing to try on fresher fruit.

## IV
# STEMS

The stem connects a bike's handlebar to the fork. Better ones are lighter and more rigid. We see two major types—while the older **quill stems** plunge down into threaded steerer tubes, the more modern **threadless stems** wrap around threadless steerer tubes instead. The pinch bolt(s) set just in front of or behind the steerer tube will always identify threadless stems. Lacking those, your excavations should reveal a quill stem.

Different stems serve different purposes. Those that set the handlebar lower and farther from the shoulders favor speed and control; those bringing the bars higher and closer may be more comfortable. We can

**Quill stem.**

**Threadless stem.**

track such tendencies by means of a few key indicators. Stem **extension** measures from the steerer tube's midpoint to that of the handlebar. The **angle** describes either the extension's distance from horizontal (angle A—for example, 0 degrees) or from the steerer tube itself (angle B—for example, 90 degrees). **Rise** refers to the extension's potential altitude in relation to the steerer; **reach** describes both a stem's angle and rise.

Stems are made further distinct by their **handlebar clamp diameter**. Dependent on age and pedigree, this may be 25.0, 25.4, 26.0, 26.4, 28.6, 31.7, or 31.8 mm. Steel stems are marginally more forgiving here—between regular 26.0 and Cinelli's 26.4 mm bars, for example—but for alloy or carbon stems, we always want to make sure we're using bars of the correct size. The fit should be snug.

Excepting carbon bars, which have their own distinct needs, it's always a good idea to smear a thin film of grease over the bar's midsection—this tends to minimize creaks. Older stems relied on solitary bolts to maintain handlebar positions: remove the bolt and grease the threads before tightening. In recent years, top-loading stems have crossed over from the BMX world to become **front-loading stems**, which enlist two or four bolts shot through a **face plate** to clamp the bars in place. Their firmer grasp allows for broader options—sweptback cruiser bars finally stay put, without suddenly rotating downward as you descend over curbs. They also simplify stem replacement; all the handlebar furniture can stay right where it is.

Make sure your stem is tight! Standing right in front of the handlebars, trap the front wheel between your feet and try to rotate the bars laterally—you shouldn't be able to. Both quill and threadless stems should always be tightened to this threshold, using the methods outlined below. Grease the bolt threads and underneath the bolt head(s) if you encounter difficulties here.

Quill stems will happily rust in place, left to their own devices—using a length of cable housing, paint a pea's worth of grease inside the steerer tube before installation to prevent this outcome. Just smear it all around. The **expander bolt** is a quill stem's spine, shooting all the way down its neck to meet a wedge-shaped nut down below. The stem's base will be angled flush with this wedge: tightening the bolt draws up the wedge within the steerer tube, bracing the stem in position. (A tiny number of older stems use keyed nuts instead, corresponding with slits up the stem's base.)

All quill stems have **maximum height lines,** warning us against raising them high enough for their expander bolts to press against the steerer tubes' weaker threaded sections. Ignore this at your own risk! If you find your bars too low, high-rise stems can be found to fit most bikes. Recumbent and semirecumbent bikes, of course, answer this question far more definitively.

Bikes with threadless headsets are often sold with at least a spacer or two stacked up below the stem: repositioning these above the stem effectively lowers the handlebars, and vice versa. The most versatile threadless steerer tubes will be tall enough to include a few wider

**Securing a threadless stem.**

spacers, allowing the rider a greater range of options when dialing in their riding position. (Bikes with shorter steerers, by contrast, might be a few grams lighter.) Most threadless stems are equipped with face plates, which provide for a further advantage: by removing the face plate and top cap, we can remove the stem and flip it upside down—this often changes the handlebar position significantly.

Whatever changes you make here, a threadless headset's preload bolt must command enough latitude to establish meaningful adjustments, and for this reason threadless stems should always overshoot the tops of their steerer tubes by 5 mm.

In recent years, various **steerer tube extensions** allow us to pair threadless stems with threaded forks, or to elevate quill stems as much as may be useful. (Note that alongside any such improvements you'll probably need longer control cables and cable housing.) We also see high-rise adjustable stems that look a lot like quill stems, lacking the preload bolt's traditional top cap, but any such creatures will have secretly swallowed their top caps entirely.

We should also discuss **adjustable stems**, which arrive in both quill and threadless versions. Most but not all are modern enough to bear face plates. The basic design splits the stem itself in half. A rear section sandwiches a forward piece; the two are separated by a splined interface. The original adjustable stems featured two bolts—one in line with the front wheel, and the other set perpendicular to it. We'd loosen the first bolt to begin an adjustment before setting the stem's angle with the other one. More modern adjustable stems are clever enough to charge single bolts with both functions. The design can be made to work with the best materials and manufacturing; alas, historically, this hasn't been nearly common enough.

I managed a bike rental shop in Minneapolis through four summers, just prior to the arrival of the city's Nice Ride bikeshare system, and most of our seventy-bike rental fleet bore adjustable stems. The cheaper versions we saw were all quills, and kind of heavy, but their central dilemma was more existential. The original design effectively channeled the lateral force generated when riding right through the solitary M6 bolt holding the sides together. This might not have been an issue in the designers' ideal world, where everyone downshifts before pedaling uphill and nobody ever needs to stand up and crank, yet in practice the stems' lateral bolts loosened with regular use. This may have been because the wrench fittings used to tighten them were curiously shallow—for aesthetic reasons, presumably—and this made them far more likely to strip out.

Once we could no longer tighten a given stem's lateral bolt, any force exerted across the handlebars was transferred to the stem itself, causing its extension to rock back and forth against the base. This widened out the gap between the two sides. And, since we're not able to cold-set such thick pieces of aluminum, this effectively ended the stem's useful service life.

The good news is that more recent adjustable stems improve on the original design by providing lateral bolts with deeper fittings for our Allen wrenches. My earlier experiences aside, this provides perhaps for a useful litmus test. If the bolt heads on an adjustable stem are just as deep as those used to attach the bike's brakes, said stem may have a fighting chance at retaining safe adjustments—provided you check in on its bolts regularly. I remain skeptical, however, given all the obvious alternatives.

# V
# HANDLEBARS

Different handlebars serve distinct purposes. Wide bars lend us extra leverage; upright or swept-back bars favor comfort; the curvaceous drop bars provide for the greatest variety of hand positions. **Mountain bars** are ubiquitous—their otherwise straight extensions trail backward only slightly. **Hybrid** or **riser** bars are similar, with bends near their stems lifting the bars' position upward; with each of these, the rearward bend is designed to be aimed up at our shoulders, rather than level.

**Cruiser bars** are longer and swept back; we mount our control levers on their lateral extensions. **Drop bars**, also known as road bars, curve forward, down, and then back: riders gain a sublime range of hand positions, as well as the potential for aerodynamic advantages.

Imagine flipping the drop bar upside down, then cutting off the bottom stretches—elongate the flat section a bit and you have **bullhorn bars**, also on the road bike standard. **Flipped and clipped drop bars** are exactly what they sound like—you shear off an old drop bar's lower sections with a pipe cutter and flip it upside down. File down the little metal ridges the pipe cutter leaves before remounting, and you have a less costly approximation of the bullhorns.

Whatever you ride, your handlebar should be clamped tightly within the stem, unable to rotate. Ditto for any control levers featuring along your bars, with the possible exception of bells or other plastic accessories, which may crack if overtightened. You should always be able to reach your control levers without straining.

The **clamp diameter** describes handlebars' wider midsections. The oldest bars bear a 25.0 mm clamp diameter, but 25.4 mm soon emerged as a new standard. It still holds for most mountain and cruiser handlebars. Italian manufacturer Cinelli produced road stems and bars with

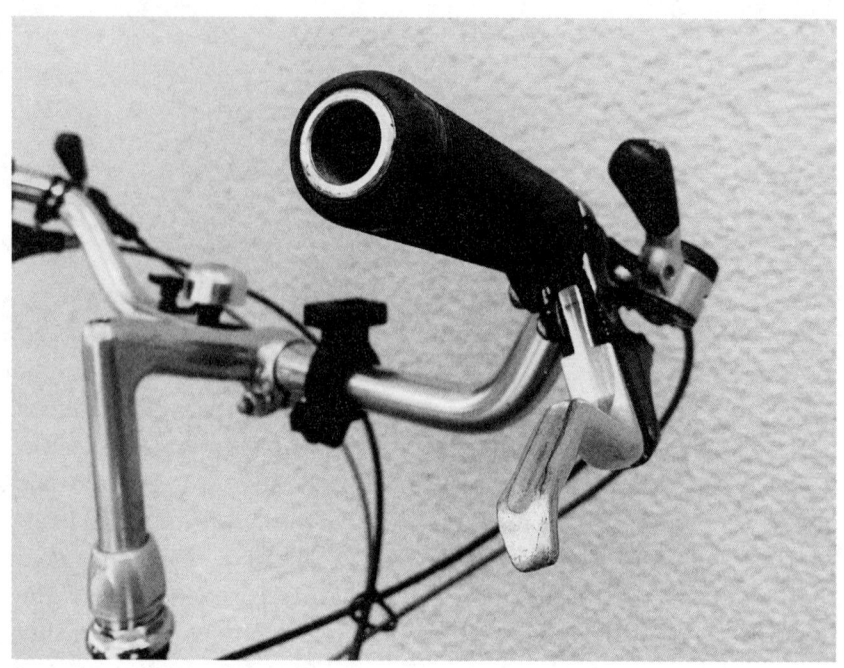

**Brake lever position for cruiser bars.**

a 26.4 mm clamp diameter for a while, but 26.0 mm became the new road standard. Steel stems allow the flexibility needed to accommodate bars just slightly too large or small—moving from 25.0 to 25.4 mm, or 26.0 to 26.4 mm—but you'll always want to ensure an exact match with any aluminum stems. The fit should be snug, not at all loose. The 31.8 mm size (also described as 31.7 mm by some manufacturers) has lately become the standard clamp diameter for higher-end road and mountain bikes.

The **brake lever diameter**, also called the **grip area diameter**, is the other major distinction. We only have two. Far and away the most common is 22.2 mm, for mountain. It is not compatible with the 23.8 mm road standard. Road and mountain control levers assume radically different profiles, given their respective domains, so this distinction makes a lot of sense. Those 25.4 mm mountain bike thumb-shifters old enough to bear steel handlebar clamps can be bent to fit 23.8 mm road bars should the need arise, but that's about it.

Truly ancient **mountain bike control levers** may also feature steel clamps, but almost all others are made of aluminum these days. (Budget bikes also once forced plastic brake levers into being: of all their lousy parts, avoid trusting these in particular.) We'll explore how brake and shift levers work in chapters 11 and 12 respectively; here we'll look at how they fit on our handlebars. This discussion applies for **BMX control levers** as well.

A control lever's position should provide for easy access: we shouldn't need to bend our wrists upward to brake, for example. Imagine lines shooting out in plane with the brake levers: on mountain and hybrid bars both, these should pass just above the front wheel, which will typically leave the levers sitting around 45 degrees below level. This angle steepens on cruiser bars, to account for their lateral hand positions, and on recumbent bikes we'll want the brake levers level or higher for similar reasons.

Dual control levers combine the braking and shifting within a single component. These are more common on road bikes, but we'll see them on mountain bikes too. They can save some space, on mountain handlebars especially. Yet others are designed to work together as matching sets. This said, not every shift and brake lever combination will sit flush against each other—see how things line up first, lest you face the uncomfortable prospect of cutting down the handlebar grips.

The steel bolts used to secure brake and shift levers will often thread into aluminum, meaning that there will be no do-overs if the threads get stripped. Add a ladybug's worth of grease to the threads to prevent this outcome, and another just beneath the bolt's head. Do not overtighten control levers: they only need to stay put. In the early 2000s, I encountered some SRAM mountain levers just slightly too loose to be fully tightened to standard mountain bars, but this is rare, to my experience. In any such cases, it's easy enough to cut a shim out of a soda can to slip beneath the clamp.

We must remove any **handlebar grips** prior to attacking our mountain control levers. You may need to remove any **bar-end plugs** first, if they're broad enough to block the grips' evacuation. The plugs may be held in place via small bolts, loosened by a screwdriver or Allen wrench. Said bolts might just thread straight out, leaving the plugs in place—tap on their heads to release the plugs' expanding sections inside the bars. No screws or bolts? Pry the bar-end plugs out with a small flathead screwdriver.

Mountain and BMX grips are meant to be snug, not loose. At the shops we'll use air guns to both install and remove them. Poke the

**A traditional Dutch bike enjoys an especially tall steel quill stem.**

tip under the edge; blast the air. Works really well. We often pretreat the bars with hair spray prior to installing grips—the air dries it out, making a kind of glue. Lacking an air compressor, poke a small flathead screwdriver under the edge and squirt some soapy water in behind it. Rotate and pull. Same thing in reverse to reinstall; they'll dry in place in a day or so.

We install **bar-end extensions** by moving everything in toward the stem rather than cutting down the grips. Tighten these a bit more than control levers: facing the bike and pushing down on them, you should be able to lift yourself off the ground. Here again, grease the bolts before tightening. The resting position typically mimics the stem's angle. Better bar ends enlist stronger threaded brass inserts within their aluminum bases, but most do not. If ever your aluminum bar-end threads strip, you might try drilling a 6 mm hole all the way through before enlisting a longer M6 bolt, a washer, and a nyloc nut instead.

Mountain bars are sometimes shortened—to better accommodate the narrows of city traffic, for example. Measure first to ensure you'll still have room for everything afterward, and use a proper pipe cutter, or a hacksaw with Park's SG-6 Threadless Saw Guide. Either

# HANDLEBARS

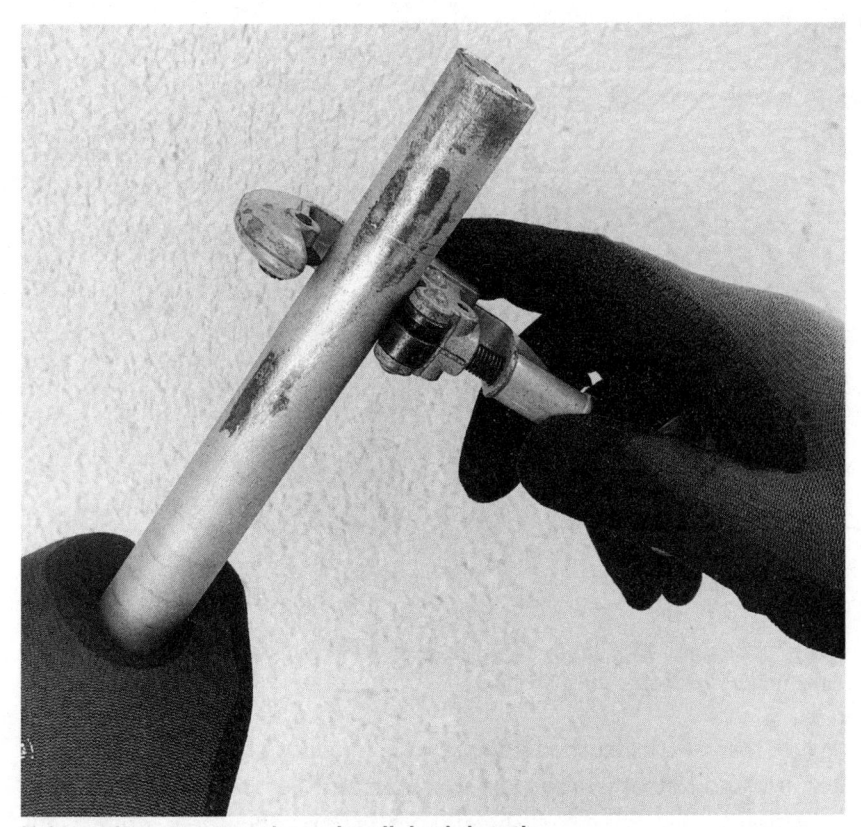

**Using a pipe cutter to reduce a handlebar's length.**

approach may flare out the edges—file them down as needed afterward, until the control levers' clamps will be able to pass.

Aluminum quill stems are ubiquitous on older road bikes. The default design clarifies their intentions: pairs of half moons cut from their sides allow the curved drop bars to pass through. The fit can be tight regardless, especially when old grip tape leaves adhesive all over the bars. Rather than try to clean this crap off—a truly tedious task—remove the stem's pinch bolt, slip a penny into the gap, and thread the bolt in backward. Once tightened, the bolt's nose encounters the coin; this broadens the gap, easing passage for your handlebar.

Prior to **wrapping grip tape**, see page 108 about road brake lever placement. We'll use electrical tape to secure any cable housing meant to travel underneath the grip tape. New tape typically arrives with a pair of road-specific bar plugs, as well as short segments of tape to wrap behind the brake levers—peel back the brake lever hoods and

**Finishing up wrapping the grip tape.**

secure these with electrical tape as well, looped right around the levers' bodies. And unless you're using bar-end shift levers, allow for a good centimeter of overlap past the end of the bars: once we're done, we'll use the bar-end plugs to tuck these in. (Absent the tape's overhang, the plugs are typically loose enough to fall out, so this is often a nice little symbiosis.)

Most mechanics I've known start the tape at the bars' lower extremities, wrapping from outside to inside, up and over toward the stem. This foundation sets the pattern for upstairs, where it matters more. Our hands will roll either with or against the tape's orientation, passing seamlessly overhead or wearing down at the edges; setting it up like this ensures the former.

The angle should be uniform, with each pass covering half the previous layer when viewed from above, and pulled just tightly enough to avoid wrinkles. The cork can rip if you yank it, so take your time. You'll run out of tape, conversely, if you double it up too much.

Reaching the brake levers, we originally wrapped up over the top, back down around the back, and then up the other side, to ensure for full coverage. Yet modern bars are often wider, as are the dual control levers, and our rolls of tape have not lengthened to account for this. We'll thus skip the classic figure eight when taping newer, wider drop bars. The hoods for dual control levers have also grown correspondingly larger, by fine coincidence, so a single diagonal pass should do it.

Up top, we wrap from back to front, nice and even, stopping just before the bar widens to greet the stem. Finish with a diagonal cut, as pictured on the previous page, before securing the roll's diminishing tail with electrical tape.

## VI
# WHEELS

The typical bicycle wheel comprises a hub, spokes, a rim, a rim strip, an inner tube, and a tire. The hubs are busy enough to merit a chapter all their own, beginning on page 61. The same holds true for the tires and tubes, as we'll see from page 54. Our purpose here is merely to understand the wheel's structure itself and how best to maintain it—what to do when the wheel seems bent, for example.

The **rim** is a big metal hoop joined by spokes to the hub. And except for the ancient tubular ("sew-up") rims and the newer tubeless (as opposed to "tubeless-ready") rims, we'll always need to involve a rim strip as well.

Bicycle rims and their corresponding tires have been made in no less than twenty diameters over the years. Wheel sizes are occasionally marked on rims, but we'll always see them on the tires. Look for three numbers in sequence along the tire's sidewall—25 × 559 / 26", for example, describes a standard mountain bike wheel. We'll dive further into tire sizing shortly, starting on page 54; suffice it here to say that a rim's size is often most easily verified by seeing what tire will fit. There's sometimes a bit more wiggle room with the inner tube sizes—slightly-too-small might puff up to just-big-enough, basically—but a tire of the wrong dimensions either would not fit the intended rim or it'd blow right off as you're inflating.

The default rim format is known as the **clincher rim**—slight lips extend inward all the way around either side, holding a tire's beads in place. **Single-walled rims** enlist single hoops of aluminum or steel, which interface with the tire on the outside and the spokes on the inside. **Double-walled rims** insert a second hoop, allowing for space between the two. Double-walled rims are mostly aluminum, though a few are made of carbon fiber.

High-end road bikes once relied on tubular tires to deliver a more supple riding experience. We literally glued these onto the rims. Now quick, before the rim cement dries, stretch the reluctant sew-up around the wheel without making a mess—but the glue gets super stringy, and it also makes your brakes wail like banshees ... anyway, there are reasons these are less common now.

Tubeless tires arrived more recently, originally on high-end mountain and gravel bikes, both of which favor lower air pressures. Their integration as high-pressure road tires has been less seamless. Within the rarefied realm of tubelessness, we must also account for the schism between **tubeless rims**, the outer walls of which lack spoke holes, and **tubeless-ready rims**, which are just a subset of the double-walled clincher rims we were already riding. Tubeless rims are rarer, and easily spotted once the tire's off: any spoke holes are drilled only through the *inner* rim walls. The outer rim wall (facing the tire) will have only a single hole, for the valve. Tubeless-ready rims are readied by means of **tubeless rim tape**, which erases the spoke holes with a barrier strong enough to retain the air pressure.

Our regular **rim strips** are less strident, leaving the air pressure to the inner tubes, with support from the tires. They merely protect the tubes from internal threats: the spokes and spoke nipples on single-walled rims, or the spoke holes on double-walled rims.

Rim strips are sized both by length and width. The fit should be just tight enough to stay in place once installed. The dimensions are usually noted at some point in its circumference—the nominal wheel size and the strip's width in millimeters, typically. Rim strips should be only wide enough to cover all the spokes or spoke holes, and narrow enough to avoid getting caught beneath the tire bead.

The worst rim strips are merely packing tape—while it protects the tubes from the spokes, it's not nearly flexible enough to be removed and reinstalled, as when replacing spoke nipples. To remove these, look for the seam and turn it over. You should see a tab—yank on it. You'll need another rim strip.

The ubiquitous big black rubber band rim strips are more flexible, but realistically these are only useful on single-walled rims. The tube's air pressure shoves a rubber rim strip right into the spoke holes on double-walled rims, increasing the odds of punctures.

We do have better options. **PVC** or **nylon rim strips** are less flexible

**Rim strip width: just wide enough to cover the valley of the spokes.**

than the black rubber bands, but they're strong enough to keep the tube out of the spoke holes. **Rim tape** is just what it sounds like: a light adhesive binds it to the rim's outer wall, and we peel that back as needed to replace spoke nipples. The thick cloth Velox tape is common—*Fond de Jante* is French for "bottom of the rim." A few distinct widths have been available over the years. New rolls are born long enough to cover 700c or 27" rims, our largest common sizes.

Our discussion so far provides a useful context for evaluating the various rim tape alternatives some may suggest. Anything such would need to be firm enough to keep the tube out of the spoke holes, straight enough to escape the tire's sidewalls, thin enough to avoid getting in the way of tire installation, and sticky or elastic enough to stay put.

The black rubber bands may tear eventually, but otherwise we should expect rim tape or PVC rim strips to last at least the life of their wheels, or more. Harvesting still-useful rim strips from dead rims is perfectly legitimate salvage. You may need to add a valve hole when repurposing cloth rim strips: fold an end back over itself and use your side cutters to remove a small V. Unfolded, this becomes a diamond just big enough to accommodate your tube's valve.

The **spoke nipples** are usually made of nickel-plated brass, but we'll sometimes see lighter, brighter, and more fragile aluminum versions as well. The standard nipple bears four flats, meant for one of a few standard spoke wrenches. Campagnolo, Mavic, and Shimano have each introduced proprietary spoke nipples, for which we'd need corresponding spoke wrenches.

Park Tool's spoke wrenches are most common within the North American market. The black-handled SW-0 is meant for 3.23 mm (0.127") nipples, the smallest common size, which is most often found on hand-built wheels or higher-end bikes. The green SW-1, 3.30 mm (0.130"), is most useful on the taller 16 mm nipples we see on some older bikes. The red SW-2 is the most likely, in that it corresponds with the 3.45 mm (0.136") nipples we see on low-end, midrange, and budget bike wheels. The blue-handled SW-3 is seeing more use with the 3.96 mm (0.156") nipples we find on various e-bikes.

Most **spokes** are stainless or zinc-plated ("galvanized") steel. A tiny elite are carbon fiber. Beginning from a flattened button we call the spoke head the eager spoke darts through a hole in the hub flange, bends at its elbow, and traces down to the rim, where it threads into a spoke nipple. Spokes most often break, when they do, at the aforementioned elbow bend, and so we also see a rarefied sect of **straight pull spokes**, which only work with designated straight pull hubs. Some of these last reverse the equation's polarity, anchoring spoke heads at the rim and bringing the spoke nipples up to the hub.

A wheel's **spoke lacing pattern** maps the spokes' journeys from hub to rim. Three-cross is far and away the most common: each spoke passes over two others, momentarily bending just enough to scoot under a third before meeting its nipple on the rim. One-cross and two-cross are less common—most useful, perhaps, when trying to build a wheel with spokes roughly 20 mm or 10 mm too short for three-cross, respectively. (With one- or two-cross, we won't even try to pass spokes under their peers.) **Radial lacing**, the great atomizer, represents the least social plan—each spoke shoots straight out to the rim, all alone, without even *noticing* the others.

The spoke holes on our double-walled rims may or may not be equipped with single or double steel **eyelets**, which also favor stronger wheels. The double eyelets are best—little spoke-pipes, basically. (These also spare us the hassle of shaking spoke nipples out of a rim, if ever we drop one inside while replacing spokes.)

**Rim with spoke eyelets and machined sidewalls.**

Hubs with disc brakes should only be built on eyeleted rims, owing to the stronger centrifugal forces involved. Disc brake wheels, however, have no use for **machined sidewalls,** the polished lateral surfaces that best accommodate rim-mounted brakes.

Seen from above, the average multispeed rear wheel's hub will be offset toward the frame's neutral side. The cogs occupy more real estate along the hub's axle; this is just what happens. Scooting the hub over like this also causes the drive-side spokes to lay flatter, more in plane with the rim. The neutral-side spokes, in turn, form more of a peak at the hub. We call this effect the **wheel dish.** We'll get it by using spokes 2 mm longer on the neutral side—once tensioned, the shorter drive-side spokes will naturally drag the rim over to their side, which, given the hub's offset, allows the finished wheel to sit centered within the frame.

The downside? Dishing weakens a wheel—a consequence of using shorter spokes on the drive side. The strongest spoked wheels feature uniform spoke tension across each side, but among dished rear wheels it's always higher across the drive side. The drive-side spokes are already under greater strain, channeling our pedaling force into acceleration and momentum, and this makes them more vulnerable yet. The steeper the dish, the weaker the wheel.

Thus do we see **dishless rear wheels**. Their camp technically includes track, BMX, and singlespeed, as well as most wheels built around internally geared hubs, but we're really talking about wheels built with **offset rims**, which scoot all the spoke holes over toward the neutral side, allowing for uniform spoke length and tension on both sides of a built wheel. Tandem manufacturer Santana has taken another approach here, centering its tandems' rear wheels around especially broad 160 mm hubs.

If your wheel is out of true, first check for **broken spokes**. The pattern on each side should be identical, without any gaps, but you should also check them individually: squeeze the spokes together in pairs, all the way around the wheel on both sides. Spokes usually break at their elbows up by the hubs, as noted, but the typical three-cross lacing pattern can hold broken spokes in place long after they're dead.

There are lots of uses for broken spokes, from making tools to making chainmail to rethreading them as shorter spokes, but they'll never resume their original missions. Merely bent spokes are often luckier—I straighten these all the time, using box pliers, so long as it's not too severe.

Spoke damage is sometimes obvious—maladjusted rear derailleurs and bent derailleur hangers are equally capable of tossing chains over the largest cog and into the spokes. The results are not subtle: you'll need to replace any spokes the chain sawed halfway through, in addition to those broken outright. This is what **pie plates**—the round plastic or metal shields, mounted behind the cogs?—are meant to prevent. Alas, these may yellow or rust with age, looking even less cool, and thus does the slaughter continue. Any decent bike shop should have a spare pie plate for you. Also see rear derailleur adjustments, beginning on page 142.

Spoke counts are always in multiples of four, and the hub and rim drillings must always match. Broken spokes should be rare: any regular recurrences would imply that a stronger wheel is needed for a bike's given purpose. Adding spokes adds strength as well—while most hubs and rims are drilled to accommodate 32 or 36 spokes, tandem and BMX hubs might fit 40 or 48. Lightweight race wheels, by contrast, reduce spoke counts to reduce weight. Best of luck with those.

Different hubs, rim sizes, spoke counts, and lacing patterns require spokes of different lengths, measured in millimeters. Proper **spoke rulers** feature small holes through which to drop the spoke head, streamlining our measurements. Alternately, hold a ruler to your wheel, measuring from elbow to the base of the spoke nipple. Various online sites, downloadable programs, and wall charts can also confirm the replacement spoke length(s) needed for a given wheel—we input the hub and rim models, spoke count, and lacing pattern.

The vast majority of standard 14-gauge spokes and nipples share the same 2 mm threading—2.2 mm × 56 TPI, officially. Like sew-up tires, 1.8 mm 15-gauge spokes are less and less common. The luckiest spoked wheels have butted 14/15/14-gauge spokes, which confer advantages similar to those we'll find with butted frame tubes.

Our spoke wrenches must be able to slide all the way down to the bases of the spoke nipples whenever we're truing wheels or replacing spokes, and the nipples must all be able to spin freely—it's very much worth it to clean up the wheel before beginning, if necessary. Add a drop of oil atop each spoke nipple's threads as well, and another where each nipple meets the rim, then spin the wheel for a minute—the oil will centrifuge down into the spoke threads. If left in place, the oil can also make rim brakes squeak, so plan to clean up again once you're done.

Unless your hub is larger than your cog—a mere handful of monocog wheels—you will probably need to remove the cog(s) prior to replacing any spokes. See page 64 or page 70 if you're working on freewheel or cassette hubs, respectively, page 216 for info on removing sprockets from internally geared hubs, and page 136 for more on track cog removal. **Bladed spokes** are also excepted here—they replace the spoke head with a second elbow bend, allowing us to insert them in reverse. These are not as strong, but good in a pinch.

What about reusing spokes? Among survey respondents who answered this question, seventeen community bike shops (59 percent) do so, while twelve do not. The split is less even for reusing rims: nineteen (73 percent) are in favor, with seven opposed.

Whether building wheels or simply replacing spokes, **spoke compound** helps to preserve adjustments agreed between spokes and their nipples. Most commercial versions are mild thread lockers; some prefer using lubricants instead. While not all community bike shops build wheels or replace spokes, twenty-six provided input on their choice of spoke compounds. Twenty-one (80 percent) regularly use spoke compounds; five do not. Of those who do, five use some kind of lubricant for this. Three use boiled linseed oil; another three leaves the choice of spoke compound to the mechanics. "We have pipe thread compound that we put on threads when building wheels," notes Santa Cruz's Bike Church collective. "After we are done with this container, we will try something that doesn't have PTFE or some other chemical that bioaccumulates."

Replacement spokes follow the same trajectory as their peers: we'll typically bend them slightly to weave under two spokes and over a third, for example, with the ubiquitous three-cross lacing pattern. Spokes falling outside the hub flanges will appear flared out a bit when first installed—the factory's default 90-degree elbow bend will never be quite steep enough for them. Press down on these just past the elbow to flatten them out.

Spoke nipples may be reused, unless the spoke threads broke off inside or excessive misadjustment has rendered them unadjustable. Their edges should also be nice and distinct rather than rounded down. You'll need to remove the rim strip in order to replace spoke nipples. The tall "aero" rims often lack double eyelets, making them great places to lose spoke nipples—avoid this by threading the replacement nipple *backward* onto a second spoke before poking it into the intended spoke hole and making the transfer, threading the new nipple up to meet the replacement spoke.

Replace any broken spokes before truing a wheel. You might make a wheel look tru*er* by overtightening the spokes to either side of a gap, using the techniques described below, but this would also leave you with drastically uneven spoke tension, and thus a deeply insecure wheel.

Using the correct spoke wrench is also crucial. You should only be able to slide it down from the top of the nipple: the fit must be snug, with no play at all. We'll typically turn the spoke wrench with one hand, making adjustments while holding the spoke with the other hand—doing so helps us avoid **spoke wind-up**, in which a stubborn or rusted spoke-and-nipple pairing simply turns together until the spoke's threads snap off inside the nipple. This happens all the time with rusty wheels—you'll need to replace both. Hold especially seized spokes with a fourth hand tool instead.

**Using a second spoke to transfer a spoke nipple.**

Certain older, wiser touring bikes demonstrate a keen awareness of their spokes' mortality, providing spoke holders with slots for three spares atop the drive-side chainstay: one each for the rear drive side, rear neutral side, and front wheel. By fine coincidence, storing the spare spokes in this location also protects the frame's paint from the chain. The drive-side spokes can usually fill in for the other two sizes, so given the odds it's not a bad idea to just triple up on those. Lacking the graceful spoke holders, you can also secure spares to the frame with a couple rounds of electrical tape. Don't forget the spoke nipples!

Our skills with **wheel truing** accrue with experience. We usually work in small increments, unless a spoke is very loose or very tight. And as you'll find, checking your work after each adjustment actually saves time.

We'll be tightening and loosening specific spokes to pull or release sections of the rim toward one side or the other, or to set them closer or farther away from the hub. Spokes too tight pull the rim too far in a given direction, and the reverse is also true—this is about finding the balance. The more you true wheels, the more you'll be able to anticipate what comes next: seeing *this*, we start by turning *that* spoke, about *so* much.

Both the depth of our adjustments and their breadth along the rim's surface will be functions of how much work the wheel requires. Our goal is always the same: in addition to making the wheel as true as possible, we also want to ensure that the **spoke tension** is relatively even across each side. Given the opportunity, this is best measured with a **tensiometer**. Lacking such, we can go by feel—squeeze the spokes on a healthy wheel and translate that to the wheel you're working on. Or, if you're more musical, go by ping: the sounds spokes make when plucked.

It's easiest to true wheels in a truing stand. Manufacturers build stands differently, but certain unifying features carry through—one dial opens and closes the calipers, another draws them toward or away from the hub. There may also be a third dial, to open and close the stand's dropouts around the hub: use your wheel's axle nuts or quick-release skewer to hold it in place, lacking such. And if you can't access a truing stand, use a bike's brake pads for reference—these don't work as well for truing, but it'll be better than nothing.

The stand's calipers may or may not be centered. If they are not, we can always remove the wheel and flip it around, to measure both trueness and the wheel dish, as we'll discuss more on page 50.

Begin by spinning the wheel slowly. Note where the rim first hits the calipers—you'll start with this largest deviation, then proceed to the next most obvious problem, and go on from there. The process becomes predictable in this sense, but it may not be strictly linear. Spoked wheels are dynamic systems; our corrections in one area may rebalance the wheel's spoke tension in ways that manifest as other, smaller discrepancies elsewhere on the rim. We'll address these in turn, using the same methods each time. The more redeemable a rim, the more its corrections come to seem intuitive.

Position the truing stand's calipers such that their tips barely graze the peak of the largest problem area. Recall that we're hoping to equalize spoke tension, across each side at least: check the spokes directly above the problem to see if any spokes are very tight or very loose compared to the others. Sliding the spoke wrench down from above, begin by turning it in half-turn increments, spinning the wheel to check your work after each adjustment.

As a wheel's problems diminish, move the caliper closer in to keep track of them. (Or, if you're using brake pads, increase the brake cable's tension as you go.)

We'll sometimes see broader bad spots without any center—a result of subpar wheelbuilding, typically. (A review of the spokes' tension may confirm this.) Our same remedy applies, only more broadly: you'll make the same sorts of adjustments, only across a wider range of spokes.

When truing, we'll also want to confirm a wheel's roundness. **Hops** describe sections where the rim bows farther away from the hub; **flat spots** appear when the rim and hub are drawn too close together. Hops are almost invariably the result of inadequate or uneven spoke tension; hits to the rim and overly tight spokes can each cause flat spots. We address either using the very same logic as above, flipping the axis from horizontal to vertical: adjust in small increments before spinning past the calipers to check your work. You may need to reposition the stand's calipers to really see these—flat spots are easiest seen with the calipers positioned above the rim, for example.

The calipers on Park and other truing stands provide for small cutouts in the corners, through which we can confirm both wheel true and roundness simultaneously—while we'll begin by focusing on each measure independently, checking them together is a fine way to finish. As dynamic systems, our wheels' lateral true and roundness are of course related.

Real flat spots—as opposed to spoke-tensioning problems—cannot really be removed, from aluminum rims anyway. Steel rims are heavier, weaker, and rustier, but in a pinch they are also more amenable to alternative truing methods. "We occasionally use a homemade wooden block for percussive maintenance on steel rims," notes one mechanic. "It is a forceful hop removal tool."

The last factor we must consider is the **wheel dish**—loosely, how centered the wheel appears when fit into the frame or fork dropouts. This detail should have been resolved when first the wheel was built, and it should generally stay that way, but any serious truing regimen may raise the point anew.

You can check for wheel dish in the truing stand by flipping the wheel back and forth, such that each side checks in with each caliper in turn, but you should also see how it lines up with the frame itself. The wheel should appear correctly dished in either location, but the stand's calipers can fall out of adjustment, and both frames and forks may be knocked out of alignment. Seriously misaligned frames and forks should not be ridden, but smaller discrepancies are more common, and this is the world we live in.

The frame test takes no effort at all—you sight down the top of the tire, using the fender hole in the frame's brake bridge or fork crown as your reference point. Adjusting for wheel dish itself is simple enough: all the spokes on the one side get the very same tweak, be that with tightening or even a little loosening. We will do a half turn or two apiece, typically, before checking the true again.

The **final tension** is the wheel's proof of enlightenment. Properly tensioned wheels ride better, and they hold their true better as well. Spokes of different gauges and materials function best at different tensions, as measured in either kilogram-force (kgf) or newtons (N), where 1 kgf = 9.8 N. At the Haight Street Freewheel in San Francisco, the first shop I worked at that actually used a tensiometer, the standard used for the 14/15/14-gauge double-butted spokes we built wheels with was 135 kgf—a figure that has continued to work well for me in the years since.

Whenever building a wheel or undertaking extensive wheel truing, it is always a good idea to finish by stressing the spokes. Grab them in pairs and squeeze hard, all the way around the wheel. And then you check the true one last time.

Most bicycle wheels are built by machine. Building them by hand allows for better control of spoke tensioning, as well as more choice in lacing patterns. And once you're comfortable truing wheels and replacing spokes, building wheels is only a few steps further. This book will not describe that process, however—word is that there are plenty of bicycle wheels rolling about already, for the present at least. "We have so many wheels, there is no need," says Paul Laudeman of the KickStand Community Bike Shop in Knoxville, Tennessee. "Only rarely does a volunteer build a wheel." Simon Batterbury sees a similar trend at Melbourne's WeCycle: "Always plenty of old wheels in stock."

Among those community bike shops that do build wheels, doing so with used parts appears not uncommon. "Our staff and volunteers almost all ride wheels they've built out of donated/used parts at the shop," notes one mechanic. "Spokes and nipples are cleaned and

**Using a Park TM-1 tensiometer.**

treated with spoke prep or a similar locking compound, prior to reuse." Toronto's Gateway Bicycle Hub makes the practice standard. "We have workshops rebuilding wheels with used parts: hubs, spokes, and rims," notes Ed Mark. As a caveat, however, we can't expect too much from the lightweight alloy spoke nipples. "Brass nipples are much better for reuse than aluminum nipples," notes Isaac at Troy Bike Rescue in Troy, New York. "Aluminum nipples crumble and corrode." Others elect not to reuse spoke nipples at all. "We don't reuse spoke nipples except on occasion for cable tips on personal projects," notes Alex Wilson at Chicago's West Town Bikes.

Our discussion to this point provides a useful context for evaluating the merits of **composite wheels**, which replace our useful spokes with nonadjustable stretches of plastic or carbon fiber. They may be great fun, unless you need to true them, because we can't. You might ask your friendly local bike shop to inquire with the manufacturer about any possibilities for warranty or repair, but that's all we can do for them.

## VII
# TIRES AND INNER TUBES

Like every other bike part, **tires** span a broad range of quality. Better examples may last longer, prevent flats better, fit more securely, or weigh less. **Kevlar belts** are sometimes inserted into tire treads to minimize flats; **Kevlar beads** on folding tires replace the rigid wire beads. Smooth tire treads are better for paved surfaces; knobby tires are better off road. And, perhaps counterintuitively, thin road tires can do quite well over the packed snow on city streets—more skis than snowshoes, basically. It's only in the unplowed hinterlands that wider or studded tires become more useful.

**Tire size** will be noted on the **sidewall**. We'll often see numbers expressed in inches or as fractions—26 × 1⅜ for old English 3-speeds, for example—but any such numbers are merely nominal, a shorthand used to describe a tire's actual dimensions. These last are best captured in the **bead seat diameter (BSD)**, a three-digit number that describes the tire's bead. The BSD is usually paired with a second two-digit number representing the rim's width. (Note that 700c and 650b are also shorthand—closer scrutiny should identify 622 and 584 BSDs, respectively.)

The tire-sizing regimens we perhaps reluctantly inherit bundle together decades of contradictory marketing gestures, such that the BSD number emerges as the key indicator. It may even reveal new possibilities—your 700c road rim might fill in on your gnarly 29" bike if needed, for example, because both are based on the same 622 BSD. (And in turn, 27.5" is simply a new name for the old 650b size.)

The tire itself will indicate how much air it needs, describing a range in bar or pounds per square inch (psi) in big block letters on the sidewall, where 1 bar = 14.5 psi. Lower pressure provides for a wider contact surface and thus a plusher ride; high pressure tires allow for greater speed.

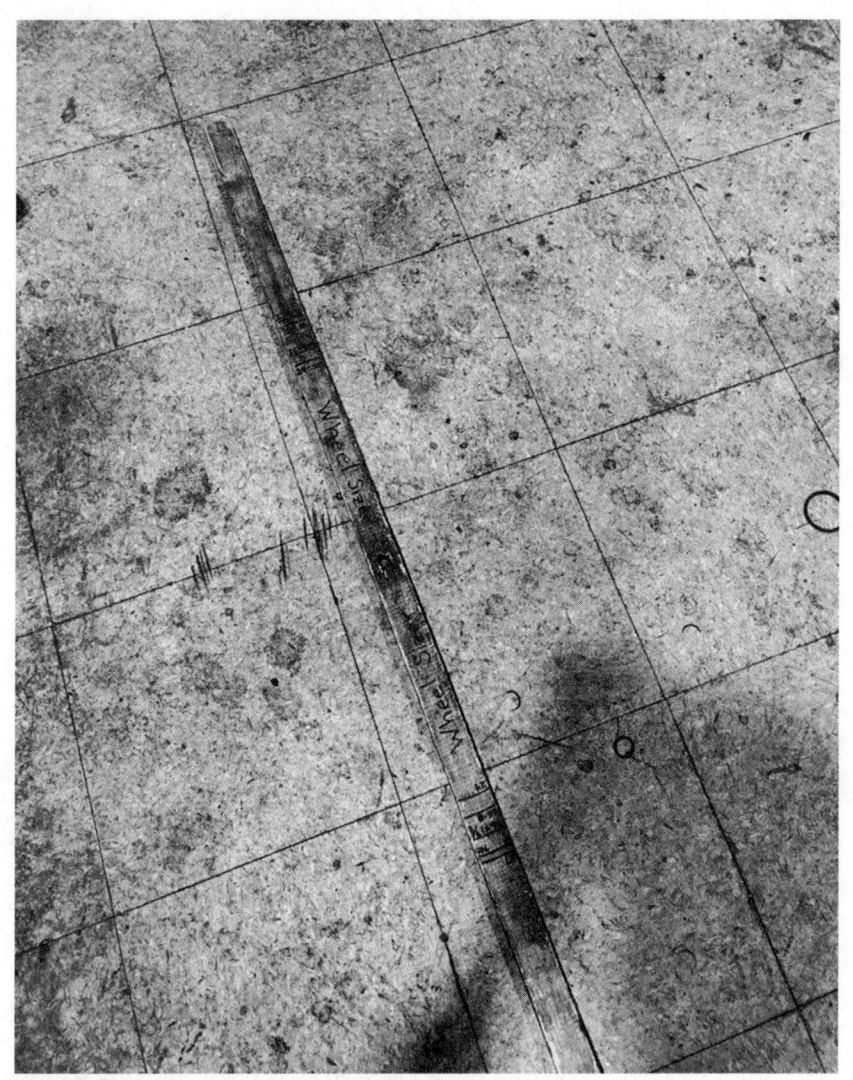

**Wheel measuring stick at the Flat Bicycle Collective, Montreal.**

Barring skids, **tire wear** is often very gradual. "We give away salvaged tires and tubes, recommending them for everyday use," notes Jack Kelleher of the Clonakilty Bike Circus. "If you're going on a long roll-about, the story is different." On kids' bikes, which tend to skid more than most, tire life can often be extended by switching the front and rear tires. Our rubber tires grow brittle and begin to crack if we don't use them for extended periods; keeping them out in the direct sun eventually does the same. We can hinder this condition, known as

**Presta (left) and Schrader (right) valves; Presta valve adapters.**

**dry rot**, but it cannot be reversed—there is no magical tire balm, great as that might be to have.

Inside most tires we find the **inner tubes**. Excepting the odd monoblade front forks, we'll always need to remove a wheel to replace or repair one of these. This involves releasing the hub, as described on page 61, and most often a brake as well; see pages 111, 115, and 124. With rear flats on derailleur-equipped bikes, shift all the way to the smallest chainring and cog in front and back, then pull back on the rear derailleur cage right below the parallelogram: the chain should form a rough triangle, allowing you to pull the wheel out. (On newer bikes, you might also need to release the rear derailleur's clutch, as discussed on page 154.)

You'll also need to mostly deflate the inner tube, if that hasn't happened already. **Schrader valves** are most common. **Presta valves**, which preserve their air pressure a bit better, have traditionally been associated with higher-end bikes. Our pumps depress the pin within Schrader valves to deflate them; we can also jam it down with a screwdriver or Allen wrench to deflate. Presta valves wear knurled caps—spinning these up unlocks the valve; pushing down opens it.

TIRES AND INNER TUBES

Twist down to close once finished. (The ubiquitous Presta-to-Schrader rim adapters allow Schrader pumps to inflate Presta tubes.)

Inner tubes can and do last for decades. "When we strip unusable bikes for parts, we have a station where folks remove tubes from wheels and inflate them," explains Sylvie Baele of Second Chance Bikes in North Charleston, South Carolina. "Then we let them sit for a week or so. The ones that have not deflated, we keep. We remove the valve core (on Schrader valves), deflate them, measure them, roll them up, put the valve core back in, wrap them up tight, label them, and then sort them into bins by size."

Tubes get punctured all the time, despite the tires' best efforts. This tendency can often be minimized, however, if not avoided entirely. "We advise that the best protection against flats is keeping tubes properly inflated and investing in a quality tire suitable for their riding," says Nicole Muratore of the Bike Saviours Bicycle Collective in Tempe, Arizona, echoing what may be close to universal common wisdom among bike mechanics. Location matters here as well—the western United States' goathead thorns, for example, are particularly notorious. "Most riders in our city get goatheads from cycling on sidewalks," Muratore continues, "so the recommendation to ride in the bike lane when possible is also at the forefront of these discussions."

Survey respondents' views on inner tube sealants were decidedly mixed—a function, often, of the goathead thorns' local prevalence. "We recommend sealant (Stan's or Orange Seal) in Utah, one state where the goathead plant is everywhere," notes one mechanic. "It really makes a huge difference in tube/tire longevity."

Got a **flat tire**? Remove the wheel and fully deflate the tube. Trace your thumbs around each side of the rim, pressing each tire bead in turn toward the valley at the rim's center. Tires and rims tend to lightly bond over time, and it's useful to break this before grabbing the **tire levers**. These are also pretty intuitive: slip two of the broad ends under the tire bead across a span of four or five spokes, above the valve. Secure one lever's hook beneath a spoke, then pull down with the other. This orientation is key—the tire will often be on there pretty good, and we'll earn the most leverage by setting things up such that we're pushing downward. Remove the bead entirely on one side before attacking the other.

Tire lever sets often come with a third, because they do break sometimes. For decades now I've thus favored the famous **Quik Stik** in

**Tire levers: one snags a spoke while the other pulls down.**

place of levers—a single, stouter implement that combines the levers' missions.

You'll need to patch your tube, if you don't have a spare. First, see if it can be inflated, twice its usual size. You might hear the hole's hiss or feel its tiny breeze while running the puffy stretched-out tube past your ear and face—hopefully so, because otherwise you'll need to dunk it underwater and watch for the bubbles.

Mark holes on dry tubes with a permanent marker. For wet tubes, I actually recommend the judicious use of safety pins, inserted very close to the original hole—the marker won't work in the wet, and we're already patching, right?

A patch needs a quarter inch of overlap all around; any hole that allows for that might be patched. Absent larger holes or breaches at the valve stem, tubes regularly outlive their tires. Once the tube is clean and dry, apply a patch-sized puddle of the rubber cement included in the patch kit around the hole. This must become *fully* dry before the patch is pressed into place. You'll need to remove the foil before applying new patches. And once you run out of those, make a lifetime's supply by cutting apart a dead inner tube—that's what people did in Mauritania at least, when I was there with the Peace Corps.

It's possible to accumulate a healthy surplus of tubes over time, allowing the carriage of spares. Patching tubes in batches, in turn, becomes more efficient—once all the glue is super dry, stack the patched sections like pancakes and press them within a quick-grip clamp for a few hours. Overinflate again, this time leaving them overnight—those still full come morning are good to go.

Prior to installing or reinstalling an inner tube, inflate it just enough to leave it less than flat. Doing so helps prevent the tube from being pinched between tire bead and rim on the way back in, which can easily pop the tube all over again. When installing it in the tire, line up the tube's valve stem with the most prominent feature on the tire's sidewall—the biggest or most colorful label, usually—and face this to the drive side. We call this **pro-setting** the tube. It gives us a point of reference when patching a tube—or, conversely, when locating debris dug into the tire tread. Finding a staple piercing a quarter past the valve stem, for example, shows us where on the tube to look for the corresponding hole.

Tuck the tube in all the way around the tire, starting with the valve, moving outward in both directions at once. Scoot the tire back and forth as needed until the valve stem stands perpendicular to the rim. Tuck each of the tire's beads in turn into the wheel, starting at the valve each time. Thread the Presta tube's knurled valve nut, if there is one, most of the way down—we'll finger-tighten it in place atop the rim once the tire is inflated, to help protect the valve.

How well the tire beads fit their rims varies greatly. Those on better-quality tires get tighter, especially with smaller wheel sizes. It's often helpful to push that first bead into the rim's central valley

**A pro-set valve stem.**

in order to create the slack needed to push the second bead over the rim's wall. This may strain the fingers, but that's just part of it—better that than getting the tire levers involved, which is an excellent way to pinch a fresh hole in the tube.

If the tire's bead slips on easily, this augurs a second caution: we need to make sure the tire is seated correctly, in order to avoid accidentally blowing it off the rim as we inflate it. Thus, when **installing a tire**, new or used—regardless of how tight the bead is—it's important that the tire sits centered on the wheel. We'll see to this by laying it flat. Pump it up to 20 psi, then pause to check how the bead is sitting—it should be even, all the way around, on both sides. Pausing here allows us to push and pull the tire as needed to even out the bead's purchase on the rim.

The sequence changes a bit with **folding tires**. Here, we'll install one tire bead completely, slip the inner tube into place, then install the second bead. Again, puff just a bit of air into the tube beforehand. Line up the tire's label with the rim's valve hole to pro-set before installing the tube.

# VIII
# HUBS

Were our wheels eyes, the hubs would be their pupils. Hubs are differentiated in several ways, beginning with their width. The distance a hub occupies between the insides of the frame or fork dropouts is officially known as the **Over Locknut Dimension (OLD)**, but most of us just call it the **axle spacing**. A hub and the frame or fork it is used with must always share this measurement. When installed, the outermost nuts or axle spacers should become flush with the dropouts, without any need to significantly expand or compress the frame or fork. The ideal fit is snug, not loose.

Your hubs will be attached to the frame in one of three ways. The **solid** or **bolt-on axles** were the originals: nuts outside the dropouts hold these in place. We'll typically use a 15 mm socket or wrench to install and remove these wheels; sometimes it's a 13 mm up front.

The **quick-release axles** are lighter, stronger, and easier to use. The **quick-release skewer (Q/R)** sprouts from a cam-and-lever assembly, then passes through a hollow axle to meet a threaded adjusting nut on the far side. Q/R axles are meant to be just slightly narrower than their dropouts; small springs at either end keep the Q/R skewer centered. Pulling the lever backward away from the hub releases the cam, and with it your wheel.

To reinstall, first center the wheel within its dropouts. Hold the Q/R lever out 90 degrees, in line with the axle, and tighten the adjusting nut on the opposite side until it is finger-tight. Our goal here is to ensure that the Q/R lever becomes tight enough: from that 90 degrees, you should need to push it into place with the palm of your hand. Less than that is too loose, and not safe to ride.

Lounging atop the ubiquitous bolt-on and Q/R standards squat the **thru axles**, another crossover from mountain-biking technology,

**Pull the Q/R skewer's lever backward to release a wheel.**

still clustered up around the high end at the time of writing. The axle becomes a pin, independent of the hub, piercing through both dropouts to skewer it. Bolts on the dropouts secure the axle ends. Thru axles also sidestep a concern we may have regarding the use of front disc brakes with regular Q/R levers, as detailed on page 133.

The industry standard 9 × 1 mm front **threaded axle** is shorter and thinner than its rearward 10 × 1 mm equivalent. (Italian manufacturer Campagnolo uses a distinct axle threading.) Front axle spacing ranges

**Tighten the Q/R adjusting nut until the lever must be pushed in by palm.**

from 70 to 79 mm for folding bikes, but 100 mm is standard for nearly all bikes sold in North America. Rear axle standards have ranged from 110 mm for the oldest BMX or track bikes to 160 mm for some tandem bikes. The standard for road bike rear axles was 126 mm for a while, but 130 mm is the modern road OLD standard. Most common is 135 mm, used for both mountain and hybrid bikes.

Were our hubs TIE fighters from Star Wars, their **flanges** would be the wings. Each flange hosts a smooth **bearing race** at its center, with the spokes falling from even holes around the edges. Loose ball bearings are standard for hubs—nine ¼" bearings for each side out back, most typically, with ten ³⁄₁₆" bearings up front. **Dust caps** cover the gaps between bearing cones and races on each side. (Caged hub bearings are truly rare, but sealed-cartridge hub bearings are more and more common.) Threaded **bearing cones** descend the axle from either side to face the bearings. We'll typically see washers or perhaps spacers after these, before each axle end is capped with a stout **locknut**.

The cones may become pitted over time, especially if ridden while maladjusted. Any such should be replaced. (The races spread the bearings' exertions across relatively broader surfaces, and thus tend to last much longer.) Note that both hub cones and dust caps are designed to work as sets and with particular hubs. In other words, you might have a hunt ahead of you to find the correct cones or dust caps your hub needs, but this would be preferable to attempting guesswork with mismatched hub parts.

Knowing a hub's manufacturer, model name or number, and production year can be key to tracking down its parts. "We have drawers of old hubs that rarely get built into wheels," Baltimore's Velocipede Bike Project notes, "but [they] are most often used to replace worn cones in matching hubs we are working on, since there is little cone standardization."

Those rear hubs bearing multispeed cogsets are grouped into two distinct camps, based on how we attach the gears. **Freewheel hubs** are threaded on the drive side to accept a corresponding **freewheel**, which combines the cogs and the coasting mechanism into a single part. Both Italian- and French-threaded freewheels have been used, but the 1.37" × 24 TPI (ISO) threading has long been the standard here.

Freewheel threads have the usual righty-tighty, lefty-loosey orientation, which in their case means that riding serves to continually tighten them in place. A multispeed freewheel's breadth also pushes the drive-side bearings back toward the frame's centerline, unfortunately, leaving the hub's slender 10 mm axle supporting our weight for a stretch—freewheel axles are famous for bending under heavier loads. (Traditional track hubs feature both right- and left-handed threads, for cog and lockring respectively; see page 135.)

We remove freewheels with the funny-looking sockets known as **freewheel extractors**, of which the world has seen at least a dozen

**Freewheel hubs. The one on the bottom is a tandem hub, also threaded for a drum brake on the neutral side.**

distinct examples. Your freewheel will pine for one in particular. A handful of the extractors are more common—all modern freewheels answer to Park's FR-1, for example, just as most singlespeed freewheels surrender to their FR-6. The FR-2 and FR-3 extractors, for two- and four-prong Suntour freewheels respectively, still see some use.

Here I must stress the importance of keeping the extractor engaged: *always* set up the hub's axle nuts or Q/R skewer on top of it to keep the tool in place. Just get it finger-tight above the extractor, then loosen it gradually once the freewheel begins to loosen. This is especially important with the shallower extractors, such as Suntour: the notches strip out far too easily, effectively cementing the freewheel in place. Also, the threads may let go quite suddenly, once they do—be ready for this.

The fact that our freewheel threads are continuously being tightened as we ride makes them difficult to remove. I had long assumed that we needed a bench vise to hold the extractor, like every other bike mechanic I've known, but Ross Willard of Recycle Bicycle Harrisburg in Harrisburg, Pennsylvania, provides us with a simpler and more intuitive method.

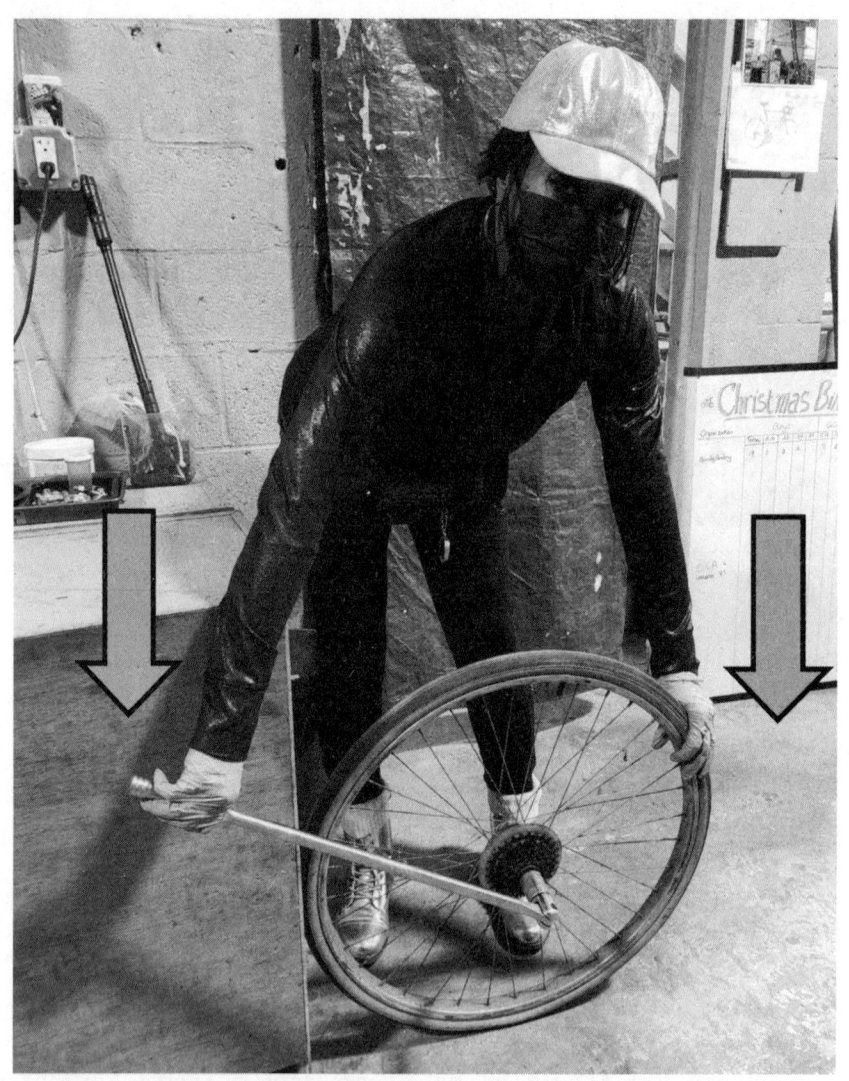

**Nan demonstrates freewheel removal at Recycle Bicycle Harrisburg.**

First, put your freewheel extractor in a breaker bar rather than a vise. The tool provides three times as many contact surfaces as the vise, Willard points out, gripping the extractor far more securely without any danger of rounding off the corners. Make sure the wheel is wearing a tire—we'll need this for traction—and face it upright and perpendicular to a wall, right there on the floor. Now we get to the real genius of this plan: you'll be pushing down on the breaker bar with one hand while bracing the wheel with the other. The wheel has

**Bracing a freewheel for disassembly at Velocipede Bike Project, Baltimore.**

nowhere to go, shoved against the wall, but you'll have all the leverage you can muster: the freewheel never had a chance. "The wheel will try to climb the wall," as Willard describes it, "but [it] cannot lift your weight." The technique is somewhat similar to what we'll do when removing cassettes, as described below, but with the wall filling in for the chain whip's role.

**Freehubs** incorporate the coasting mechanism into the hub itself, pushing the drive-side bearings back out toward the dropout, a design that better supports the axle. We can also replace the hub's splined **freehub body** independently of the cogs, which now slip down the freehub body's splines as a **cassette**, held in place with a **cassette lockring**.

Cassettes are routinely replaced when worn, often alongside their chains, as detailed on page 228. Freehub bodies rarely expire. You may or may not be able to replace yours—the cheaper the hub, the less likely this is. Freehub replacement involves a hub overhaul, which we'll discuss just ahead, on page 72.

Shimano was first to mass-produce splined freehubs and cassettes, in a then-impressive 7-speed range. The smallest cog threaded down atop this original Uniglide cassette to hold it in place. Yet the successive cogs' orientation to each other becomes important for fluent shifting, as it turned out, and the original approach effectively randomized this detail—up top, anyway. The design became popular regardless—the axles fared far better than they had with freewheels.

Suntour followed with their own freehub about a decade later, using a noncompatible format, but they went under a few years after that—your odds of finding replacement cassettes for their hubs are slim, in other words. This was arguably too bad; some of their parts were made quite well. Surviving Suntour freehubs might be set up as single speeds across one of their surviving cogs, as described on pages 212–14, but realistically that's about it.

Shimano set a new standard with their 7-speed Hyperglide (HG) freehub, which enlists a distinct lockring: the top cassette cogs' teeth could now be better aligned, to better facilitate smoother shifting. We see this clearly when looking down at the splines around our Hyperglide freehub bodies: one spline will be narrower than the others, in alignment with matching features within the cassettes, ensuring that each cog lines up as intended.

We must also discuss **freehub compatibility**. SRAM freehubs and cassettes, for a time, marched in faithful alignment with Shimano's standards. While the two companies' derailleurs and shift levers are not cross-compatible, as discussed on page 150, many of their respective cassettes and freehubs were designed to work well together. Cracks began to appear with the advent of 10-speed, however, before becoming full-on neuroses at the 11-speed and 12-speed levels.

Shimano's 8/9/10-speed HG mountain freehub provides a useful point of departure here. The 7-speed HG freehub is a bit shorter, meaning that we'd need to add a 4.5 mm **cassette spacer** to accommodate a 7-speed cassette on the 8/9/10-speed freehub. Conversely, Shimano's 10-speed cassettes are actually *thinner* than 9-speed; we'll add a 1 mm spacer to make these work with an 8/9/10-speed HG freehub. Their 11-speed mountain cassette fits 8/9/10-speed HG perfectly, however. Mountain and road otherwise begin to grow apart at 11-speed, for Shimano.

**Freehub, freehub body, and freehub fixing bolt.**

The company's HG 11/12-speed road freehub will also accommodate 8-, 9-, and 10-speed Shimano cassettes, using a spacer or two, as well as their 11-speed mountain cassettes. In 2018 they introduced the 11/12-speed MicroSpline (MS) freehub body, which uses almost twice as many splines, both thinner and shorter; a design change that allows for lighter aluminum to be used in cassette construction. MS freehubs only align with Shimano MS or MS-compatible cassettes and hubs. Coming full circle, we arrive at the Hyperglide+ standard. In this context, the + sign signals a strong preference for 12-speed.

SRAM and Shimano freehubs and cassettes tend to be cross-compatible up through 10-speed, and sometimes 11-speed, give or take a spacer or two. Beyond this point, we find SRAM's XD 11/12-speed freehub, as well as their XDR road version, either of which will require distinct XD-compatible 11-speed or 12-speed cassettes.

As a rule, unless explicitly specified, we can always assume that Campagnolo parts—from cassettes to cables—will only work with other Campagnolo parts. Their Ultra-Drive freehub body works with Campagnolo cassettes ranging from 9-speed to 12-speed. Always pay close attention to the spacing whenever installing Campagnolo cassettes—spacer width can vary, going up the gear range, and they need their original pattern to make sense of the world.

Whatever their particular affiliations, and with the exception of the aforementioned Uniglide and Suntour pioneers, cassettes are installed and removed in the same way. The lockring threads into the freehub directly atop the cassette; any required spacers sit back by the spokes. Splines radiating out around a lockring's underside ratchet away against matching features found atop the cassette's final cog as their gap begins to close; we continue tightening until they can ratchet no farther. This should leave the cassette just loose enough to spin with the freehub. Any lateral sliding would indicate a problem with the spacing.

Beyond all the tedious internecine bickering outlined above, the sad truth is that some generic hub manufacturers don't hold to standards quite as tightly as we might like—a cassette ostensibly meant to fit a given hub just might *not*, in other words. If a cassette still has lateral play after its lockring has been fully tightened—or, conversely, if tightening the lockring makes the freehub spin more slowly—try inserting a 1 mm spacer or two behind the cassette. (The diameter here is the same as an ISO bottom bracket spacer, should you have any of those kicking around.)

Various manufacturers produce **cassette lockring tools** to fit the standard 12-spline Shimano/SRAM lockring; Park calls theirs the FR-5.2. In the likelihood that you're working on a Q/R hub, you'll want to use an extractor with a guide pin instead, such as Park's FR-5.2G. The torque required to install and remove cassette lockrings is far less

**Cassette extractor with guide pin for Q/R axles.**

than what we need to take freewheels off; extractors with guide pins spare us the tedium of enlisting the Q/R lever to hold our sandwiches together. Similar tools are available for use with thru axle hubs.

To install a cassette, set your lockring tool in the lockring and finger-tighten it until you hear a ratcheting sound. Grab a big adjustable wrench—the extractor socket in Park's SR-12.2 chain whip also works—and use it to continue tightening until the ratcheting stops.

Cassette removal requires both a **chain whip** and a large adjustable wrench, or the socket on a second chain whip's handle, to hold the extraction tool. We'll maximize our leverage by pushing down on both.

**Chain whip in action.**

Set up the chain whip at the two o'clock position, pushing clockwise, and your other tool (holding the extractor) at ten o'clock, pushing counterclockwise. Bear down on both at once; the cassette lockring should release easily enough.

It's all a bit much to carry in your road kit, of course, but both Pamir Engineering's Hyper Cracker and Stein Tool's Mini Cassette Lockring Driver are small tools that allow us to remove cassettes on the road, in either case using only the chain and the frame itself for leverage.

Spin the axle in your fingers: how does it feel? Those merely a bit loose might simply be adjusted, as described on page 77, but any grainy- or sandy-feeling bearings merit a proper **hub overhaul**. After removing the freewheel or cassette, you will discover what tools are needed to disassemble the hub: a 17 mm box wrench and 15 mm cone wrench out back, typically, with a 15 mm box and a 13 mm cone up front.

In each case, we'll establish one cone-and-locknut pairing as our control, making our adjustments on the other side. The cassette hubs make this determination for us by hiding the drive-side cones within their freehubs; the drive-side cone and locknut become our control. And unless we're replacing the cone, we can just leave them be. For freewheel hubs, use the side with the most axle spacers as your control—our final adjustments become easier when translated through a single washer rather than a whole stack of spacers.

Some **sealed-bearing hubs** are pretty obvious—we'll see the bearing cartridges, looking at them—but others are more circumspect. Regardless, we'll want to replace any bearings spinning less than smoothly. Sealed-bearing cartridges come in many different sizes, as delineated by the alphanumeric codes marked on their dust caps. Either your friendly local bike shop or a bearing distributor should be able to obtain a replacement, given the details.

Given the option, it's best to use a designated tool such as Park's SHX-1 Slide Hammer Bearing Extractor for removal. The home method enlists a hammer and small punch shot through the hub body to patiently tap-tap-tap on the bearing cartridge's underside, hitting all around the circle to gradually ease it out.

Prior to installation, smear in a thin film of grease around each cartridge's socket on the hub flanges. Various manufacturers produce hub bearing presses, and when possible it's always best to use one of those. You might assemble your own, alternately, using a longer solid axle, locknuts, and various washers. If none of that is happening, position the cartridge nice and level atop its cave, lay the flat face of your box wrench over it, and slowly tap-tap-tap until it's all the way in, evenly around the circumference.

Most bikes awheel in our world enlist **loose bearing hubs**. Use a small magnet to draw these out, then use a rag dampened with lightweight oil such as WD-40 to shine them up. Clean the bearing races and cones thoroughly, looking closely for any scars or pitting. Pitting is effectively contagious, for cones and bearings alike: replace everything as a set, on either side. "We also use the pitted ones for educational purposes, to show as a representation of what pitting looks like," says Danni Limonez of Chicago's Bikes N' Roses.

So can you reuse hub bearings if they're looking pristine after cleanup? Among respondents who answered this question, twenty-nine (90 percent) said yes, while only three said no.

Most metal dust caps may be removed by using our 3 mm flat tip screwdrivers as levers, but take care when doing so—bent dust caps are not easily straightened. Press them back in place with the face of a box wrench.

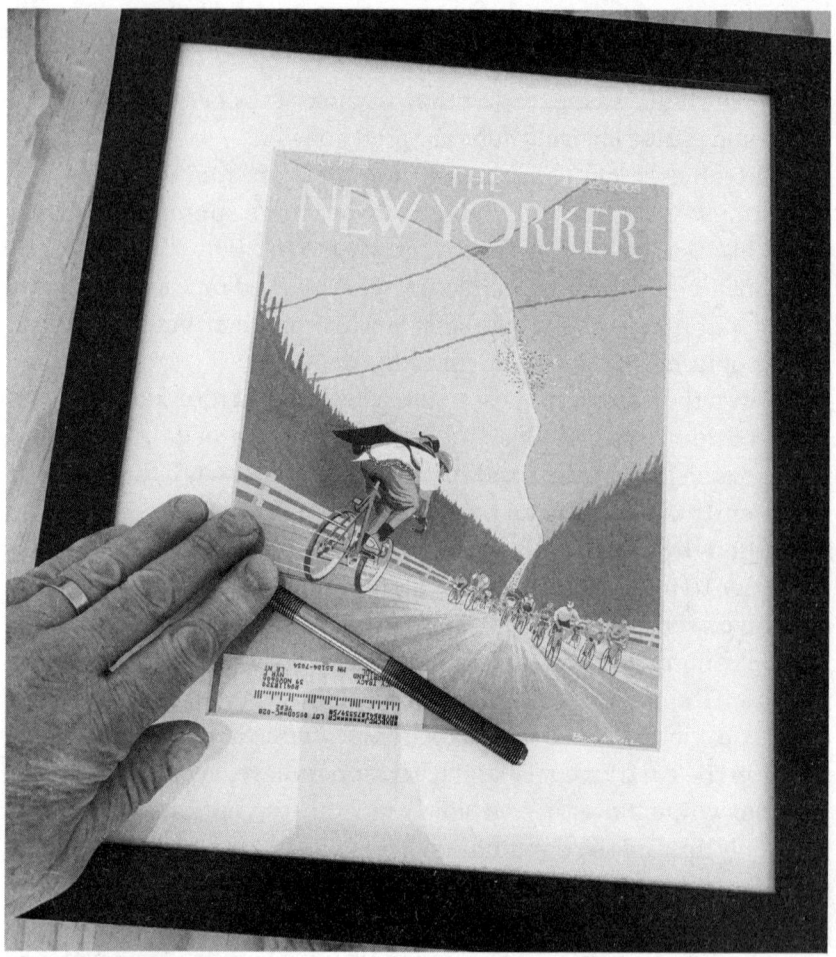

**Rolling an axle on glass.**

Is the axle bent? Possibly: it'd bind on one spot when spun, rendering the hub's adjustment on-again, off-again. Confirm by removing all the axle's fittings and rolling its naked length on a glass pane. **Bent axles** become obvious in this context, and these should be replaced with an appropriately threaded solid or Q/R axle as needed.

Are you **replacing a freehub**? This would be the time to do it, with the hub disassembled. Shimano holds its freehubs in place by means of a hollow bolt, through which the axle passes: peering within, you'll see fittings that will accept your 10 mm Allen key. Turn counterclockwise to loosen. When installing the replacement freehub, be sure to get the fixing bolt nice and tight.

**Spin the axle with a rag to help the bearings settle into the grease.**

Once the cones, bearings, and bearing races are clean, grab your grease gun and shoot a nice fat donut into each bearing race, about as wide as the bearings themselves. Plop the bearings right in, one by one. The grease will hold them while you're putting the hub back together.

Once all the bearings are in, slide the axle back in place. Using the tightened cone-and-locknut set as a point of reference, finger-tighten the opposite cone and locknut atop its bearings. Use a rag to spin the axle a bit, to help the bearings settle into place—even a buildup of grease can throw off the adjustment.

We'll begin our hub adjustment with the cone slightly overtightened. Back it off toward our ideal—neither loose nor binding. Working

**Using leverage to finalize a hub adjustment.**

in decreasing increments, you'll be countertightening the cone and locknut against each other to finalize the adjustment. Keep an eye on the axle end to determine whether the cone or locknut is turning.

Our hub adjustments are always easier with a vise and an **axle vise,** an inexpensive but quite useful tool any bike shop should have. The correct hub adjustment may take a couple tries, but it gets easier with practice. Hub adjustments are key—spending a couple extra minutes to get this right will be worth your time. We'll typically finish with very small measures. The cone and locknut should become tight indeed: you'll get the best leverage by positioning your wrenches such that you're squeezing them together.

You may find yourself tempted to enlist the opposite locknut to get the adjustment just right—bearing down on both locknuts simultaneously, to tighten the adjustment—but doing so risks bending the axle, especially when done in larger measures.

The final bearing adjustment requires precision. The axle should not bind when spun; once installed, we also shouldn't be able to move the rim laterally. The best adjustment, however, varies by just a hair within this narrow spectrum. The Q/R lever's cam mechanism compresses the axle assembly, so thusly equipped hubs should be adjusted just *slightly* looser. Conversely, and for the opposite reason, solid axles should be adjusted just *slightly* tight. A fine distinction, but one that gets easier with practice.

## IX
# SADDLES AND SEATPOSTS

Bike seats, also known as **saddles**, invite controversy. It just depends what you're looking for. Many find the broader and softer versions more comfortable; others prefer the firmer and thinner saddles, which allow for a more efficient transfer of power. Leather saddles last longer, for better or worse. Synthetic saddle covers rip more easily—this is why some wrap their rear corners in Teflon. And, as I learnt with the Peace Corps in Mauritania, prolonged exposure to sunlight tears great cracks through the synthetic covers.

Modern saddles are built around pairs of parallel hollow metal tubes we call the **saddle rails**. With only a few exceptions—ancient flat-railed saddles, the odd mono-railed BMX saddle—the rails are wonderfully cross-compatible. The seat from one bike will almost always fit on the next one, in other words. The rails' diameter is usually 7 mm, or perhaps 8 or 9 mm—a range the average seatpost will have no trouble accommodating.

When installing or removing seats, we will use the **seatpost hardware**. As a rule, all metal seatpost hardware should be greased: dab a pea's worth on the threads, and smear a bit more under the bolt head(s) as well. You might need to take things apart for this to happen.

The original **seat clamp** fits atop a **straight seatpost**: a chrome-plated steel tube, the top of which narrows slightly to accept the clamp. A threaded rod runs across the top; nuts at either end loosen or tighten the mechanism. These will answer to a 14 mm box wrench, typically. Pairs of contoured washers on either side accommodate the seat rails and also provide for two sets of facing radial splines, which allow us to ensure the seat is installed at the appropriate angle. The clamp should sit behind the post when mounted.

**Laprade seatpost.**

Get the hardware nice and tight. Loose seat clamp nuts allow the splines to grate against each other, which erases and effectively wrecks them.

The **Laprade posts** are more common, for decades now. These will be aluminum, or perhaps carbon or titanium. Laprade posts render the splined adjustment horizontal, which helps a lot. It's also much simpler. We'll look for a pair of contoured plates atop the post, held in place by an elongated nut. A single bolt pierces this sandwich; it'll answer to your 6 mm Allen key. The Laprades hold up far better, but their splines will erase themselves as well if ridden loose.

**Micro-adjust seatposts** are similar to Laprade posts, but they add a second bolt—our adjustment seesaws between the two, basically.

**Suspension seatposts**, like most other components, come to us at a range of different quality levels. The cheaper versions may feature a broad splined nut across their midsections, which can be hand-tightened if the suspension mechanism loosens—a chronic problem across many first-generation suspension posts. The early shock-post manufacturers further economized by limiting the sizing runs to a few general sizes, such as the ubiquitous 27.2 mm. When sold with cheaper stock bikes, suspension posts often arrived with aluminum adapters we call **seatpost shims**, which allowed for their deployment within wider seat tubes. The shims bear fat lips up top, lest our seat tubes swallow them whole. And when the measurements line up, they can be used with regular rigid seatposts as well.

**Seatpost sizes** currently in use range in size from 22.2 to 38.6 mm, *mostly* in even 0.2 mm increments. It's not quite as complicated as that, fortunately—nearly all bikes awheel today will anticipate seatposts with 25.4, 25.8, 26.2, 26.4, 26.8, 27.0, 27.2, 31.8, or 34.9 mm diameters. It's even more so with the newest bikes; sizes below 25.4 are nearly extinct already. The size will be etched on the front, just above the seatpost's **maximum height line**, an important notice we ignore at our own peril—the seatpost must be installed to a certain depth within the frame's seat tube in order to maintain its structural integrity. Longer posts are often available for some of the common sizes, such as 27.2 mm, but when possible a larger bike would probably be the better move.

We adjust the seatpost height through a Q/R lever or binder bolt at the top of the seat tube. Older bikes accommodate this bolt directly; most newer ones send it through a removable **seatpost collar** instead. The bolt or Q/R lever usually sits directly behind the seatpost, straddling a gap at the top of the seat tube; occasionally it'll be up front. Wherever it is, the seatpost collar's bolt or Q/R should sit directly over the gap in the seat tube.

It is equally important that the gap's edges, which we call the seat tube ears, are precisely parallel: any angling-in toward the top would point to a seatpost a size too small, which could bear very negative consequences for aluminum or carbon fiber frames in particular; neither material possesses the flexibility to safely accommodate discrepancies in this regard.

Here again, steel is more resilient. Bent-in seat tube ears in steel frames can often be straightened, given patience and a large flathead screwdriver. Pull the post out and use the tip to gradually widen out the gap as needed, being careful not to flare out the ears. Vise-Grip

SADDLES AND SEATPOSTS

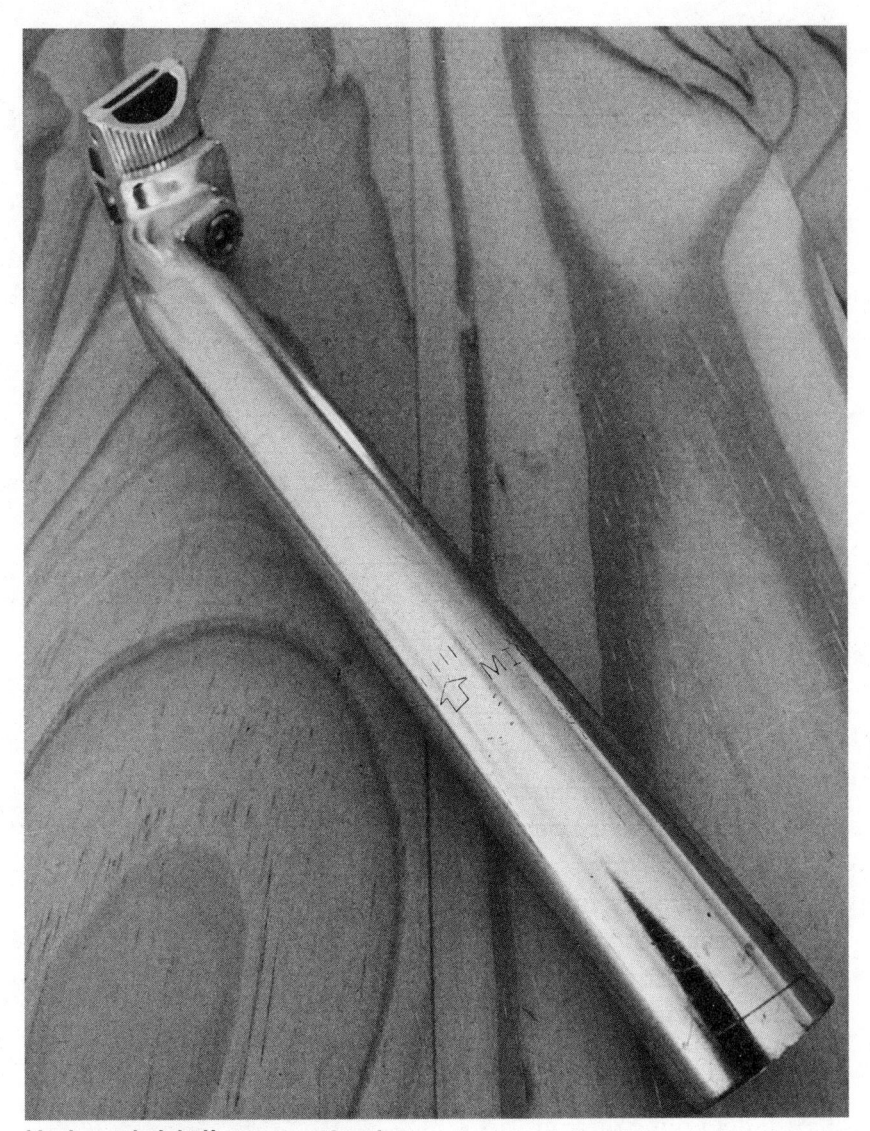

**Maximum height line on a seatpost.**

pliers are useful for returning flared ears to the rounded profile we like, but they won't do much for your paint. And as mentioned above, so long as we respect the max height lines, seatpost shims can help us accommodate narrower seatposts in wider seat tubes as needed.

Assuming a frame has the correct post—not overly loose, and with the seat tube ears perfectly parallel—the best way to confirm seatpost size is to copy it from the original. Lacking such, the **seatpost**

**Install your saddle at a comfortable midpoint along the rails.**

**sizing gauges** are fairly ubiquitous now; your friendly local bike shop should definitely have a set. These are just stepped metal pipes with the sizes etched in a row down the front—slide it into the frame, see where it stops.

The **seatpost fit** should be snug: we can move it up and down by hand, but the post should not slide down into the frame on its own. The accumulation of rust can tighten this equation over time, but this rust can also be safely removed in various ways. At the furthest extremes, we encounter seized seatposts—those allowed to rust in place, basically. An ignoble fate we'll explore further in the chapter on rust, beginning on page 231.

Seats and their posts are sometimes stolen, owing to their Q/R levers. Regular seat bolts are better in this respect, the locking versions especially. Seat leashes are also good—we can even make our own by using a brake cable, a P-clamp, and some other basic hardware.

There's only one more detail to mention with regard to **installing seatposts**... and if you thought "grease," you guessed correctly! Use a length of old cable housing or similar to smear a blueberry's worth of grease all around the interior of the seat tube. Also slide the post up and down and all around to help ensure said grease gets everywhere. We do this precisely to prevent seized seatposts, and where applied it works quite well. (Use carbon paste or similar, rather than grease, for carbon frames or posts.)

In terms of the final **seat position**, saddle manufacturers design their wares to be level. The seat rails' length provides for some additional rider discretion. It is safest to keep to the middle of the range here. Farther-reaching fit adjustments might be better pursued through changes to the stem or handlebars, as discussed in previous chapters. **Crank forward** frames may also bear consideration—the design pitches the pedaling axis forward of the seat, leaving the rider with a flat-footed purchase in the ground when seated; the handlebars reach up and back in compensation. **Recumbents** bring this tendency to its logical conclusion, seating the rider in something like a flying lawn chair. The pedals move up by the front wheel, either close to the ground for easier transitions or raised to various elevations to provide for greater pedaling torque.

# X
# CONTROL CABLES

The tiny fraction of high-end bikes with electronic shifting systems is growing incrementally, at the time of writing, just as hydraulic brakes allow a handful of downhill racers and trials riders to stop faster than anyone else could possibly need to, but all the other bikes continue to rely on steel control cables for braking and gear reduction. The cables associated with old 3-speeds are of a fixed length, but more generally we have three distinct possibilities: **road brake cables**, **mountain brake cables**, and shifter or **derailleur cables**. Their original lengths are denoted in millimeters, typically—road brake cables are 1700 mm; mountain brake cables are 1800 mm; derailleur cables are 2100 mm. Tandem brake and derailleur cables are also available, measuring 3500 mm and 3000 or 3100 mm, respectively.

"Universal" brake cables feature a road brake head at one end and a mountain head at the other; you chop off the one you don't need. For this—or any other bike-related cable cutting—you'll need a set of **cable cutters**. These are not exotic, or even expensive, just specific. **Cable housing cutters** are more useful, in that their jaws are wide enough to cut cable housing as well.

While derailleur cables are 1.2 mm wide, brake cables of either sort are 1.5 mm wide—a discrepancy easily spotted by eye. But what really set them apart, as the picture on the next page illustrates, are the cable heads. Campagnolo derailleur cables are 1.1 mm wide, which is fine, but their cable heads are also just a hair narrower, and this renders their shift levers *incompatible* with our standard derailleur cables. A regular cable head still zips right into place, as I learnt exactly once, but then it'll get stuck there, until you drill it out at least. Have fun with that!

Campagnolo cables are identified by a small *C* etched into the cable head. Generic versions are available, with the same marking. We

CONTROL CABLES

**Top to bottom: Road brake, mountain brake, and derailleur cables.**

can always check to confirm—poke the cable head in *backward*, just to make sure it slides right back out.

We replace cables when they become frayed or excessively rusty; we may also need to do so if handlebar or other component changes render the originals too short. Otherwise we'll only draw them out every few years for lubrication, when undertaking overhauls for example. (These should come more somewhat frequently, of course, if you're regularly riding in the elements.)

Cable removal abides by the same pattern, in each case. You'll probably spot either a **cable ferrule** or a tangle of frayed cable wire at the very tip of the cable's tail—we'll need to snip this off with the cable cutters before loosening the binder bolt on the component and pulling the cable back out through its cable housing.

We make an exception for uncut cables: those that lack a ferrule, but somehow are not frayed either. Closer inspection will reveal a tiny dot of welding, sharpened to something like a point to better navigate through the housing. These are worth preserving as is, whenever feasible.

The particulars vary, but the different components' binder bolts are typically released with a 5 mm Allen wrench or a 9 mm socket. Each one pins a distinctly contoured washer to a particular point on the component. Looking within, you should see a telling cable-sized groove across the washer's inner side, and perhaps a matching feature on the component as well. Such washers are specific to their components—there's no standard version—and the little grooves do wonders for our cables' longevity. After making any necessary adjustments, make sure the cable falls in line between the grooves as you tighten the bolt. Crushing a wound-steel bike cable between two flat pieces of metal will fray it, past a certain point.

We'll always look for two things when **installing cables**: a recess just big enough to accommodate the appropriate cable's head in the control lever, and a tiny cable-sized hole extending beyond this. Most modern control levers hide their cable heads, with varying degrees of sophistication. But we can find them.

With the exception of Gore's specially coated Ride-On cables and similar products—identified by the paint-like coating all along their lengths—we'll always want to oil a cable when installing it. The slender plastic straw extending from our classic black plastic Tri-Flow oil dropper bottles is just the right size for this: poke it right into the housing and squeeze, just a bit. Rock "N" Roll's Cablemagic probably holds up better over the long run—it's thicker, so we'll just squeeze a bit onto the cables directly before installing them.

Cable installation is simplest with mountain brake cables, which typically provide direct cable access on their undersides: we'll see a perfect mountain-cable-head-sized cavity, with an alley for the cable leading suggestively away toward a knurled knob we call the barrel

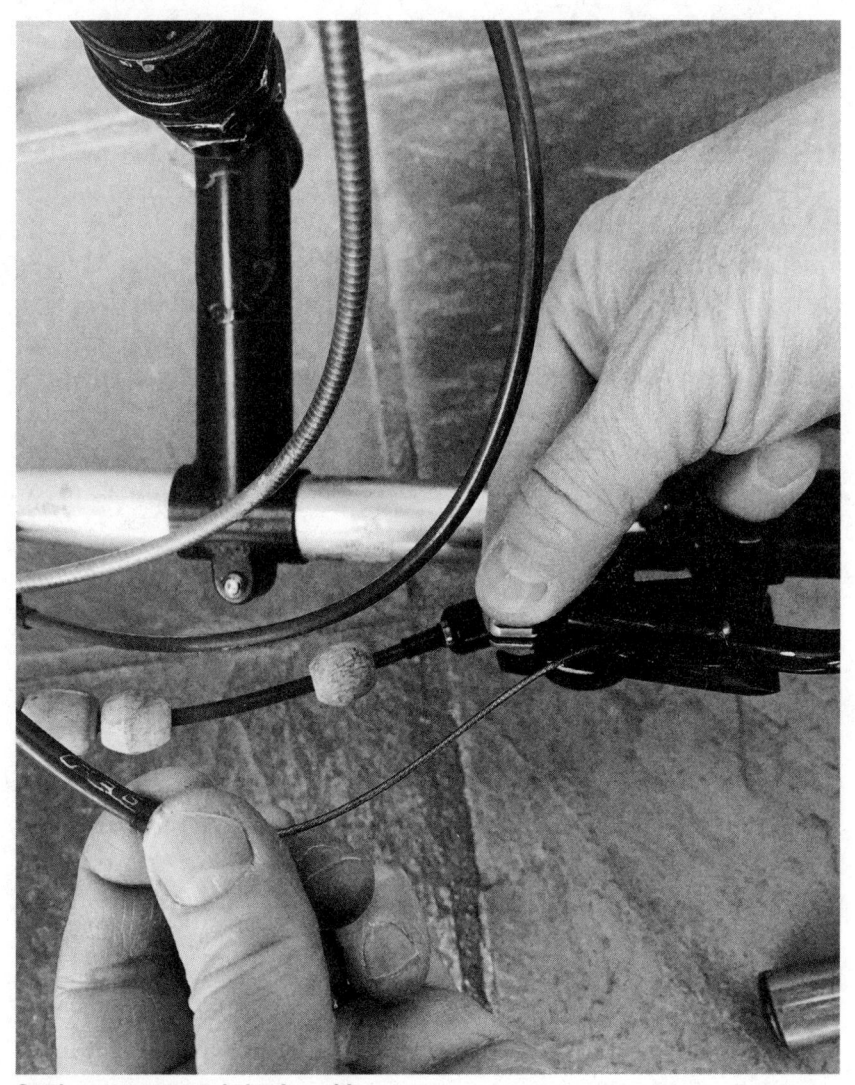

**Setting up a mountain brake cable.**

adjuster. The barrel in turn will bear a knurled collar of its own: both feature alleyways for the cable at some point in their circumferences. We dial these into alignment like a combination lock, allowing the cable to pass through. We'll return to the barrels shortly, when discussing cable adjustments.

Road brake levers are often nearly as simple, but their design has typically precluded the use of cable alleys or barrel adjusters—on the levers themselves, anyway. (We'll find barrel adjusters at points farther back along their cables' lengths.) Squeeze the brake and look inside the lever: the cable head's recess will be mounted on a short pivoting bar, only one side of which will be wide enough to fully accommodate it. Some levers slice an alley for the cable's installation into this pivoting bar; others require us to thread the cable through and directly into the cable housing. This last will sprout directly from the lever's peak, among the older **nonaero brake levers**, which to my awareness have not been mass-produced since the 1980s. Road bikes built in the years since typically bear **aero brake levers**, with which the cable housing sneaks in under the handlebar grip tape at the stem, emerging only to meet a corresponding hollow in the aero lever's base. (In addition to peeling back any handlebar grip tape, we'd also need to remove the aero lever itself in order to examine this transaction in detail; see more on page 94 ahead.)

When removing brake cables from Shimano dual control levers, it bears mentioning that brake cable installation on older models may require an extra caution. The company's original design parked the cable head within a pivoting bar that falls right out, absent the cable. Worse, said bar was fit with a total of four super-tiny plastic washers, two to a side, each of which loves nothing more than "accidentally" falling out and disappearing forever beneath the workbench.

I suppose replacements might be 3D-printed, given the access and schematics, but otherwise you're kind of screwed. So let's avoid this, shall we? *Whenever pulling a brake cable from an older Shimano STI lever, be sure to hold the pivoting bar carefully in place while doing so.* Push the cable forward from below to get it started, such that the head pops out of its recess—you might need a small pick or screwdriver to draw the cable head out—and then hold a finger atop the pivot assembly until the cable is fully removed.

Our control cables travel through **cable housing**. The original housing was simply long, flexible coils of stainless wire—we could run an oil dropper along the exterior for lubrication. Newer 5 mm **brake housing** is built around coils of flattened galvanized wire, which rusts, wrapped inside and out with plastic. More rigid, but also more waterproof. Eventually, it was noticed that these lengths of coiled housing compressed under tension, in measures large enough to throw off the careful calculus of the then-emerging indexed shifting systems. Thus do we have the compression-less derailleur or **shifter housing**, which followed a similar format, but with the wires arranged in a linear pattern. The original shifter housing was also 5 mm wide, but the thinner derailleur cables' responsibilities are less strenuous, so we also see 4 mm shifter housing.

The brake and shifter housing are *not* cross-compatible. While using brake housing might simply confuse our most particular indexed shifting systems—anything above 9-speed, really—a sudden panic-yank on the brake lever could cause the linear-wrapped shifter housing to splinter.

We'll sometimes be able to spot the 5 mm brake housing away from 5 mm shifter housing: the coil's profile may be visible beneath the ubiquitous plastic blanket. The brake housing is also more flexible; the linear-wrapped shifter housing is more rigid. If nothing else, pull off a housing cap and look inside.

We see Campagnolo's signature idiosyncrasy anew with their brake cable housing, which—in coordination with their marginally thinner brake cables—is just *slightly* narrower than the standard. If your Campagnolo brakes suddenly feel sluggish in their new housing, in other words, you probably need to redo everything with Campagnolo housing.

We'll always want to ensure that cable housing wears a **cable housing cap** anytime it ends—at barrel adjusters, cable housing stops, or in the components themselves. Both 4 mm and 5 mm housing caps can be had. Don't crimp these in place; the cable's tension should hold them still just fine on its own.

The **cable housing stops** guide the cables and housing in their journeys along the frame; only the cable itself gets all the way through. **Cable guides** are also common: these are smaller loops, just wide enough for the cable itself. Most multispeed bike have a pair of these directly under the bottom bracket, for the derailleur cables. Cooler still are **cable housing guides**, which are wide enough to accept the housing itself—a function that allows for **full-length cable housing**, from control lever straight down to component. Both grit and precipitation can work their way into the housing via the cable housing stops—witness rusty cables—and only the full-length housing fully responds to this perennial phenomenon.

The cable housing is almost always too long on the smaller frame sizes of new bikes. Manufacturers necessarily default to the lengths

**Cable housing just long enough.**

required for the largest frame runs; few shops find it cost-effective to correct this oversight. Overlong housing is always getting in trouble, snagging on branches or railing posts—bad things can happen if we rush and yank it free.

The **cable housing length** should be just long enough. We're talking about the segment between a control lever and the first cable housing stop it encounters on the frame, mostly—this should *only* be long enough to avoid binding at any point in the handlebar's rotation.

Think "just slack enough." (The balance of a bike's cable housing segments—those stretching between cable housing stops, or from cable housing stops to the components—are more static in their measurements. These lengths also change less between different frame sizes.)

We'll use this same formula to determine if a bike's full-length housing is too long. In such cases, we'd pull the cable out and trim any excess from the housing segment tail end. We can also expect a bike's cable housing length to change when switching to handlebars or stems of different dimensions—upgrading to high-rise bars, for example, will require longer cables and housing throughout. Whenever replacing bars, stem, or control levers, set everything up as you'd like it to be before finalizing the housing length.

If you're traveling internationally, it also bears mentioning that the control levers and their cables are positioned differently in different places. The front brake is expected to be on the right in the 54 Commonwealth countries, which is mostly the UK and its former colonies—places where people drive on the left, basically. And we look for the front brake on the left elsewhere.

The particular **cable routing** used might merit further discussion when setting up a new-to-you bike or handlebar. Specifically, it's worth it to set things up such that we avoid extra bends in the housing—features that gravity inevitably bends downward, where they attract water and eventually rust. The default cable routing sees the two derailleur cables routed back to the first cable housing stops on their respective sides of the frame: right to right, left to left. This may look organized, or predictable at least, but it actually adds length and a redundant bend to those first housing segments. If we cross the derailleur cables in front of the head tube instead—right to left, left to right—the housing length can shrink a bit, with no worries of rusty valleys further down the line.

The crossed cables will then recross in an X beneath the down tube—or across the top tube, depending—rushing to meet the next sets of cable guides or housing stops. Everything returns to normal from there, with each cable proceeding as originally intended. The X looks nice and odd, but it makes not the slightest difference in terms of cable performance. (Note that we can only do this where cables will not drag across any frame tubes when crossing—those few early

**X marks more ideal cable routing.**

mountain bikes with laterally mounted cable housing stops are necessarily excluded.)

Switching out for a high-rise stem or wider handlebars often means updating our cable housing length as well, and here it bears mentioning that disparate lengths of housing can be linked together, in the event you're just working with scraps. The double-ended connecting or "junction" housing caps allow us to join segments of 5 mm brake cable housing in sequence, as do Jagwire's EZ-Bend housing segments. We can even make our own versions, using either flexible or rigid V-brake noodles, should you have access to any surplus of those. Pull the nosepiece off one with your pliers and replace it with the housing cap from another noodle.

The increasingly strident demands shot forth by our modern indexed shifting systems preclude such remedies for shifter housing, sadly. Speaking of which, in time you may also notice another tendency specific to shifter housing: the inner wires' length may appear to grow, suggesting haircuts. Removing the housing caps, it's common to discover that the wire suddenly extends an eighth-inch beyond its plastic sheathing. But this only means the wires' long, gradual coils have settled in and straightened out just a bit; no big deal. Trim the housing down just another eighth-inch below the original cut, set it up again, and off you go.

Following on any measurements you've made—and after removing the cable itself, of course—**cutting cable housing** becomes a three-step process. We'll first give our cable housing a nice and even 90-degree chop with our cable housing cutters. This action tends to flatten the shifter housing where it is cut, you'll notice: rotate the housing 90 degrees, put it back in the cutters' jaws, and give a gentle squeeze to round things out. Cutting also flattens out the plastic inner liner, so we'll need to stab this back open with a **pick**. These are easy to find—years ago I somehow managed to connect with a Snap-on version, actually—but it's also easy to make your own by sharpening a spoke to a point via a grinder wheel. Adding a couple 90-degree bends to your new poker's tail makes it easier to use.

Klein was among the first bike manufacturers to introduce **internally routed cables**. The trend has resurfaced again more recently, across broader numbers of road bikes—looks nice and svelte, marginally more aerodynamic. The challenge, as one might expect, comes with cable replacement: after plunging into a frame tube, the blind cable won't easily find its way back out.

Manufacturers plan for this eventuality, inserting a thin sleeve known as cable liner or cable sheathing between a pair of cable-sized holes in the frame. Lacking such—or if this lining is detached at one end—it is not a good idea to remove the cable. Cut off the ferrule or frays at the cable's end instead, slide off any cable housing behind the cable's exit hole from the frame, and slide a new segment of cable liner up from the back end. Circumstances will vary, but it's possible you may also need to chop off the cable's head as well, as a means to move around the front cable housing and install a new sleeve from that direction. Bottom line is that before replacing anything, we'll always want to see either a cable or some kind of cable sleeve extending fully through one frame hole and out the other.

If that's not happening, look inside the frame to check if the tube's tail end is internally sealed at the seat tube: inserting a new cable from the front end, it may be possible for you to use a flashlight and your finger or a screwdriver to guide the cable's tail to its exit hole inside the tube. Bend and twirl; scope it out; do it again. This may take some time. Alternately? It's easy enough to use tape, hose clamps, or zip ties to secure full-length housing to the frame's exterior—which, in terms of cable performance, repairability, and theft deterrence, would arguably provide for the better option.

Returning briefly to the aero road brake levers, note that you'll want to remove them from the handlebars prior to replacing any cable housing routed beneath the grip tape—specifically, we need to make sure the housing ends up flush with the lever's base. A pair of **aero brake lever cable housing issues** also bears mentioning here. Firstly, the cable housing socket at the rear of some aero brake levers may be too narrow to accept a standard 5 mm cable housing cap. Or—worse—maybe it's just wide enough to let one get stuck in there forever, where it might ultimately end the lever's useful service life if ever it gets bent. Test for this first, preferably with the lever removed from the handlebar: will a housing cap slide easily into place and back out again, or does it run into resistance farther back?

Our second issue relates to certain older Dia-Compe aero levers, which will anticipate distinct DC cable housing caps—shorter, thicker, and with correspondingly round faces. These sorts of levers feature brake cable holes that are somewhat wider than the cables themselves, with the idea that the charming round-faced DC housing caps would be able to settle in at the best possible angles. With these, we'll *always* want to use a cable housing cap of some kind. Lacking such, using the brake gradually drags the cable housing forward into the lever's base: while the housing's internal steel coil will creep forward around the cable, its plastic sheathing will bunch up back outside the brake lever. The braking will start to feel all weird and spongy.

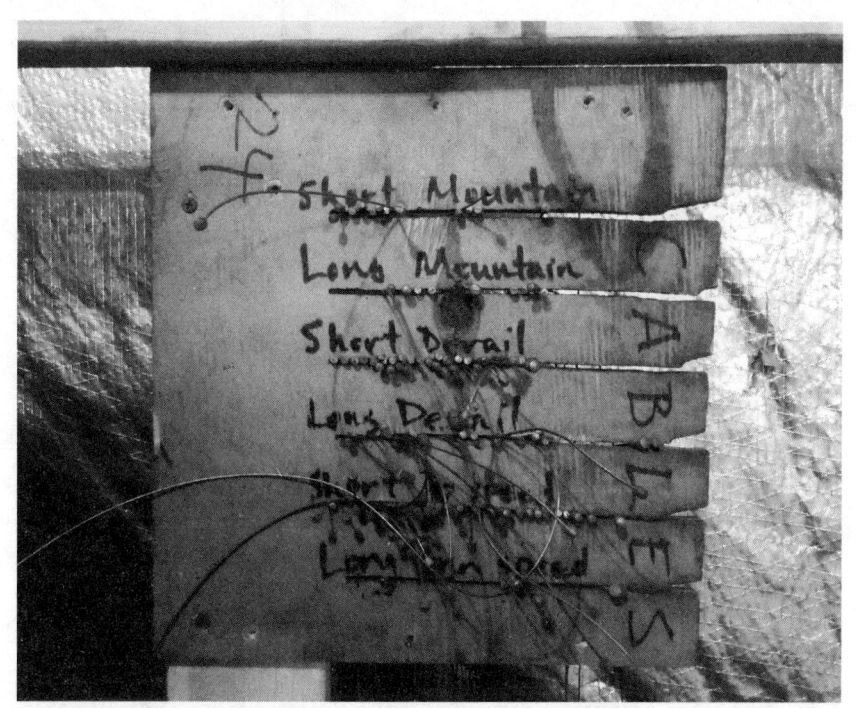

**DIY cable organizing system at Wheels for Winners in Madison, Wisconsin.**

Old rear brake and derailleur cables are typically still long enough for reuse up front. What about **reusing cables**, though? Depends who you ask. Among survey respondents who answered the question, twenty-five (78 percent) regularly reuse cables in good condition, while seven do not. The breakdown was similar for reusing used cable housing—twenty-one respondents (65 percent) regularly do so, while nine do not. Nicole Muratore of Bike Saviours Bicycle Collective provides a useful method here: "Cables are reused if they are at least 2 feet in length with no rust or corrosion. Housing is reused if it is at least 1 foot in length with no kinks or signs of rust."

"Often I can make a housing work better just by snipping off a bent or damaged bit at the end, recapping, and putting the inner back in," notes Jeremy White of Community Cruisers in Canmore, Alberta. "At one point," notes another community bike shop mechanic, "we had a volunteer super-glue the ends of the cables to help them from unraveling as one puts them back through the housing." Some community bike shops make used cables available to the public as well. "There is a wooden rack with slots for used cables utilized by people who do not want to buy new cables," explains Greg Garneau of the Durham Bicycle Cooperative in Durham, North Carolina.

Cables troubled by grit or corrosion can often be rescued with a bit of lightweight oil. Drip some on a rag; squeeze the cable through a few times. Frayed cables must be trimmed down nice and neat before reuse. You'll also want to make sure a reused cable doesn't have any sharp bends, especially as it passes through the housing—iron these out with a box pliers first. Nor should any of the short segments flattened by binder bolts end up inside any cable housing; there'd be too much friction.

Reused cables can fray when reinstalling, lacking the nice pointy soldered ends new cables have. We prevent this from happening by twisting them continuously as we edge them into the cable housing. Don't let up! And if the cable must pass through any sharper bends within components, ramp this up to the extreme—the cable spins easily across the fingertips, but it also happens that you're gradually nudging it forward as well.

Our cables must be set up correctly in order for the components they control to perform as intended. We'll first ensure that all cable housing segments are seated correctly where they meet control levers, cable housing stops, and components. But this is easy—we just yank on them, basically. For brake cables, release the brake's binder bolt and set up your fourth hand tool just beyond that point, giving the tool a few good squeezes. (This method also works for shifter cables traveling through full-length cable housing.)

Shifter housing is even easier to seat—we don't even need tools. This works equally for traditional derailleur and 1× ("one-by") setups, on regular steel bikes anyway; don't even try this with carbon fiber frames. Your wheels will need to spin, however, so the bike should be in a stand or upside down. Return any shift levers to their slackest positions—on the smallest cog in back and the smallest chainring up front, typically. (This trick works in reverse with Shimano's Rapid Rise rear derailleurs, described beginning on page 155, which reverse this polarity out back.) Start the pedals turning, letting the chain fall into its resting position, then grab the shifter cable(s) at a midpoint along the frame tube and yank: the derailleur(s) should carry the chain right up the gear range(s) as you turn the pedals, seating the respective length of shifter housing firmly in place.

CONTROL CABLES

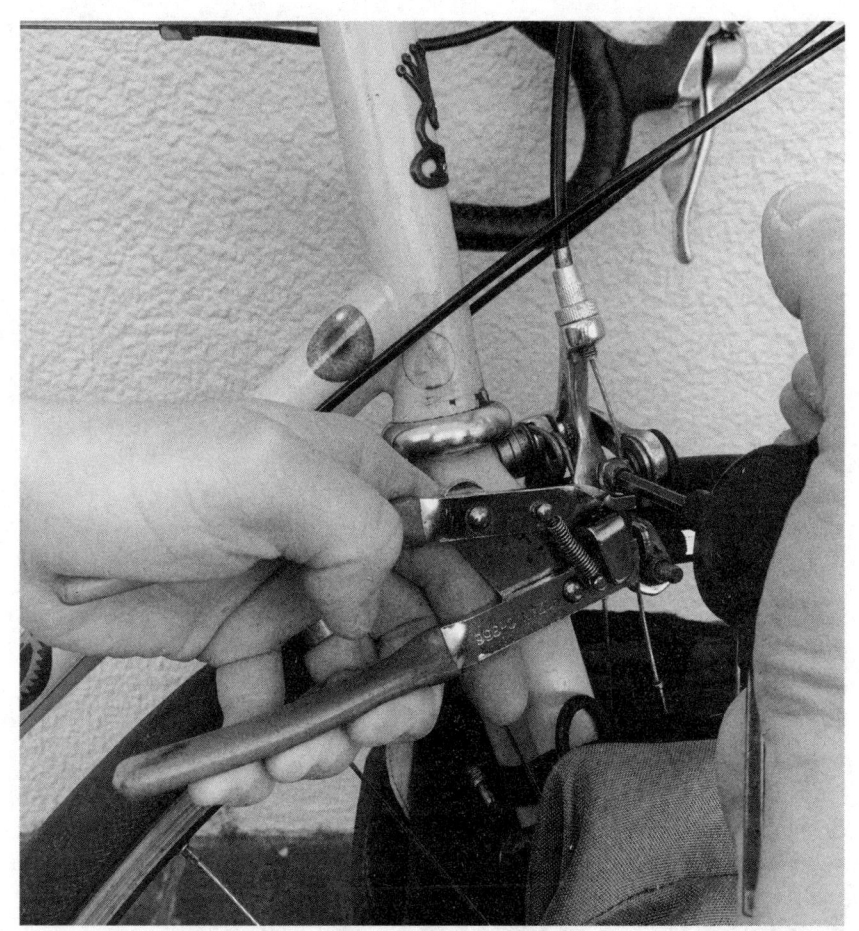

**Using a fourth hand tool to seat brake cable housing.**

This technique serves two additional purposes as well. Brand new cables inevitably stretch out lengthwise just a bit; yanking on the cables helps frontload this process. It also tests the accuracy of your derailleurs' limit screws: should the chain jump off either the largest cog or the largest chainring when you're doing this, see what's noted about limit screws (pages 149 and 143, for front and rear respectively) before proceeding.

Despite their opposing purposes, we'll find many commonalities among the brake and shifter cables in terms of making **cable adjustments**. Each cable must be installed and routed correctly, lubricated sufficiently, and adjusted to a correct tension for our bikes to perform at their best. The cable head should be fully seated in its control lever;

**Seating shifter housing, even as we stretch the shifter cables.**

the housing should be just long enough; the cable should be carefully routed through its binder bolt's cable guides.

Prior to tightening our cables' binder bolts, we should always check in on their **barrel adjusters**. These are effectively threaded cable housing stops; we'll find them at least once along the run of any remotely modern bike control cable. Dialing the barrels in reduces the housing's overall length, effectively reducing cable tension, and the reverse is also true. Barrel adjusters allow for quicker and more gradual adjustments than what we'd be able to get with our wrenches on the binder bolts, and in so doing they also save the cables some wear and tear.

**Down tube barrel adjusters.**

When installing a cable, thread all the barrel adjusters it encounters almost all the way into their fittings on the control levers, frame, or components before tightening the binder bolt. (We'll probably enlist a fourth hand tool as well when tightening the brake cables, as described in the chapter following.) Cables do stretch, but only rarely do they end up overtightened, so beginning with the barrel adjusters dialed at least most of the way in provides for the most useful range of adjustments. Thread the barrel all the way into its threads, then turn it back out a full turn or two.

We'll next route the cable down its alley beneath the **binder bolt** hardware, typically a pair of cable alleys, one on the component's body and the other on the inside of a contoured washer. (Binder bolts are also sometimes called **cable pinch bolts**.) Manufacturers' torque specifications actually vary a bit, in the event you do have a torque wrench, but in general terms we're hoping to tighten the cables just enough to prevent independent movement. We don't want to crush the cable flat, as this can lead to fraying. Finally, use your cable cutters or cable housing cutters to cut the cable a hand's width past the binder bolt, then use the elbow of some pliers to crimp a **cable ferrule** at the end.

**Installing a cable ferrule.**

The steps outlined above will apply almost universally, with the obvious exceptions of Sturmey-Archer's fixed-length 3-speed cables, Rohloff Speedhub cables, and so forth. The specific adjustments required for our various braking and drivetrain systems are detailed in their respective chapters.

# XI
# BRAKES

Our brakes should stop us quickly, effectively, and with minimal effort. They should also release from our rims as soon as we ask them to, and they should avoid complicating our wheels' release from their frames as well. Finally, it's generally reasonable to ask that the brakes work quietly.

Our bikes' various braking systems necessarily share many similar characteristics, parts, and performance issues, as we'll see, but each variant takes a distinct approach. We'll begin here by reviewing certain important traits many braking systems share in common, before moving on to consider each system in turn.

Brakes are activated by means of brake levers, most of which we pull by hand. (A coaster brake fixes its lever to the frame—we "pull" it by pushing backward on the pedals.) And while the materials used will vary, all brakes will feature both **brake pads** and **braking surfaces**: activating the lever presses the former into the latter. All our mechanical braking systems rely on **spring tension** to maintain the distances between the two. Most modern braking systems will additionally feature quick-release hardware of some kind, allowing us to remove the wheels without deflating the tires.

The roots of braking performance problems will most often trace back to a narrow set of commonly recurring issues—rusty cables, poor spring tension, and a lack of lubrication within the brake pivots can each cause them to feel less responsive. This chapter will discuss methods to isolate and resolve dilemmas such as these. That said, we should begin with some basic ground rules.

**Before working on hub or rim-mounted brakes**, first confirm that the wheel concerned is correctly centered and installed within its frame or fork. The tire's centerline should line up nice and straight with the fender hole above—your frame alignment or wheel dish may need correction if this picture is not resolving for you. This done, see if you can push the wheel's rim back and forth laterally against the seatstays or the fork blades. This would indicate a loose hub—review the treatment on hub adjustment, beginning on page 75, before proceeding. Once the hub is adjusted correctly, also confirm that the wheel is true, as described beginning on page 48.

**After working on hub or rim-mounted brakes**, spin the wheel and give the brake lever a few solid pumps. We're testing a few different things here—the brake lever should not be able to touch or bottom out on the handlebar, and all the cable and brake pad hardware should be tight enough to hold their respective adjustments. The brakes should also be correctly centered, and the pads should have no contact with the tires at any point in their rotation.

All our rim-mounted and disc brakes work best when both their pads and braking surfaces are clean and dry—a fact that affords sealed systems such as coaster or roller brakes advantages that may compensate for their lack of quick-release options. These same sealed systems, of course, may also be the quietest. **Squeaking brakes** do not in themselves indicate a performance problem, unless you're needing to sneak around or something. To the contrary, they might arguably be useful in alerting other road users to your approach.

Noisy brakes result from two essential conditions: either the brake pads or the braking surfaces are somehow contaminated or the brake was produced in such a way that it is less rigid and more vulnerable to minute vibrations, sometimes called brake chatter. Maladjustments might contribute to either. Grease and oil are the worst contaminants for rim-mounted or disc brakes—keep this in mind when oiling your chain—but even a coating of dust can make them squeak. The structural issues are more existential: some braking systems will be more likely to squeak simply by virtue of their design or the materials used in their construction. V-brakes will squeak more than dual pivot caliper road brakes, for example: while the former can work well, they're also long and wispy in comparison to the latter.

We address squeaky rim-mounted brakes by means of the same basic steps across each of our braking systems. First, clean up the rims: brush any mud off with a dry rag before cleaning up any finer residue with rubbing alcohol. This will also remove any oil on the rims, if present. Hitting the brake pads with any liquids would be counterproductive at this stage, so mind the fence. Lacking rubbing alcohol, you might use dish soap diluted in water. The same liquids are also effective for cleaning disc brake rotors, which—owing to the compounds used in their brake pads—are especially vulnerable to oil contamination. Best not to touch the rotors at all, especially after pizza.

We can take the same dry rag to the pads to remove any surface debris. Use a small screwdriver to dig out any dirt ground into the channels cutting across the brake pads' faces, if present. Next, grab a basic metal file—the fine-tooth semicircular side of a garden-variety four-way hand file, for example—and shave down any shiny buildup you may find streaked across the pads' faces. You can do this while they're still mounted in their brake arms, given enough light to work, but with practice it's often just as easy to remove the pads and clamp them face-up in a vise, which allows for a more thorough job. If you're lacking in vises, set your file on the bench and run the pads across it.

Brake pad wear is inevitable, especially in the elements. Riding through snowy winters, we can expect to replace our brake pads come springtime. With rim-mounted pads, it's crucial we do this before the erasure reaches the **maximum wear lines** etched into the pads' sides, lest their steel spines carve lethal canyons in our softer aluminum rims.

Our brake pads' faces tend to be slightly narrower than the rims they meet. As a rule, it's best to set them up with their bottom edges just a hair above the edge of the rim walls, leaving the most space above the pad—this reduces the chances your pads will rub against the tire, which would do no good at all. Techniques for installing and removing our various brake pads are described in the pages following.

**Cartridge brake pads** are an option for road calipers, V-brakes, and cantilever brakes, though you'll probably have a hunt ahead of you for the last. The cartridge carriers increase rigidity, reducing the potential for squeaking. The pads' mounting hardware stays put; you're simply removing the retaining hardware for the cartridge inserts. This will be either a small bolt or a pin we can pull out with pliers, which we'll also use to extract the old pads. Note that the orientation is important here: always set up cartridge brake pads such that we install and remove their inserts from the *rear*.

Dab a red ant's worth of grease on the hardware prior to installing brake pads—the threaded posts, with caliper, centerpull, or V-brakes,

**Maximum wear lines.**

or the threaded ends of the brake pad holders we find on most cantilevers. Both of these systems feature vertical windows allowing us to position the pads in alignment with the rim walls and at a sufficient remove from the tire.

    The brake pads' **toe-in** is the angle at which they encounter the rim. As a default, the pads' front ends should contact the rim just slightly before their tails: imagine a dime wedged out back under each side. The object here is to enlist the wheel's rotational force to reduce brake chatter, dragging the pads' faces forward as they connect. Alongside cleaning and filing the pads, correcting their toe-in is often a solution for noisy brakes. Not always the trick that does it, but something to try.

V-brakes, cantilevers, and modern road caliper brakes each provide distinct toe-in hardware for the brake pads. In each case, we'll be holding the pad in the correct position with one hand while tightening the hardware with the other. Another one of those things that becomes easier with practice. Jagwire's Brake Pad Tuner tools for setting toe-in may be helpful when getting started, for the V-brakes and calipers at least: install both pads loosely, fit these tools between the pads' faces and the rim, cinch down on the brake cable with your fourth hand tool to hold everything in place, and then tighten down the brake pad hardware.

Older road calipers and centerpull brakes did not provide any specific toe-in hardware. And if these are working well for you, there's not necessarily any reason to bother with the toe-in. We'd otherwise have a pair of options if the pads are squeaking or if the braking is less effective—we can substitute modern road or V-brake pads with integral toe-in hardware, or we can remove the old-school aluminum-backed brake blocks and bend the brake arms just a bit with a big old crescent wrench.

We will return to the specifics for toeing in each distinct braking system over the coming pages, but as another general rule, those brakes still squeaking after undertaking the regular toe-in regimen will sometimes benefit from a **reverse toe-in**. This is exactly what it sounds like: the pads' tails hit just slightly before their front ends. Alternately, the slightly firmer pads offered by manufacturers including Shimano and Tektro might be an option—softer pads such as Kool-Stop can work better, especially in the elements, but they can also be noisier. The old-school aluminum-backed brake blocks, of course, are also plenty rigid.

Having covered the basic elements, we're now positioned to spell out a more universal process for **installing rim-mounted brake pads**. While the hardware will vary, *the following holds for all rim-mounted braking systems, including cantilever, caliper, centerpull, and V-brakes.*

Prior to setting up any brakes, always make sure any barrel adjusters along their cables' length are dialed fully into their respective threads—or, for the cantilever brakes, a couple turns shy of that. For each brake arm in turn, we'll hold the pad in place with one hand

**Old-school aluminum-backed brake blocks—smooth post, in this case.**

and tighten its hardware with the other. *The pads should always be set perfectly parallel with the rim walls.* Again, as a rule, it is simplest to line them up just above the inner edges of the rims' braking surfaces. Brake pads will wear right through our tires' sidewalls, given the opportunity. Pads set too close toward the hubs are less of a safety concern—they'll wear unevenly, though, if allowed to overtop the rim walls, and this can complicate their reuse. *In all cases, brake pads should be tightened securely.* The brake pads' front ends should hit flat against the rim, with the pad's tails following about a millimeter later. It's only when the brakes still squeak after cleaning the rim and filing the pads' faces that we may opt for the above-mentioned reverse toe-in.

Our **brake levers** will fit either mountain or road handlebar grip area diameters: 22.2 or 23.8 mm, respectively. And—excepting the curiously short and straight **cross brake levers** destined for the upper straightaways on road bars—our levers' profiles will indicate their inclinations as well: straight levers for mountain, curved levers for road.

The brake cable head's distance from the lever pivot further divides our brake levers, directing them toward certain braking systems in particular. **Short pull levers**, the originals, work with caliper, centerpull, and cantilever brakes. **Long pull levers** work with V-brakes and disc brakes.

As a category, all brake levers must abide by one important rule: neither wear nor adjustments should allow their tips to bottom out on the handlebars when engaged, which would compromise our ability to stop. To avoid such scenarios, we'll tighten the cables and replace the brake pads as needed.

Among mountain brake levers, all but the most basic examples provide a means to adjust the **reach**, which is what we call the resting distance between brake lever and handlebar. We reduce the reach to better accommodate smaller hands, and the reverse is also true. Look for small **set screws** threading in from the front: dial these in to decrease reach. Note that changing the levers' reach may require corresponding cable adjustments as well.

Excepting again the curious cross brake levers, we'll always need to remove any grips or grip tape prior to installing or replacing brake levers. Grip tape is typically unwrapped from the stem, depending on how it was applied—we'll start at whichever ends we find the tape holding the tails in place. Procedures for removing rubber mountain grips are detailed on page 35.

Before riding, tighten any loose brake levers until their bases cannot move. Older brake levers enlist stainless steel bands to secure their positions on the handlebars—look for a bolt head inside the lever or under or behind the cable: we'll need to release the cable to adjust these. The original **road levers** and early dual control levers adopted this approach, following various prototypical examples on the original 22.2 mm (later mountain) standard. In recent years, however, the dual control levers' bolt heads tend to hide beneath the **brake lever hoods**, the rubber cowlings covering the levers' bases. The bolt will still be

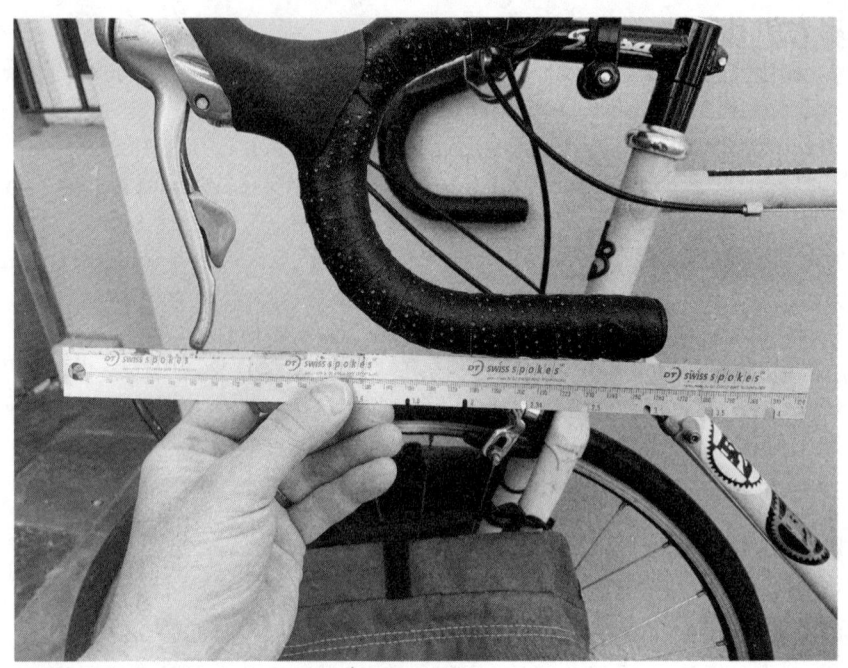

**Best position for drop bar road levers.**

pointing at the handlebars; pry up the hood's edge with your 3 mm flat-tip screwdriver for access.

As a rule, we set the **road levers** in the same position on the drop bars—the location that maximizes the range of comfortable hand positions above and below the lever. All we need is a ruler. Holding its edge flat against the bar's lower flat section, the lever's tip will just touch it, when correctly positioned. Looking down from above, the levers should also be in line with the drop bars' lower extensions, not angled inward.

We should never need to twist our wrists up to pull the brakes, and for this reason the **mountain levers** should shoot downward at 45-degree angles when mounted on flat or riser bars. Their plane passes right over the front wheel. For the same reason, we'll tilt the angle farther downward when mounting these laterally on cruiser bars and the like.

The **cross levers** we find on some drop bars' upper sections should also be installed at this same 45-degree angle, with their plane shooting out straight over the front wheel. These can be set up to manage the brakes independently or as pass-through surrogates sharing the responsibility with regular dual control or other road brake levers.

**Fixed gear**, also known as **fixed wheel**, provided the original approach to braking. And unlike the penny farthings' spoon brakes, it is still in common use. The principle is simple: there is no coasting. This was before coasting, actually. A cog is attached to a hub without any intermediaries; the two always move together. You pedal faster to go faster, and you push backward on the pedals to slow down. Riding becomes an exercise in speed control, and maintenance becomes about as basic as it could be. We'll discuss the fixed approach in greater detail in the chapter on drivetrains, beginning on page 135.

---

**Sidepull** or **caliper brakes** provide our first enduring model. The brake attaches via a bolt shot through the frame or fork's fender hole, directly above the wheel. The cable descends into the brake on the frame's neutral side, pulling the brake arms together in a tight smile; a spring mounted behind the brake arms draws their pads back from the wheel.

This basic design has been stretched in various directions over the decades: some caliper brakes can work well indeed even as others never really will. The compact aluminum renditions we see on nicer old road bikes have the best odds. The long and flimsy steel versions found on older budget bikes never had a chance—their brake arms flex too much, displacing force meant for the brake pads, greatly diminishing our stopping power.

Put more scientifically, calipers are differentiated by their **brake reach**: the distance from the center of the mounting hole to a brake pad. Caliper arms feature elongated windows, allowing us to slide the brake pads up and down to better accommodate different frames and forks, and brake reach is thus typically expressed as a range. Tektro, a popular choice for replacement caliper brakes, offers options with 39–49 mm, 47–57 mm, and 55–73 mm brake reach. Modern road calipers will favor the former two, and older road bikes the latter ones. Old 3-speeds and older budget bikes will be more inclined toward extra-long 63–78 mm or even 75–91 mm calipers.

The caliper's individual pieces stack up along a spinal bolt: the base holds the spring; the arms fall in sequence. Thin brass washers typically separate each part. The caliper's nose should feature a pair of nuts countertightened against each other, using the same principles we find on headsets and hubs. Our maintenance here follows the same

**Road caliper brakes.**

precepts: the ideal caliper should be clean, sparingly lubricated, and just loose enough to pivot freely. After cleaning, add a drop of Tri-Flow or similar lightweight oil atop each of the brake's pivot points and wipe away any excess. And if the spring seems weak, we can often improve responsiveness by popping its ends out momentarily, using a 3 mm flat-tip screwdriver as your lever, and stretching the spring laterally.

Tighten the mounting nut firmly against its frame or fork whenever installing a caliper brake, centering the two sides visually as best as possible while doing so. Older and cheaper caliper brakes are attached via M6 nuts, answering to 10 mm wrenches. Sub a nyloc nut here if you can, if it's not there already. Newer and better road caliper brakes enlist **recessed brake nuts** instead, addressed by 5 mm Allen wrenches, which otherwise disappear into a larger 8 mm diameter hole out back. Newer road frames will have planned for this; older ones can be drilled to accommodate recessed nuts. (We'll always keep the front hole at its original 6 mm diameter.)

For many years, better road caliper brakes set narrow wrench flats back by the spring, just before the frame or fork—once the mounting hardware is fully tightened, we'll grapple these with an **offset brake wrench** to fine-tune the centering. Park Tool's OBW-4 may be the most useful example; its 10, 11, 12, and 13 mm flats will correspond with nearly all caliper brake wrench flats. Their OBW-3 scoops up the rest, bearing 14 mm flats at one end and hooks to grasp a caliper's tension spring at the other. (The hubs' cone wrenches are also narrow enough to reach the slim caliper flats, but the lower headset cup typically prevents us from accessing them up front; we'd need to remove the wheel and work from below.)

Lacking such hardware, the alternate approach to centering a brake caliper grips the nuts at either end of the brake's spine, slowly turning both simultaneously. We'll begin with the mounting nut tightened 90 percent, tightening it fully once the caliper is centered.

Next comes the cable. Dial the caliper's barrel adjuster to rest two or three turns out from its base, and then pull the cable taut with your fourth hand tool. Caliper brakes require **threaded post brake pads**, one of our two broad camps for rim-mounted brakes. These are exactly what they sound like: a washer and nut caps each threaded post, fixing the pad to its brake arm. This category includes both road brake pads and V-brake pads, either of which can *usually* be made to work with road caliper brakes. (Especially modern road forks may lack the clearance to accommodate the longer V-brake pads.)

More current road pads feature pairs of facing concave and convex washers, which facilitate our toe-in adjustments. V-brake pads have twice as many washers per pad; they all typically end up on the outsides of the brake arms when paired with compact road caliper brakes. The thinner washers may be accommodated better inside the brake arms on older calipers.

From this point, we'll follow the usual rim-mounted brake pad installation process, as described back on page 103. Should they be so equipped, the calipers' quick release will be a pivot around the one arm's cable housing stop: flip up to release and down to engage.

Most road brakes produced since the 1990s have been **dual pivot calipers**. The brake pivot splits in two, giving us improved leverage and thereby improved braking performance. A small bolt drilled down into one shoulder of the brake will control the brake centering; we'll use a #0 Phillips screwdriver or a small Allen key to make our adjustments. The far ends of these bolts actually bottom out on the brake springs, which makes them very difficult to tighten—push down hard on the handle, if you are using a screwdriver, to avoid stripping these out.

**Dual pivot caliper brake.**

A dual pivot's action may be tightened, if needed, but the process is more complex compared to that we'd use for a regular caliper brake. First, remove the brake, then look for a set screw on the underside of its base: if you see one, loosen it. Next, use a flathead screwdriver to pop the spring free—keep it that way while you tighten things up. (Depending on the dual pivot's manufacture, the spring's end may be fit into a small plastic box meant to facilitate this very step.) Cable and brake pad setup will mirror what we'd do for regular caliper brakes.

**Cantilever brakes** predate the 1980s mountain bike boom, but that's when they first became popular. They were the first rim-mounted brakes to escape the fender hole, alighting instead on a pair of **brake posts** mounted on the fork blades or seatstays about 2.5 cm below the rim walls. These pivots are not painted, and they'll happily rust, given the opportunity—we'll see this, sometimes, restoring older bikes. Use emery cloth or light sandpaper to remove any rust from the brake posts. As a rule, all our brake posts should benefit from a thin coating of grease before accepting their cantilevers.

Anchoring the brake pivots to the frame and fork further improves our stopping power. The brake posts are threaded internally to accept the M6 bolts that secure the cantilever arms. Manufacturers dip these M6 brake bolts in thread-locking compound, reminding us to keep them nice and tight. No grease inside any brake posts ever, okay?

Cantilevers rely on coiled springs to return to their resting positions. One end of the spring plugs into a hole in the brake arm; the other end usually fits into a **spring hole** at the base of the brake post. These holes may appear in pairs, one per brake post, or we might see a vertical stack of three spring holes on each side—this is usually kind of a false choice, however, because we'll *almost* always be putting the brake springs into the middle holes. Anchoring them in the top or bottom holes would dramatically increase or decrease spring tension, respectively; both options are typically unworkable. *Maybe* the top set, sometimes, for especially old and tired cantilevers. Rarely, though.

The cantilever's brake cable should come right down the center from above—right through a hole in the stem, in the old days. More modern examples use a **brake cable hanger**, sandwiched in with the headset up front or dangling from the seatpost binder bolt (or Q/R lever) out back. Cable hangers for threaded headsets will feature a small tooth meant to line up with the keyway cut in the rear of the steerer tube; those destined for threadless headsets will instead use a pinch bolt to ensure they remain centered above the brakes.

A junction of some kind just above the frame or fork's fender hole shares the cable out to the cantilever arms on each side. The original recipe here involved a **straddle cable carrier**: the brake cable dives into a hole shot through a short bolt, which in turn passes through a triangular structure, the bottom edge of which supports a **straddle cable** connecting the brake arms. We'll tighten the carrier in place on the brake cable such that the straddle cable carrier rests level with or just above the fender hole.

For the low-profile cantilever brakes most riders use, the angle formed by the straddle cable's two sides should be about 90 degrees. Anything less than this reduces our leverage, and with it our braking power. Conversely, setting the straddle cable carrier too low may

**Front and rear brake cable hangers.**

assume more tension than the cantilever springs are able to provide. We will make exceptions for wide-profile cantilevers, which require longer straddle cables with broader angles.

Set up the carrier first, with the straddle cable disengaged, before getting the mighty brake springs involved. The base of the straddle cable carrier's bolt will typically require a 9 mm box wrench—a 9 mm socket's rounded embrace won't catch its edges. We'll use that same 9 mm socket or perhaps a 5 mm Allen wrench to tighten the nut. The brake cable shoots through a hole in the pinch bolt. Give it a good hand's width before clipping and capping—we'll appreciate this extra length the next time we're adjusting the brake cable. The straddle cable itself shoots through the gap between the brake cable and the carrier, trapped in place front and rear. Once the straddle cable is set up, bend the brake cable just past the carrier's pinch bolt such that its length shoots out right next to the straddle cable.

The **cantilever quick release** allows us to disengage the brake without tools, greatly simplifying wheel removal. Looking from the front, we'll spy a small cone or flat section in line with the straddle cable on one side—the left, most typically—just next to the brake arm. Something just big enough to grasp with the fingertips. That end of the straddle cable will terminate in a flat metal button, which corresponds with a cavity of similar dimensions on the brake arm. The cable slips through an alley on the brake arm, leaving the straddle cable's end nested within. Push the cone or flat section and brake arm together to release the straddle cable. If it's too tight to release, the brake's cable tension is probably a bit too tight.

Replacing the cable's quick release in the brake arm is just as easy. The same slack that allows our cantilever pads to rest at a slight remove from the rim also grants us the latitude to pull the straddle cable head just past its nest atop the brake, before bringing it back and slotting it into place. This same quick-release method holds true for the other cantilever straddle cable methods noted below.

After routing the straddle cable through its carrier, we'll slip its far end beneath a contoured washer and pinch bolt we'll find atop the opposite brake arm. Here again, tiny grooves within their embrace show us where to lay the cable. And this is where the cantilever brakes in particular demonstrate the unrivaled utility of our fourth hand cable pullers—there's just no better way to secure their cables. Pull the straddle cable through until its two sides form the angle appropriate for your brakes—90 degrees for the low-profile cantilevers most riders have, a bit wider for wide-profile—and then tighten down the pinch bolt.

The next canti straddle cable assembly to gain traction was somewhat less intuitive. Industry giant Shimano offered their Low Pro cantilever brake for a time, a system that featured one-sided straddle links: we see the expected quick-release features at one end, but only an odd circular junction at the other—the brake cable was meant to zip through this last and then head straight down to the opposite brake arm, leaving us to judge (a) where exactly on the brake cable to tighten the junction and, (b) as a corollary, where then to tighten the brake cable to the brake arm.

It came to a lot of math, for a brake. Happily, Shimano provided a cheat sheet of sorts with its TL-CB10 Pro-Set Cantilever Brake Adjustment Tool Gauge Set, a collection of six color-coded plastic templates. We'll select the brace corresponding to our brakes, route the cable through the assembly, and then tighten both bolts, using the fourth hand tool to keep the cable under tension as we work.

Nearly all cantilever brakes yet pining for the surety of these TL-CB10 relics will be happier with a **link wire**, a much simpler and more intuitive straddle cable option. Both Shimano and Tektro offer these, in a range of sizes. A quick-release cable end extends from the left; the brake cable itself shoots down a thin straw on the right. The button connecting the two will have a diagonal line etched or drawn to its front, aligning with our optimal 90-degree straddle cable angle. Flip this button over and you'll see a pair of cable-sized channels separated by a small nub: the brake cable shoots down the one lined up with its straw before the mighty fourth hand tool yanks it into position beneath the cantilever's pinch bolt. Last thing is to nudge the cable over the nub on the button's backside, landing it in the central channel.

Note that link wires are not always going to be an option—they'll need to reach their full extensions for the brakes to work well, basically, and smaller frames will not be able to accommodate this. Rear cantilever brakes on smaller women's or children's frames in particular may work better with a straddle cable and carrier.

We'll also want to center the cantilevers before setting up their brake pads. The original versions, first produced in volume by Dia-Compe and Shimano, lacked any specific centering capacity. Cantilevers have since taken up the centering mission with enthusiasm, applying a couple different methods. The most common approach admits a small **brake centering bolt** to manage the process—it will appear at the base of the right brake arm, seen from the front. This bolt bottoms out on the end of the brake spring: using a #2 Phillips screwdriver, we'll turn it in to increase spring tension, and the reverse is also true. Note that the spring effectively keeps this bolt's threads under tension as well, and this makes it difficult to tighten—push down hard on the screwdriver to avoid stripping out the bolt's head.

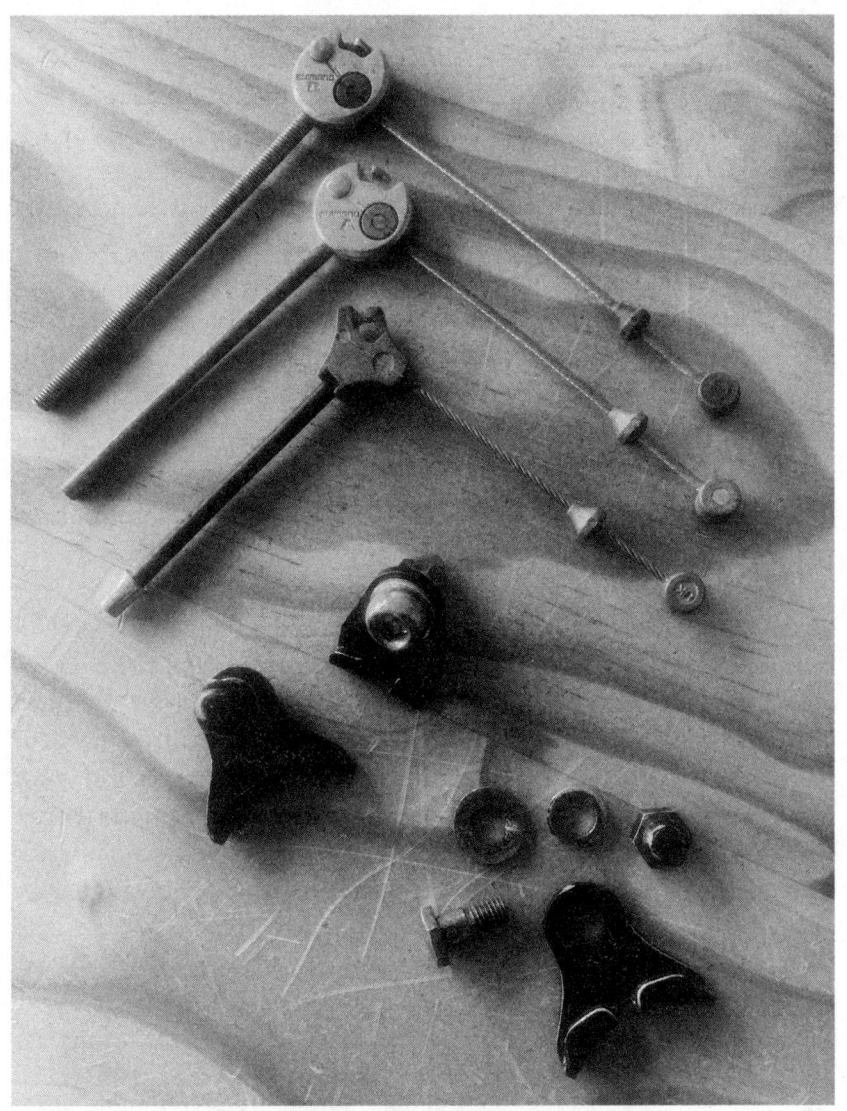

**Link wires (above) and straddle cable carriers (below).**

Centering adjustments applied via this bolt would eventually be noticed by the opposite caliper, moving it to compensate accordingly, but we can dramatically accelerate this process by jerking the brake arms back and forth laterally. Squeezing the lever a few times also helps. We may even repeat this sequence once or twice before arriving at the final adjustment: dial the centering bolt to increase or decrease the spring tension as needed, work the brakes laterally, then squeeze the lever a few times to better distribute the adjustments.

A smaller number of manufacturers have taken a different approach here. Dia-Compe 987 cantilevers, Suntour Self-Energizing SE brakes, and Paul Components' Neo-Retro cantilevers are among those that anchor one or both of their brake's springs within distinct **adjuster nuts** rather than sending them directly into the frame or fork's spring holes. These nuts sit right at the back of the brake arm, against the base of the brake post. We'll adjust these with a 13 mm cone wrench, usually—note that you'll need to loosen the caliper's anchor bolt prior to doing so. You'll also want to hold the adjuster nut's position with the cone wrench as you tighten the brake arm's anchor bolt back down again, in order to retain the adjustment. The adjuster nuts thus come to oversee both centering and spring tension, basically. What's it called, streamlining?

Once your cantilever brakes are centered, thread the nearest barrel adjuster a few turns out of its threads before beginning work on the brake pads. We set the pads up flush against the rim, and then we return the barrels to their starting positions, to provide for the slack our brakes need to work.

Most cantilevers use **smooth post brake pads**, and the sad truth is that we don't really have any shortcuts for setting these up—there's literally nothing holding them in place until their hardware is tightened. For each side, you'll need to hold the brake pad in position with one hand while tightening the hardware with the other. This, too, gets easier with practice.

The brake pad's post fits into a hole atop a curious banjo-like bolt, which in turn pierces concave and convex washers bracketing the brake arm's vertical window before being capped with a nut on the far side. The brake post hardware may have accumulated dust and dirt in its travels—clearing this crap out can greatly simplify your adjustments, even if it means taking the mounting hardware apart for a second. (Leaving the opposite arm intact while doing so will of course provide for a handy template for reassembly.) Add a red ant's worth of grease to the bolt's threads when putting things back together.

The sides of our brake pads will often feature small arrows specifying which end should face forward: when in doubt, we can assume that the pads' longer ends should trail to the rear. We'll grasp the

BRAKES

**Smooth post brake pads with cantilever brakes.**

banjo-bolt with a 5 mm Allen wrench, most often, and turn its nut with a 10 mm wrench. Rolling the nut as tight as you can with your fingers first ("finger-tight") will save some time. Continue tightening the nut until the brake pad can no longer be moved.

A few cantilevers use threaded post brake pads, which set up similar to V-brake pads; we'll discuss V-brake pads on page 124.

Once our cantilever brake pads are set up, thread the cable's barrel adjuster back down into its socket and pump the lever nice and hard a few times to test that the brake's cable and pad hardware is all sufficiently tightened. Also spin the wheel, to both confirm the brake's centering and the pads' clearance from the tire. As a rule, if anything's rubbing you should readjust as needed.

... And that might have been it, but circumstance requires that we also discuss **automatic toe-in**, a misguided effort from the 1990s meant to "assist" us in setting up our smooth post cantilever brake pads' toe-in by inserting springs into the brake pad hardware. The opposite is more often true, unfortunately. Should you find anything looking like a spring in your brake pad hardware, I would thus strongly encourage you to remove it.

Shimano provided the first version of automatic toe-in—conspicuous gray or black plastic washers, each containing an odd spring. Easy to spot, and to remove. Later examples replaced these goof-gaskets with thin metal washers bearing radial cuts, the edges of which bent in opposing directions to approximate springs. Nor did it stop there—overcome, perhaps, by feelings of inherent futility, the automatic toe-in springs eventually snuck away, hiding within the cantilevers' brake arms themselves. If your pads end up at bizarre angles, far from what you had intended, it's probably worth checking for this. Take them apart, ditch the little springs, and try again.

Automatic toe-in misapplies an original approach to thread-locking, from the era before nyloc nuts and Loctite. Sprung washers effectively force nuts and bolts together, placing their adjustments under tension. We can still find valid uses for this technique—both pedal reflectors and standard kickstands employ washers with these radial cuts—but it has no legitimate business with the brake pad hardware.

o=o=o=o

**Centerpull** brakes have not been current for decades, but they were once common enough, and many continue to serve. These mount via M6 bolts sent through the frame and fork's fender holes, much like the caliper brakes. Almost all, save the old Mafac Racer centerpulls, use threaded post brake pads.

While the centerpull preceded both the dual pivot calipers and the cantilever brakes, its prescient design pulled elements from each. The brake's pivot points are relocated from the center to its shoulders. Its cable reaches down the center to grasp a straddle cable carrier of fixed length; buttons at either end slot into the brake arms, quick-release style. We'll set up our fourth hand tool directly below the straddle cable carrier in order to tighten the centerpull's cable. The carrier's bolt is often the weak link for centerpulls—be sure to tighten it securely.

Encountering such relics in the wild, the brake cable's housing will typically end at a cable housing stop sandwiched either into the upper headset stack or dangling from the seatpost binder bolt out back. Anything such should include a barrel adjuster, our only option for fine-tuning centerpulls' cable adjustments.

Centerpulls also lack any dedicated centering hardware. We'll use a 10 mm box wrench to tighten the M6 nut out back; hold the brake level as you do this. Here as well, sub a nyloc nut if possible. We fine-tune a centerpull's centering by means of impact adjustment—line up a 6 mm flat-tip screwdriver on the side that needs to move inward, with its tip hitting the brake spring, and tap on the screwdriver's tail with your hammer until the brake is centered.

The bodacious 1980s witnessed a burlier version of the centerpull design, known as the **U-brake**. These appeared on BMX bikes and a handful of mountain bikes—GT, most famously. U-brakes pivot atop cantilever-style brake posts, but they are not cross-compatible with cantilevers or V-brakes—U-brake posts are mounted *above* the rim rather than below it. This reduces the leverage, and with it the brakes' power. Worse, out back, the Us are often mounted on the undersides of the chainstays—the best possible place for them to get splattered with any mud or dirt we ride through, presenting significant maintenance challenges. The U-brake's lower profile may have made some BMX tricks easier, but mechanically they're otherwise more of a liability.

Frames anticipating U-brakes also need longer rear tringles, in order to accommodate their pivots above the rear wheel—another tendency marking them as a doomed 1980s fashion item. Mountain bikes have long since moved on to the more efficient shorter stays our modern braking systems make possible.

The U-brake's rear cable terminates in a straddle cable carrier out back; up front, its housing runs directly into a barrel adjuster on the brake arm. Our cable adjustments will follow those previously described for use with centerpull and caliper brakes, respectively. U-brakes anticipate brake pads with threaded posts.

It also bears mentioning that the U-brake's posts are perfectly positioned to accommodate another 1980s breakthrough, the **roller cam brakes**. These were not without their advantages, but at this point they're very, very uncommon, so we're just going to move on. I mention them only to note that the roller cams and U-brakes are cross-compatible, if ever either runs into problems. Two cranky, troublesome characters with only each other to lean on—a perfect plot for a 1980s movie.

∞∞

Linear pull or **V-brakes** began their inevitable takeover in the 1990s. Shimano's Parallel Push units were the original shock troops—they succeeded in proving the concept, but we see now how their design was rushed and understand why this doomed them. Parallel Push incorporated odd parallelogram-like linkages within the brake arms, and these inevitably loosened: the brakes' performance began to diminish, even as their squealing grew ever louder. The basic format, however, once improved, soon became nearly ubiquitous: two long sticks rise to either side of the wheel, linked overhead by a cable shot through a curved aluminum straw known as a **brake noodle**. Dashing out the noodle's tip, the brake cable immediately disappears into a rubber boot, the toe of which reaches the binder bolt on the far side.

The improvement in leverage V-brakes provide is truly striking: so much so, in fact, that some manufacturers actually sought to reduce its stopping power—ours being a wantonly litigious society and all. The noodle's tail section suddenly becomes conspicuously wider and taller, alerting us that a small spring hides inside, pushing off contentedly against the cable housing cap and sapping our V-brake of its strength. It's insidious, really.

Our bikes' front brakes are always considerably more powerful than the rear brakes—deceleration shifts our weight forward, granting the front wheel more traction—and for this reason, these cheesy decept-o-noodles were only spec'd up front. They targeted low- and mid-range mountain bikes and hybrids specifically—as if to imply that more sophisticated riders were expected to know better. Entry-level rear brakes often feel squishy on their own, owing to their longer cable

**V-brake.**

runs and their diminished production values, so the two brakes might not even feel that different. Fortunately, it's easy enough to get in there with a pick and dig the springs out.

Looking at the frame and fork, the Vs anticipate the same brake posts we'd use for cantilevers, in the same positions. And much like their elder siblings, given a choice the V-brakes' springs will prefer the brake posts' middle holes. Here as well, the upper and lower spring holes, if available, are essentially symbolic—again, we might even call them false choices. The brake posts' exteriors should also be rust-free and lightly greased.

The linear spring running up each brake arm becomes a defining feature of modern V-brakes. Small bolts threaded into the base of each arm face off against their brake springs, leaving them expertly positioned to govern the springs' tension. The brake noodle ends with

**V-brake pads.**

a conical ridged nosepiece, which slots precisely into a hole at the end of a long, boxlike carrier pivoting atop the left brake arm. The boot then slips over the noodle's nose, keeping the cable warm and dry.

It's easiest to set up the V-brake's pads with the springs tension released, a status we here achieve while the brake is disengaged. To release the V-brake's quick release, use one hand to push the left brake arm's boxlike carrier forward and slightly down while pushing the brake noodle back and slightly upward with the other. The springs' long tails can usually be pushed aside with the fingers once the brake is open; at most, you might need a small flat-tip screwdriver to pop them out.

The V-brake pads' taller threaded posts allow room for two sets of concave and convex aluminum washers: one thicker set, one thinner. The two convex washers form a small metal pea, which the brake arm slices neatly in half. The concave washers swoop in from either side, forming bowls for our split-pea soup—one tall, one shallow. A thinner steel washer and an M6 nut then slips over the end of each brake post. Finger-tighten these last, and you are ready to toe in the V-brake's pads.

The setup is reasonably intuitive, especially compared to cantilevers. We must only attend to the two washer sets' sequence, with the goal of positioning them such that the brake arms sit parallel to each other when resting. Doing so optimizes the design's available leverage, and with it the brakes' stopping power.

When sold as new, the V-brake pads have a default setting with the taller (broader) bowls set closer to the pads and the shallow (thinner) bowls out toward the nuts. This arrangement typically works best up front, where the brake posts on forks are often spaced wider apart. Chainstays are often closer together, however, and thus we'll generally need to switch things around out back, setting the thinner pair inside the brake arms, with the broader pair on the outside. When making changes, we'll always follow the same split-pea soup recipe noted above.

V-brakes largely escaped the automatic toe-in phase, which dates more to the cantilever era, but there were a few unlucky exceptions. The original Shimano STX V-brakes, for example, featured smooth post brake pads with the sly radial-cut spring-loaded washers. As with the cantilever versions, just get rid of these.

The same principles, previously described on page 103, regarding the installation of rim-mounted brake pads apply with V-brakes as well. Hold each pad to the rim where you'd like it to sit; tighten the nut all the way down while you're holding the pad.

Finish by bending the cable under the brake spring, such that its tail falls in line with the brake arm—the end of the spring should hold it right there as you ride. Clip the cable right past the brake bosses and cap it with a ferrule.

Routing used cables back through the brake noodles can be challenging—shoved straight in, the cable will want to fray. For this reason, it's best to continuously rotate the brake noodle as you're putting the cable back through, twisting it in the direction the cable is wound. Move slowly, spin vigorously, and you'll do fine. Renoodling the cable also provides extra incentive to get the cable lined up correctly in its alleys beneath the pinch bolt—flattened segments of cable can be difficult to get back through the noodles. You may need to yank it through using the fourth hand tool.

We'll finalize the V-brakes' centering, once the pads are set up, by using the bolts at the base of each brake arm. Small adjustments

**Clipped and capped V-brake cable.**

here do a lot—turn the bolts half or even quarter turns. Their threads will be under ever-greater tension as we dial these in; press firmly on your screwdriver's handle when making adjustments. And with the V-brakes especially, rock the brake arms back and forth laterally after each adjustment—this will help to more efficiently distribute any spring tension adjustments across the two brake arms.

○•○•○

**Coaster brakes** have been with us for more than a century, as their antique 110 mm axle spacing suggests. We're able to broaden this historical distance by involving longer axles and hub spacers, but the basic formula doesn't change—depending on which way the pedals are turning, a cone swimming in grease within the hub shell either transfers the energy into forward momentum or pushes metal brake shoes out against the interior of a steel hub shell, which slows us down. Coasters are still spec'd on some smaller children's bikes, which likely remains their best use. Other braking systems will be more responsive.

We're able to adjust coaster brakes' bearing cones, or even crack them open to supply fresh grease, but their central requirement is wonderfully straightforward: the arm connecting the hub to the frame just needs to stay tight. It shouldn't be able to move at all, actually. We'll find it bolted to a metal bracket wrapped around the neutral-side chainstay—the bracket may have multiple bolt holes to better accommodate stays of different widths. Fill in any gaps between the bracket and chainstay with rubber or metal shims, nice and tight. You might even replace the coaster's dusty old hardware with an M6 bolt and a proper nyloc nut.

○○○○

Arai's **drum brakes** externalize this same approach, transferring the process to a removable component threaded onto a rear hub's neutral side and putting an actual brake lever in charge of it. These things mark a fairly specific moment in the development of cycling technology, sandwiched between the continuing evolution of rim-mounted brakes and the rise of disc brakes. They were never common, appearing principally as **drag brakes** on tandems. We'll call on these to passively decrease our speed while heading down the mountain pass, leaving the regular rim-mounted brakes free to address more immediate concerns.

Coming down the mountain can generate a lot of friction heat once you hit the brakes, and the drag brakes at least succeeded in pulling this away from the rims—where, according to lore, it sometimes became hot enough to pop inner tubes. This exchange exposed the drag brakes themselves to more *concentrated* friction heat, unfortunately—enough to even dissipate their grease, sometimes. Overly dry drum brakes are vulnerable to either seizing up or ceasing to function altogether. (Coaster brakes share this same liability, but few are ever charged with speed management on epic descents.)

The drag brakes thread onto the same 1.37" × 24 TPI right-hand threads we'd be using for freewheels. The hub would need to be threaded on both sides, in other words, or threaded on one side with a freehub body on the other—a rare bird indeed these days, before we even factor in the 140, 145, or 160 mm rear hub spacing most tandem frames will require. Said frame would also need the bracket or braze-on needed to accommodate the bolt securing the drum brake's arm.

Both thumbshifters and bar-end shifters can be used to control drag brakes. The cable's pinch bolt provides for a partial kind of quick release, popping in and out from its perch on the brake—you'll still need to undo the brake arm's fixing bolt in order to remove the wheel, but that math's often simpler than rewiring a cable. And if you do break a spoke, or otherwise need to remove a tandem's drag brake, have one rider sit in the stoker position while the other pushes the bike backward with the drag brake engaged. It should thread right off.

---

Shimano's latest take on this theory is the **roller brake**. These are fairly common on Dutch bikes, and various others like them, for front and rear wheels both. They were also stock equipment on the 1,800-plus Devinci BIXI bikes I repaired for Capital Bikeshare in Washington, DC, from 2016 to 2018. Not the world's strongest brakes—nor the lightest, if anyone's counting—but they do work consistently through all weather conditions, and they famously require very little in terms of maintenance. We'll see a grease port on the brake's flat face; its rubber cap pops off with a flat-tip 3 mm screwdriver or similar. Rotate the wheel slowly while greasing the brake. Shimano recommends we hit this with their specific Roller Brake Grease every second year, or more often if riding in hilly areas or with heavy loads.

The roller brake's barrel adjuster sits on a quick release—loosen the cable tension a bit to remove it before popping out the cable's anchor bolt. Shimano provides two versions of the roller brake: the brake arm will either attach to the frame through a bolt and a brake arm clip, just as the coaster brakes do, or its nose will dive into fittings frame manufacturers provide on the fork blade and chainstay. Fins radiating out around the hub flanges help the roller brakes shed their heat. Roller brakes were designed to work with Shimano's internally geared Nexus hubs and their Nexave cassette hubs, both of which provide the unique splined interfaces roller brakes require. The hub's neutral locknut holds the roller brake in place.

Shimano provides a Wear Out Measurement Tool to help us determine if a given roller brake is worn beyond useful service—it measures the distance between the barrel adjuster and the pinch bolt when the brake is engaged. Alternately, we might ask: does the brake still work? If not, does an injection of Roller Brake Grease appear to help the situation? Failing this, it's safest to assume the brake is toast. We're able to find basic repair parts for roller brakes—dust caps and pinch bolts and so on—but not the guts. Roller brakes are replaced when they wear out.

○─○─○─○

Whatever acreage among the bikes the V-brakes may have missed, the **disc brakes** have long since claimed. Their objective appears to be full-spectrum dominance—while proponents trumpet their arrival aboard "performance" road bikes, the sad truth is that we now find vaguely suspicious disc brake subvariants bolted to $200 budget bikes as well. They're no longer necessarily performance gear, in other words. But neither are they going away anytime soon.

Most disc brakes are designed to work with long pull brake levers, but short pull models are also available—Avid's BB7 is available in both versions, for example. The basic plan definitely has its advantages: at their best, disc brakes can provide as much stopping power as a bike might reasonably need. Their broad rotors also allow friction heat to dissipate far easier than drum brakes ever managed. And should they ever get warped beyond repair, we're able to replace them independently of the wheels. The disc brake pads do not last long, however, and beyond a handful of more common examples there really aren't any standardized replacements. And while oil and grease generally undermine braking surfaces—excepting coaster, drum, and roller brakes, of course—disc brakes are basically allergic to lubricants. They're also effectively a kind of poison, for the organic and semi-metallic brake pads at least. This means we'll always need to avoid touching the rotors' braking surfaces: wear clean gloves or grab them by their interior edges, if you even need to.

Bike racks and other fixed objects can also knock the rotors out of true fairly easily—even minor bends can put disc brakes out of commission, pending repair.

We replace the disc brake pads once they've been reduced to a thickness of 1.5 mm. In terms of their materials, we find three broad categories. Organic disc brake pads are made of rubber and other fibers in a resin base: they make less noise, but they don't work as well in the weather and require replacement every 500 to 700 miles. Organic pads also absorb oil, making any such contact essentially fatal from a performance perspective. Sintered or metallic pads are composites of ceramics and metal particles—they're louder, better in the wet, and may last up to 1,250 miles, dependent on riding conditions, but they also require a bit of warm-up time before they work at their best. Sintered pads can, however, come back from minor oil spills: remove both pads and sand them clean with fine sandpaper. Semimetallic brake pads draw elements from both camps—they last longer, warm up more quickly, and make more noise than organic pads. And no oils on these ones either, please.

Our cunning manufacturers have avoided standardizing disc brake pads—for their own reasons, quite literally—and as a result we now see *dozens* of different disc brake pad profiles in circulation, few of which are cross-compatible. Best to know the brand, model name, and perhaps even model year when hunting yours down.

Disc brake rotors are more reasonable. We'll find these in 140, 160, 170, 180, 200, 203, and 220 mm diameters, last I checked. The larger rotors have the extra leverage required to stop us more effectively, but they're also more vulnerable to getting bent. Smaller rotors are better in this respect, and marginally lighter as well. Some manufacturers offer further refinements in the forms of floating or two-piece rotors, which incorporate aluminum or other materials to help rotors dispose of friction heat more efficiently. This, in turn, can also extend brake pad life.

Did your disc brake suddenly start making more noise? Stop to check if the pads need replacement, and also clean it up. **Cleaning disc rotors** is easy—just use a clean rag and some isopropyl rubbing alcohol. Be thorough.

You'll want to confirm the wheel alignment and hub adjustment, as well as the brake caliper's positioning, before evaluating the straightness of a disc brake rotor. Like their wheels, disc rotors are most easily trued off the bike. Park's DT-3 Rotor Truing Gauge is an attachment that bolts to Park truing stands. We can then use a rotor truing tool such as their DT-2 for truing warped rotors up to 2 mm thick. If no stands are available, we can also use the brake pads to true rotors on the bike. You'll want plenty of light either way, with something bright and visible as a background to provide for contrast. Badly bent rotors should be replaced; those beset with less drastic variations can often be straightened. Lever very slowly, checking your work with a spin past the pads or caliper with each adjustment. Cracked rotors are much rarer, and these should always be recycled and replaced.

Note that disc rotors wear as well, albeit much more slowly than their pads. Shimano warns us with machine script etched to their rotors' faces to replace them if they become thinner than 1.5 mm; other manufacturers provide parallel recommendations for their own wares. Truly worn rotors can develop lowered flood plains, extending across the braking area, with minor plateaus remaining up by the hubs—our (gloved) fingertips would run off tiny cliffs, scaling down to reach them. Both Cycartis and Birzman offer rotor wear indicators covering the most common brands.

Disc rotors attach to their hubs in one of three ways. The most universal standard is a circle of six M5 bolts accessed via a T25 Torx wrench. Beyond the novel tool—its first deployment, among the bikes—disc brake manufacturers always treat such bolts with thread locker as well. Rotor bolts must always stay tight! Loose rotors can shear off their bolts, given the opportunity. Install their bolts in a star pattern, skipping one bolt all the way around the circle until they're all snug.

Shimano saw fit to offer a five-bolt disc rotor for use with their Nexus range, but the company has otherwise abandoned bolt-on rotors altogether with their Center Lock system, which assigns matching splines to both the rotor's interior and its designated hub. We'll use one of two lockrings to hold such sandwiches together, addressed with either a standard sixteen-notch bottom bracket tool, for those with exterior splines, or a standard twelve-spline 23.4 mm cassette lockring tool, for lockrings with internal splines.

Take your time when **routing disc brake cable housing**. The pads sit very close to their rotors, eliminating all discretion, and this makes it important that the cable housing doesn't bind when turning the handlebars—a too-short or poorly routed segment of shifter housing can effectively "pull" a disc brake's lever just by dragging across some other piece of cable housing.

**Replacing disc brake pads** generally requires a new set: the pads wear relatively quickly. It is only the outboard pad that actually moves on regular cable-activated disc brakes—the outsiders press the rotor into their inboard kin, which just sit there and take it. All the same, they both wear. Finger-turnable knobs or small Allen bolts centered over the pads allow us to set the outboard pad's resting position, and perhaps the inboard pad's remove from the rotor as well. We'll begin by removing the wheel and backing both of these all the way out, to make it easier to pull the old pads out with our pliers.

Some manufacturers, such as Shimano, hold their pads in place with retaining pins—yank any such out with a pair of pliers prior to attacking the pads. The other common approach here, as we see with the popular Avid brakes, for example, is to frame a wispy boxlike spring around the edges of the brake pads. New pad sets come with new springs—the hinge always faces away from the rotor. A further minority of manufacturers use magnets to retain disc brake pads.

We install disc brake pads as pairs. They should snap into place once they're correctly positioned, assuming you're using the correct pads for your brakes. Each disc brake pad tends to leave a finger hanging down—we'll grasp these firmly with pliers and pull to release the old pads, or push to install the new ones.

**Disc brake caliper setup** begins with the cable. First, use a fourth hand tool to confirm that the cable's housing is fully seated, then route the cable under the caliper's pinch bolt and tighten it. The brake arm should be fully extended when we do this—anything less undermines braking performance. (We'll address any latent cable slack later, either with the pad positioning or via the cable's barrel adjusters.)

Loosen the pair of M6 bolts attaching the caliper to the frame or fork just enough to allow it to move around freely. Install the wheel, and then dial the piston bolts or knobs in until both pads are pressed right up against the rotor. Their embrace confirms that the caliper is as parallel as possible with the rotor—go ahead and tighten down the caliper's fixing bolts right there. Give the lever a few squeezes to flush out any remaining slack, then back the outboard pad away from the rotor. Next, start backing the inboard pad away from the rotor until it stops rubbing on the rotor. Now we dial in the outboard piston, here again stopping just before it begins to rub. At this point, both the cable's barrel adjuster and the piston bolt will be able to change the outboard pad's distance to the rotor, if the caliper provides you this option—given the option, it's best to use the latter. The truer your rotor, the tighter the lever's resting position can be.

One last caution about disc brakes: *If you're riding an older disc-equipped bike with Q/R hubs, keep an eye on the front Q/R lever's adjustment.* Years past the advent of bicycle disc brakes, researchers discovered that the standard downward-facing front fork dropout design fails to consider the downward force that results from the disc brake caliper's position—which, as it turns out, can be enough to gradually loosen a Q/R lever. In extreme cases, this in turn could be enough to cause a front wheel to drop out of its fork.

More modern disc-specific forks sidestep this problem, reorienting their dropouts to a forward orientation. The various bolt-on axle arrangements likewise avoid it.

My Surly Big Dummy came with an old-style disc brake fork, for what it's worth, and the front Q/R lever has not yet loosened unexpectedly—because I tighten it appropriately, perhaps.

○◯⬤◯○

The breadth and scope of existing methods for controlling speed on our bicycles provides a context useful for evaluating the **hydraulic brakes**, which are available in both rim-mounted and disc versions. Beyond the small but colorful cliques of trials riders and serious downhill racers, hydraulic brakes provide more stopping power than most other cyclists will ever need.

In terms of their maintenance, every piece of a hydraulic braking system will need to align with the manufacturer's recommendations. Most systems use a DOT fluid; others, such as Shimano, use mineral oil. Glycol-ether-based DOT fluids are hygroscopic, which is to say that they absorb water from the environment, which in turn eventually weakens and rusts any hydraulic systems this water may be inadvertently smuggled into—no use saving the half-empty bottles of brake fluid for next time, in other words.

Hydros are supposed to be bled every six months. You'll need to buy a new bleed kit each time. Different manufacturers have different versions—these will typically include a syringe to pump new fluid into the brakes and a drainage hose to release the old fluid from the levers, as well as hardware to prevent leaks along the brake lines. Braided stainless steel lines are more durable, but they're not yet standard.

The smallest pinprick anywhere along the line will suspend a hydraulic brake's stopping power entirely, until the damaged segment is replaced, which means another bleed kit. Hang a can or something off the handlebars to collect the old fluid while the brakes bleed. We're trusting gravity to sort out any air bubbles that may want to get in there.

"Used" hydros is not really a thing—they've always been rare, mere wedges of fractions within the vast spread of our regular cable-activated (so-called mechanical) brakes. More to the point, there's never been a time when we've been unable to replace a hydro system with a mechanical one.

## XII
# DRIVETRAINS

The drivetrain encompasses everything that makes a bike go. Moving past balance bikes—still the best starter bikes ever—the **fixed gear**, also called a fixed wheel or a track bike, provides for the simplest approach. A single cog is fit to the rear wheel, and the bike does not coast—the pedals and wheel always move together. We manage speed with our feet: pushing forward for more speed, backward to slow down. All things being equal, fixed gear bikes can be good hill climbers—riding one, we'll quickly understand how much energy we use to keep a coasting gear engaged. Coming back down can be more challenging—absent a front hand brake, anyway.

Beyond your local topography, the **gear ratio** will determine how easy it is to slow down a fixed gear bike, or how fast it might go. Gear ratios too low find your legs spinning faster than you'd like them to, at speed; those too high can hurt the knees, and they can also be more difficult to stop with. We'll divide the number of chainring teeth by the number of cog teeth to find the gear ratio: 46-tooth by 16-tooth, for example, makes for a 2.75 gear ratio. This would fall in what is generally seen as the 2.7–2.8 sweet spot for bikes with 700c wheels. (Smaller wheels will measure things differently.)

A threaded **track cog** is best accommodated aboard a **track hub**, which bears two successive but short stacks of threads. The slightly smaller top set is left-hand threaded for a **track lockring**: 1.29" × 24 TPI, most often. Below these, we'll find a narrow, cog-width band of standard right-hand 1.37" × 24 TPI threads. (The track lockring threading can vary—Campagnolo, Miche, and Phil Wood track hubs use 1.32" × 24 TPI Italian-threaded lockrings; Mavic hubs use the 33 mm × 1 mm French standard.)

**Track lockring tool (left) and chain whip (right).**

As with cassettes or freewheels, it's easiest to remove threaded track cogs and lockrings when standing over the wheel with its neutral side facing our legs. We apply a light coat of grease to both cog and lockring threads before installation. Most track lockrings only provide us with a pair of openings for our track lockring tools, most of which are equipped with only a single tooth. For this reason—in order to

DRIVETRAINS

**Track hub (top), track lockring (below left), and track cog (below right).**

avoid stripping the lockring out during installation or removal—you should always hold the tool's tooth firmly in place with one hand while pushing on its handle with the other.

Once the lockring is off, we'll use a **chain whip** to remove a threaded track cog, engaging its central segment with the cog's teeth and wrapping its extension clockwise to grip more teeth. With the smaller cogs at least, you may want to wrap a toe strap or rubber band across the handle and the tool's chain extension, hugging them to either side of the cog. Once the chain whip is set up, push counterclockwise on the handle to remove the cog.

Track cogs share their ISO cog threading with freewheel hubs and bottom bracket lockrings—for their manufacturers' convenience, perhaps—and this striking coincidence sometimes generates speculation. Why not run a track cog on a freewheel hub, using a BB lockring to hold it down? *Because the steel cog would inevitably loosen.* The cog would erase the aluminum hub threads as it went, rocking back and forth between pedaling and backpedaling before spinning free and just letting go, all of a sudden. Thread-locking compounds might slow such a process, but they'd be powerless to prevent it.

Besides, a more recent innovation provides a far simpler and more reliable alternative, should a threaded track hub be unavailable. While Miche, Sugino, and White Industries have each offered proprietary splined track cogs with their own special hubs, we also now enjoy the miracle of **bolt-on cogs**, which take advantage of the established ISO six-bolt pattern with which we'd otherwise attach rotors to disc brake hubs. This new sorcery provides these hubs the potential to become fixed gear hubs, in other words—replace the Q/R axle with a bolt-on solid one and you're good to go.

We can identify dedicated **fixed gear frames** by a few key characteristics: the rear track dropouts, the 120 mm rear spacing, and the shorter **bottom bracket drop**. Imagine a plane running between the front and rear axles: BB drop describes the BB spindle's distance below this line, center to center. Most road and mountain bikes have 65–75 mm BB drop; fixed bottom brackets are more typically up in the 55–65 mm range. Thus do we avoid **catching a pedal**, which is the explosion that happens when a fast-moving fixed gear pedal encounters the pavement when banking a turn.

**Fixed gear pedals** must be narrower as well, for this very same reason. Dedicated track pedals can be found, but they won't have much to offer in terms of grip. The various svelte clipless pedals, which we'll discuss on page 205, are often good candidates. We can also use tin snips to cut down the aluminum pedal cages we'll find on older mountain bike pedals—cut the ends flush with the axle end and then file the edges down nice and smooth.

The default width for **fixed gear chains**, also called track chains, is ⅛". Their cogs and chainrings share this same wider ⅛" (BMX) standard, but narrower ³⁄₃₂" (7/8/9-speed) cogs are also available. These ³⁄₃₂" cogs are often used for fixed gear conversions, as they can allow the convert's existing chain and chainring to continue participating—absent any derailleur-compatible master links holding the chain together, that is. SRAM, ConneX, and other chain manufacturers provide these, also sometimes called quick links, for use with multispeed bikes, in which context they work splendidly. Not so with the fixed gears—the abrupt changes in momentum can loosen the derailleur-compatible quick links, especially when the chain is not sufficiently tensioned. However, ⅛" BMX-style master links are ideal for ⅛" fixed gear chains. We'll use a chain tool to connect ³⁄₃₂" fixed gear chains, as described on page 173.

**Chain tension** is critical for the fixed gears. You'll feel a loose chain, riding one—it's that millisecond of uncertainty, between pedaling and backpedaling. Hop off and check; this just takes a second. Pressing down from above, we shouldn't be able to push a correctly tensioned fixed gear chain more than ½", or 1 cm. Chainrings are sometimes a bit ovalized, so it's best to do this test at each of its four compass points.

We tension a track chain by walking the hub backward in the dropouts. Fully tighten the neutral-side locknut, leaving the drive-side locknut loose. Grab a handful of spokes just behind the seat tube, and use these to pull the wheel toward the drive-side chainstay—as you do, the axle end on that side will edge back in the dropouts. Clasp the spokes and drive-side chainstay together to maintain the new position, and then fully tighten the drive-side locknut. Loosen the neutral-side locknut, recenter the wheel, and check the chain tension again—it should be higher.

Repeat these same steps as needed until the chain reaches the tension described above. Get the cranks spinning, then let go—a properly tensioned fixed gear chain will stop the wheel's motion after just a rotation or two. It may look too tight up in the repair stand, in other words, but out on the street that's actually about what we want. Your chain is too long if the axle reaches the end of the dropouts—you'll need to remove a link with a chain tool, as described on page 173.

**Chain tension adjusters** can help with this, on bikes with track or BMX dropouts at least, but they are not strictly necessary. We'll see these on one or both sides—a washer with a long threaded tail hoops around the axle, directly under the locknut. Tightening the nut above the collar on its threaded tail section draws the axle back toward the dropout ends.

Fixed gear chains wear a bit faster than others, having nowhere to run, and their tension will begin to fade as this happens. Their cogs and chainrings wear as well, and it's best to replace all three simultaneously. An old cog will grind away noisily at a new chain, wearing it down prematurely.

**Fixed gear conversions** are an option for any frame with horizontal dropouts. In addition to the disc hub conversion mentioned previously, it's often possible to update fixed gear hubs with the spacers and longer solid axles needed to fit wider frames. **Flip-flop hubs** are another popular choice here—these are threaded on both sides, for fixed gear or a singlespeed BMX freewheel, and they can be found in various hub spacings. Both gears would need to be of similar sizes—within a couple teeth, at least—in order to use the same length of chain.

Multispeed bikes tend to arrive with 175 mm cranks; we'll substitute shorter 165 mm cranks when converting to fixed, to avoid catching a pedal. Chainline is the other major consideration—the cog should end up directly behind the chainring, such that the chain run between the two is perfectly straight, not angled to one side or the other. We'll mount our chainring on the crank arm's inside or middle shelf, for example, while placing any needed hub spacers over on the neutral side and redishing the wheel accordingly. The double-ring chainring bolts your multispeed bike probably came with will be too long, so you'll likely need to use a set of **single-ring chainring bolts** instead.

Chainline, chainrings, and cranks will all be described in more detail farther ahead—see pages 184, 185, and 176, respectively—but here it also bears mentioning that not all chainrings are round. This is obvious enough, sometimes—neither Shimano's Biopace nor Sugino's OvalTech egg-rings are fixed gear compatible, but the rest we can work with. Many crank-chainring combinations also leave a bit of wiggle room, allowing the rings to scoot around laterally on the crank arms' shelves. For both reasons, it's important to center the chainring on the crank when converting to fixed (or singlespeed). Leave the chainring bolts finger-tight until you achieve the desired chain tension, as described above. Spinning the cranks through a few rotations will nudge the chainring to its most central position—fully tighten the chainring bolts at that point.

Frames with smaller wheels can make ideal candidates for fixed conversions—they are easier to start and easier to stop. And given the fixed wheel's sustained momentum, the small wheel's most famous shortcoming—its tendency to shed speed—begins and ends as a nonissue. BMX frames begin with the correct dropouts and hub spacing, if not (originally) the optimal seat height. Note that gear ratios are a function of wheel size—a 58-tooth/13-tooth combination with a 4.62 ratio might sound overwhelming, but on a 16"/349 wheel, it feels similar to the 2.75 standard for 700c wheels.

I'm a big fan of front brakes on fixed gears. Their position leaves them far more powerful than rear brakes. Their pads stay cleaner, and the cable is shorter, so they're easier to maintain as well. You might not even use the front brake in your daily rounds; many fixed riders find they prefer controlling speed with the legs instead. The brake might just hang out, ready if you need it.

☉☉☉☉

Singlespeed bikes were next in the evolutionary sequence, yet more so than with the fixed gears, we'll need to develop a better understanding of additional drivetrain technologies before getting into their specifics; we'll pick them up again on page 210. We can resume here with the **friction derailleurs**, the first devices to convince a chain to hop between cogs. The name comes from the sensation: **friction shift levers** provide no tactile click or other signal to mediate the process—we're trusted to find the gears ourselves. The chain becomes quieter once we settle on the gear we've selected, which will be different than the one before.

Many of our modern indexing drivetrains' key attributes first appeared on their friction forebears, beginning with the **rear derailleur**, the pulley-powered parallelogram through which the chain climbs its little stairway. The top part of this wondrous machine, anchored to the frame with a mounting bolt, is called the B-knuckle. It hangs from the frame's **derailleur hanger**, an M10-threaded fitting extended below or bolted just beneath the drive-side dropout. The two **derailleur pulleys** spin within a **derailleur cage**, which pivots beneath what we call the derailleur's P-knuckle. The lower of the pair is the tension pulley; the upper one is the guide or jockey pulley.

The derailleur's cage must be long enough to access its cogs. For the old friction systems, we'll use **short cage derailleurs** to cover road cog ranges up to 26 teeth or so, and what we'd now call **medium cage derailleurs** for any cogs up to 34 teeth. Longer-caged derailleurs can manage smaller gear ranges as well, if more slowly. (We once had only two distinctions—short and long cages—but indexed shifting, as we'll see, has brought longer rear derailleur cages yet. Shifting into the present, what were once called "long cage" derailleurs in the age of friction shifting have effectively been rendered "medium cage" by comparison.)

The commands our shift levers bark down through their derailleur cables are taken up by springs within the derailleurs they control. The first of these, wrapped around the derailleur's mounting bolt within

**Derailleur hanger, extending below the dropout.**

the B-knuckle, pushes off against a tooth in the derailleur hanger's base: its tension rotates the derailleur cage back away from the cogs, giving the pulleys room to operate. Coming back down the gear range toward the smaller cogs, this same spring also returns the derailleur to its resting position—beneath the smallest cog, originally. A second spring is charged with dragging the chain up toward the bigger cogs, expanding the derailleur's parallelogram as it goes. In this original iteration, moving a shift lever away from its resting position sends the chain up toward the bigger cogs; returning the lever to its resting position does the opposite.

Always confirm the derailleur hanger's alignment before undertaking any **rear derailleur adjustments**. Looking from the rear of the bike, pull the derailleur cage down and compare the pulleys to the cogs—we want them all parallel, rather than seeing the pulleys angled in toward the wheel. Bent derailleur hangers can almost always be fixed, one way or another, and we'll always want to take care of this before proceeding, as described on page 146.

We'll begin adjustments with the **limit screws**. We'll always see these in pairs on old friction derailleurs, most often marked $L$ and $H$—drilled into the B-knuckle or the face of the parallelogram itself. They bottom out on opposing teeth within the derailleur's parallelogram, effectively confining its movements within specific parameters. They have no other function.

With the rear derailleurs, the low (L) screw governs access to the largest cog, while the high (H) screw polices the smallest one. Limit screws use very small threads, you'll notice, which hold their adjustments quite well. We set them up when installing the derailleur, or when modifying the gear range, perhaps. They just stay put otherwise.

The rear derailleur's H limit screw also establishes the reference point for the derailleur cable's tension. Once the cable is bolted beneath the derailleur's binder bolt, loosening the H screw increases its tension. Past a certain point, in other words, you'll need to disengage the cable before further loosening of the H limit screw has any visible effect.

Both the pedals and the wheels will need to turn when **testing limit screw adjustments**—set the bike up in a stand or flip it over on its handlebars. Turn the pedals forward and press on the rear derailleur's parallelogram, pushing it up the gear range. We want it to stop above the largest cog—if it doesn't get there, loosen the L limit screw in half or quarter turns, checking your work at each interval. Conversely, if the chain hops over the top cog and into the spokes, fish it out with gloves or a stick and dial the L limit screw in, until it does stop above the largest cog. Our goal here is to forestall any possibility of dumping the chain into the spokes while riding, when it could really do some damage.

There may be another, quicker way to test a derailleur's limit screws, if its derailleur cable is connected. (Don't even try this with carbon fiber frames.) Pedal forward again and yank hard on the cable, right in the middle along the down or top tube—the derailleur will be moved to demonstrate how far it can bring the chain in the low direction. Adjust the limit screws accordingly, if necessary. Next, continue

**Rear derailleur limit screws.**

pedaling, but let go of the cable—the derailleur will fold down to show you its resting (high) position. Here again, make any adjustments necessary. This test has the additional benefit of more thoroughly seating the cable housing.

The *L* and *H* markings can sometimes be hard to read, but we can figure it out. Release the cable and spin the pedals, allowing the derailleur to settle into its resting position. Next, press the parallelogram to further compress it. Turning one of the two limit screws out will allow the derailleur to compress even further—that one will be the H limit screw.

Standing behind the rear wheel, imagine lines radiating out in plane with the cogs' teeth: when setting our limit screw adjustments, we're effectively comparing these lines against those extending from the derailleur pulleys. As a default, we'll allow the pulleys to *barely* move past their ultimate cogs, at both the low and high ends. This departs nominally from the orthodoxy, which has us limiting the pulleys' range precisely at the L and H cogs, but to my experience the rear derailleurs do better with just a whisker's more breathing room.

We'll see three principal formats with friction shift levers. In the olden days, **down tube levers** fit atop **shifter bosses**, a pair of laterally mounted threaded posts set near the down tube's apex. Cheaper road bikes often instead use bolt-on chromed brackets fit with shifter bosses—a small metal plate under the down tube prevents these from sliding down. And while some newer road bikes get all self-conscious and hide the cables inside their tubes, any such machines would also lack the confidence to go with regular old DT levers.

**Bar-end levers** sprout from the ends of our road bikes' drop bars, sending their cables down through housing stops mounted to the shifter bosses—or, with some of the oldsters, through chromed bolt-on brackets. What we call **thumbshifters** first became common aboard the early mountain bikes' chromed bullmoose handlebars—these, too, relied on bolt-on cable housing stops. **Stem mount levers** are meant for use with the old 22.2 mm (⅞") road quill stems, also most often with the same bolt-on housing stops.

All friction levers are bult around threaded bases, found either in the shifter bosses on the frame or in similar elements incorporated into the bar-end, thumbshifter, or stem mount hardware. Friction levers will equally possess a means to tighten their mechanism, right up top—a folding wingnut sometimes, or perhaps a broad flat-faced screw. We want these all a touch more than finger-tight, just enough to hold the derailleurs in position.

**Using friction shift levers** may involve a learning curve, coming over from the clickbait of modern indexed shifting systems, but they were fine enough for decades. Micro-ratcheting friction levers, still a modern standard for front derailleurs, remain the best among them. You'll need to be pedaling to shift, like any other derailleur system, and likewise we'll want to avoid **shifting under load**: ease up the pressure when shifting. Stop actively *pushing* the pedals while shifting; use only enough force to keep them in motion. Shift into easier gears before challenging a hill.

The original shifting orthodoxy also warns us against **cross-gearing**, which is what we call riding with the chain in either of the extreme low-to-high or high-to-low combinations—that is, with the chain on either the smallest cog and smallest chainring or the largest cog and largest chainring. Doing so stretches the chain laterally—a tendency that many suspect causes them to wear more quickly. (This theory, once broadly accepted, is lately more disputed. Not being an engineer, I can offer no further clarity here.)

Do not lubricate friction shift levers—just clean them up if you need to. Friction levers can be paired with indexed rear derailleurs, but gear ranges spanning more than 9 speeds arguably diminish the advantages they may have offered. Friction derailleurs, conversely, are not familiar with indexing.

The omnipresence of replacement rear derailleur hangers among modern aluminum and carbon frames points to the centrality of **derailleur hanger alignment** among rear shifting concerns. Rear derailleurs can become miniature levers anytime a bike takes a hit down around the drive-side chainstay, bending the hangers in toward the spokes. Such injuries can instantly negate any advice the limit screws may wish to provide, leaving the chain free to jump right over the last cog and into the spokes.

Bent hangers are easily identified, seen from the rear. A healthy derailleur cage should track nice and parallel in relation to the cogs—pull the cage's tail downward to see this more clearly. Any angle less than parallel would indicate that the derailleur hanger is bent.

There is a slight possibility the derailleur's cages may also be bent, but this is far less common. The two pulleys' teeth should appear on the same plane when seen from the rear or beneath. Bent rear derailleur cages can often be straightened with patience, a stout pliers, and a vise. Remove both pulleys; flatten each cage plate in turn.

The best way to straighten a bent derailleur hanger is with a **derailleur hanger alignment tool**. Every bike shop should have one. A hefty lever rotates in plane around an M10 fitting, which threads into the bent hanger. The lever comes to reflect the derailleur hanger's misalignment; we position and press on it as needed to make things whole. You won't need much force—the tool's leverage absolutely dwarfs the diminutive hanger. In fact, it's best to lever *slowly*, especially with aluminum hangers—these will happily snap if pushed too far or too fast. Lacking this tool, slot the short end of your longest Allen key into the derailleur's mounting bolt and grip the derailleur's lower knuckle with your other hand, pushing both simultaneously.

In other respects, **rear derailleur maintenance** is pretty basic. Oil dropper bottles are perfect for lubricating their various pivot points—oil spray cans leave overspray everywhere, which picks up grit, which gets into the pivots and slowly undermines them from within. The chain, derailleurs, cassette cogs, and chainrings will often benefit from a thorough spring cleaning, or perhaps less often, dependent on your local conditions. Drivetrain cleaning is described more fully on page 225.

Cable tension is much more of a concern with indexed drivetrains, as we'll see, but an excessively slack derailleur cable will also affect friction systems' performance. Rusty cables and sharply bent segments of cable housing can create problems as well. Cogs, chainrings, and chains all wear out eventually; the consequences and remedies here are detailed beginning on page 228.

The rear derailleurs' return springs can grow tired after extended use—the journey back to the resting position slows down, irrespective of cable adjustments or lubrication. In such cases, it often helps to insert a 1 mm M10 rear axle spacer under the derailleur's mounting bolt: by moving the resting position out just a bit, we effectively grant the tired old spring a bit more tension. (You'll need to readjust both limit screws as well when doing this.)

While some rear derailleurs made by Campagnolo, Paul Components, and others were designed to be rebuildable, in practice this is just not very common. "I'd say that very old Campagnolo was famously rebuildable, but Campy from the last twenty-plus years not so much," says West Town Bikes' Alex Wilson. "Perhaps from a design perspective it's rebuildable, but from a supply/parts availability [perspective], Campy is the worst to work on."

Moreover, for shops, rebuilding individual components often isn't feasible. "We have an overwhelming surplus of everything due to the many bikes which are donated, so this level of work is unproductive for us, because it takes time away from doing routine, conventional jobs with quicker turnaround," says Community Bike Hub's Glen Mason. "With only so much time, we have to pick our battles." The Bike Kitchen's Jesse Cooper expresses a similar sentiment: "We can't justify the cost of rebuilding a shifter for an hour when the resulting performance is still diminished and new component and labor may be the same cost as labor to repair."

⊙⊂⊃⊂⊃⊙

You'll need to get the rear derailleur set up first before working on the **front derailleur**. Friction shifting up front has enjoyed a longer term of service—the crank's two or three chainrings are easier managed than the multispeed cogsets out back, and the element of friction is very useful when adjusting the front derailleur's **trim**. Our chainrings must be equally ready to accept chain runs coming in from both of the cogset's poles, but the front derailleur's cage must also be narrow enough to focus on one chainring in particular—trimming describes the minor finishing adjustments that move the cage clear of the chain. We hear it rubbing; we move the lever a hair.

The original friction front derailleurs were attached to their frames in one of two ways. The great majority enlist 28.6 mm/1" clamps wrapped around the base of the seat tube. Some higher-end road bikes featured **braze-on front derailleurs** instead, which rely on small curved brackets brazed, bonded, or welded to the frame in the same positions. Clamps bearing such brackets allow us to transfer braze-on front derailleurs to frames that lack them, but a frame with the braze-on bracket will not accept a clamp.

The indexing front derailleur cages have been pulled and prodded in various directions, as we'll see, but the friction front derailleurs were more predictable. The cage was all of two mostly parallel fins back then, the lower edges of which faithfully shadowed the largest chainring's profile. The idea was to allow for just enough movement to avoid dumping the chain. The **front derailleur positioning** was thus a wonderfully simple measurement back in the friction era: the cage must clear the top of the largest chainring by 2 mm, and the longest section of its outer plate must be parallel with the chainring's face.

Note that some of the bolts securing older clamp-on front derailleurs were positioned such that fully tightening them can rotate the derailleurs slightly out of alignment. For this reason, hold the derailleur in place with your free hand while securing the derailleur—get the bolt 90 percent tightened, double-check the derailleur's lateral alignment against the chainrings, then hold it there as you tighten the bolt fully. The braze-on's mounting setup is lighter and more streamlined, but this attachment method isn't as secure as a clamp; using a mild thread locker can help the derailleur retain its position.

The front derailleur's limit screws reverse polarity: the L screw now governs the smallest chainring, with the H screw overseeing the largest chainring. (The limit screws' labeling tracks low and high gears, in other words, rather than cog or chainring size.) The narrower rear gear ranges associated with older friction systems simplify our adjustments here as well, among the standard double-ring cranksets of that era. In the small chainring, the L screw should be set so that the chain does not rub in any gear combination, low to high. After adjusting the L screw, set up the cable beneath the front derailleur's pinch bolt and then use the test described on page 143 to set the H screw. Triple-ring friction cranksets are less common, and these may be better served by the extended inner cage plates associated with indexed front derailleurs.

○○○○

The **indexed derailleurs** have been with us for more than four decades now. The original 5- and 6-speed systems have long since been overshadowed by their more complicated descendants, which in recent years have managed to fit 13 cogs on a single hub. This treatment will cover cable-activated indexed drivetrains up to 12 speeds.

Whatever performance advantages they may offer, indexed systems are also far more particular than friction derailleurs. At this point, all the major component manufacturers take steps to limit the interoperability of their various wares with relation to competing systems and technologies—and increasingly, as we'll see, with regard to their own product ranges as well. Reconfiguring the length of cable pulled per shift, cog widths, cog spacing, and the derailleurs' design can improve shifting performance, even as each such step also serves to further develop a handful of essentially parallel and redundant subscription models. We see this over and over again with indexed drivetrains, from the cogs and derailleurs to the bottom brackets and chainrings: only one or perhaps a couple products might satisfy, and they're all increasingly expensive. Our industry's standard-bearers continue to cater to the imagined heroic pursuits of individualized fulfillment, always in their own special ways, even as they exemplify the fading and transactional compromises of late-stage capitalism.

Shimano Index System (SIS) 7-speed levers and derailleurs first appeared on new bikes in the 1980s. Both Campagnolo and Suntour offered versions of their own soon thereafter. Suntour's Ultra freewheels aligned with Shimano's nascent 7-speed indexed cog spacing standard, but their MicroDrive set out on its own standard. The company repeated the gesture as the world moved on to 8-speed, and it went out of business shortly thereafter.

Suntour made some really nice shift levers in their time, and with a bit of patience their 7-speed levers might be matched with 7-speed Shimano gear. These early systems can sometimes approximate cross-compatibility; it depends who you ask—or perhaps who is riding. "I actually have old 8-speed Campag shifters on my road bike and run a 7-speed Shimano cassette with that, because the spacing is the same as the old 8-speed Campag cassette," says Glen Mason of the Community Bike Hub. Yet while such off-the-books remedies may work for some, they may not be everyone's cup of tea. "The most common pitfall is trying combos that are okay for an experienced mechanic or rider," the Bike Kitchen's Jesse Cooper explains, "but the shifting nuance can be a turnoff for less experienced riders who aren't satisfied with the performance."

These differences in cog spacing were only an early conflict within the ongoing struggle for **indexing compatibility**. As a rule, it's always best to match like with like when setting up or replacing indexing drivetrain components. If that's not in the cards, JTek Engineering offers a wide range of Shiftmate pulleys, which allow cross-compatibility among Campagnolo, Shimano, and SRAM levers and derailleurs within the 7-speed to 12-speed ranges. Wolf Tooth's Tanpan performs a similar function, allowing Shimano's 10- and 11-speed road shifters to work with the company's otherwise-incompatible Shadow and Shadow+ mountain derailleurs, about which more shortly.

The indexing shift lever determines the **cable pull**, a measurement that has varied both across manufacturers and over time. Reaching the derailleur, each indexed shift will move its parallelogram a defined

DRIVETRAINS

distance up or down the cogset. This distance, known as the **shift ratio**, is a function of both the cable pull and the parallelogram's dimensions—SRAM's flagship levers pull more cable, for example, in anticipation of the squat and boxy SRAM parallelograms they hope to find below. The shift ratio in turn is meant to coincide with **cog pitch**, which is the distance from the center of one cog to the next. Everything must always line up and match, within each of our manufacturers' parallel utopias.

The most substantial divisions between our different indexing systems began with the addition of extra cogs to the gear clusters out back—manufacturers took diverging approaches, basically. The default hub spacings were held as sacrosanct—originally, anyway—and this required each slice of a 10-speed cogset to become relatively narrower, crammed into the acreage previously filled by 8- or 9-speed clusters.

Almost all 6-, 7-, 8-, and 9-speed Shimano shifters and derailleurs are cross-compatible. They are all designed around the same 1.7 mm shift ratio distance, which the company marketed under the 2:1 label. (Shimano's Dura-Ace rear derailleurs used a different shift ratio prior to 1997.) Shimano's 10-speed road range carried over this same friendly-sounding 2:1 shift ratio as well, with the exceptions of the Tiagra 4700 and GRX groups, both of which align with Shimano's 11-speed road range instead.

The Shimano hairs split further with their 10-speed Dyna-Sys mountain line, which only works with other Dyna-Sys mountain. The company carried over the Dyna-Sys name to 11-speed mountain, but *not* its shift ratio—we'll need to specify Shimano Dyna-Sys *10-speed* or *11-speed* when seeking replacements, in other words. Shimano's 11-speed road line introduced yet another shift ratio, with which only the aforementioned 10-speed Tiagra 4700 and GRX sets align. Hyperglide+ again redefined things anew for more recent 11-speed and 12-speed systems. (The name may sound familiar: Shimano originally presented products labeled "Hyperglide" in the 1980s. The two systems are not compatible.)

In 2021, Shimano introduced Linkglide, a new standard for 10-speed and 11-speed built around a redesigned cassette the company claims will provide for longer service, owing to thicker materials and a stouter finish. This thickness also confronts cog spacing, unfortunately, and thereby the shift ratio and cable pull as well. Other

10-speed or 11-speed chains will work with Linkglide, but the cassettes will only pair correctly with Linkglide derailleurs and shift levers.

While SRAM chains and cassettes are broadly cross-compatible with Shimano through 11-speed—across each successive level, at least—their shift levers and rear derailleurs may or may not be. In the late 1990s, SRAM introduced their ESP range, with what they called a 1:1 shift ratio: the rear derailleur's longish parallelogram was reconfigured as more of a squat box, an update that greatly increased the cable travel associated with each shift. This was actually a really good idea—it allows for a far more generous range of useful adjustments, basically—but Shimano retained its dominance regardless, so in the early 2000s SRAM also began producing various Shimano-compatible shift levers, for which they adopted Shimano's 2:1 label. These Shimano-aligned levers all had letter names: MRX, Attack, and Rocket. SRAM assigned numbered names—3.0, 5.0, 7.0, 9.0, X9, X0, and so on—to parts using their own 1:1 shift ratio.

SRAM's 7-, 8-, and 9-speed 1:1 components are all cross-compatible. SRAM 10-speed moved on to a different standard, Exact Actuation, for both road and mountain. Their 11-speed road range is on this same Exact Actuation standard, but SRAM's 11-speed mountain began anew with its X-Actuation standard, which sounds similar but is not cross-compatible. "I constantly have to look up which SRAM parts are Shimano-compatible," notes a mechanic at Santa Cruz's Bike Church. "I am deeply frustrated by Shimano's choice to diverge their road and mountain lines."

Some older Shimano indexing rear derailleurs attempted to improve shifting performance by means of **floating derailleur pulleys**: the guide pulley is rendered just slightly narrower than its internal bushing, allowing it to scoot back and forth on the bushing's lateral axis. These "Centeron" pulleys were an evolutionary step, used on indexed rear derailleurs up to 8 speeds, after which point they were effectively crowded out by the indexed cogsets' increasingly strident demands. SRAM pulleys don't float—laterally, at least.

Various rear derailleurs basic and sophisticated have featured **large derailleur pulleys** over the years, as you may have noticed, in both the guide and tension positions. These larger pulleys enlist greater numbers of teeth in shuffling the chain back and forth, and in so doing they also dilute its wear across broader surfaces, but as mere lieutenants the pulleys are ill-positioned to meaningfully change shifting performance either way.

Rear derailleurs have evolved in more substantive ways as well. Shimano's **direct mount derailleur hanger** has recast the derailleur hangers we multispeed riders already knew as **standard mount derailleur hangers**. The company's 2012 Shadow rear derailleur heralded this change with its **B-Link** pivot, a longish and extra-sturdy can tab that shifted the derailleur mounting bolt's position back and a bit down by about an inch. The direct mount rear derailleur, introduced the following year, cut out this middleman. The B-Link or direct mount approach simplifies rear wheel removal and installation. It also repositioned the rear derailleur to a somewhat safer position, one that also foreshadowed the introduction of thru axle hubs.

Shimano's road range went direct mount in 2017. Campagnolo picked it up the year following; its **Rear Derailleur Joint** allows users to switch back and forth between standard and direct mount hangers, much like a B-Link. Wolf Tooth Components calls their version of this the GoatLink—it also moves the derailleur hanger down and back, convincing Shadow+ 10-speed rear derailleurs to wrap their chains around cogs up to 42 teeth in size. Their RoadLink derailleur hanger extension, by contrast, drops the derailleur pivot down but not back, allowing 10-speed and 11-speed road derailleurs to manage cogs up to 40 teeth. SRAM's **Universal Derailleur Hanger** is specific to thru-axle setups, at the time of writing; hubs with Q/R skewers are not compatible.

The rear derailleur hanger's repositioning was only one campaign within what we might call the war on front derailleurs. The conflict is most visible among higher-end mountain bikes, where vast new cogsets and further rear derailleur modifications on 1× drivetrains are increasingly trusted to provide the gearing ranges front derailleurs had previously offered. The enmity is not surprising, unfortunately—indexed front derailleurs famously require more particular adjustments. And as we'll see, variables including cable direction, mounting parameters, and chainring size have brought forth literally *dozens* of potential replacement options, all up and down the quality spectrum. Ultimately, the front derailleur, shifter, cable, chainrings, and extra chain links can also add weight, complexity, and expense, seen from a certain angle, and some of the gearing combinations they offer are also redundant.

We'll soon return to the beleaguered indexed front derailleurs—they still feature on some majority of bikes in the US market, after all, and most can perform well enough with proper adjustments. Continuing here with the indexed rear derailleur's journey of self-discovery, a handful of imaginative brands enlisted superb micro-ratcheting friction shift levers as a hopeful compromise for front derailleur management—Shimano's excellent indexed-in-rear/friction-in-front bar-end shift lever sets remain a solid choice for tour bikes to this day, for example. The broader industry had other plans, alas; its newly repositioned derailleur hangers anticipated cassettes of ever broader dimensions. Ranges of 9 to 52 teeth suddenly became not uncommon among newer mountain bikes above a certain price point.

Disposing of the front derailleur left the chain without guidance when passing over the chainring, a circumstance that perennially threatens derailment. Recumbent manufacturer BikeE, in an early experiment, went with the most obvious remedy—their single-ring cranks bolted **chainring guards** to either side, giving the chain literally nowhere to run. The **chain guide**, presented later in various iterations, might even be elegant: the chain was made to pass through an inconspicuous bracket, which was adjustable laterally to accommodate varying crank profiles. We bolt these to the seat tube, about where a front derailleur might otherwise have sat. More recently, as we'll explore further on page 187, narrow-wide chainrings have also been instrumental to the success of 1×11 and 1×12 drivetrains.

The front derailleur's last remaining argument was lost to the **clutch derailleurs**, which allow us to add or remove spring tension from a derailleur's P-knuckle by turning an Allen bolt. Or, with Shimano's versions, by literally flipping a switch. Increasing the tension here makes it very difficult to move the lower (tension) pulley forward, which greatly assists the chain in staying put atop its chainring. Releasing the clutch's tension returns the derailleur to what we'd otherwise recognize as its regular spring tension, allowing us to remove and replace the rear wheel more easily.

Clutch derailleurs make downshifting marginally more difficult, but their intervention reduces drivetrain noise considerably. They also make it far easier to ditch the front shifting apparatuses altogether. Shimano calls theirs a Chain Stabilizer; for SRAM it's the Cage Lock.

DRIVETRAINS

**Chain wrap**, also sometimes called **rear derailleur capacity**, describes how large a cog a rear derailleur can accommodate. Chain wrap is a function of the gear ranges, front and back, and we measure it by adding the difference between the smallest and largest chainrings to the difference between the smallest and largest cogs. An old standard road crank with 42-tooth and 52-tooth rings paired with a 12–23-tooth cassette, for example, would give us a capacity of 21. We'd need to use a road derailleur with at least that much capacity, which would be all of them. An old 28/38/48-tooth triple mountain crankset paired with a 12–28-tooth cassette, by contrast, would have a capacity of 36, for which (on a standard mount derailleur hanger) you'd need a long cage derailleur.

As a rule, using the smallest cage possible for your cogset will give you the best shifting experience. Thus do we set the long cage rear derailleurs aside for triple cranksets, or cogsets reaching 36 teeth and above. Shimano short cage rear derailleurs have a capacity of 21. Their medium cage capacity is 34, and their long cage capacity is 42. For SRAM it's 32, 37, and 45, respectively, and for Campagnolo it's 27, 36, and 39.

Prior to beginning any **indexed rear derailleur adjustments**, recall that all cables must be correctly routed, and the non-Teflon ones must also be kink-free and well-lubricated, before reporting for work. We must also attend to the rear derailleur's setup, maintenance, and hanger alignment, as described beginning on page 142. These promises made, our focus narrows to consider the **cable tension**, the principal factor responsible for governing the accuracy of our indexed systems. We'll adjust the cable tension by means of a barrel adjuster—look for one on the derailleur itself, at the frame's cable stop, at the shift lever, or in-line on the cable housing.

Set the bike up in a stand or flip it upside down, start the pedals turning slowly, and shift up one gear. The chain should hop into the next gear. Seen from the rear, both pulleys' teeth should be in plane with those on the second highest cog. This first shift sets the pattern—once the adjustment is correct here, it will echo up and down the gear range.

Here I'm compelled to mention Shimano's indexed **Rapid Rise** rear derailleurs, also known as Low Normal, which flip things upside

**B-tension screw.**

down, from the chain's perspective: the resting position moves to the low/largest cog, leaving us to shift "up" to the high/smallest cog. Shimano has offered such devices off and on since the 1990s, originally as an entry-level package. Working with such fruit, we'll conduct the aforementioned indexing test on the second *lowest* cog instead.

The desired result is the same either way—shifting from the rear derailleur's resting gear to the adjacent one, the chain should make the jump, stay put once the lever is released, and avoid riding up against the next cog. Adjust the cable tension as needed to obtain this result. We'll twist the barrel adjuster in or out in half-turn increments, checking our work each time. Turning it out increases tension, moving the cage position away from its resting position, and the reverse is also true.

The **B-tension screw** traditionally threads into the B-knuckle, perpendicular to the mounting bolt, where it presses against the tab we see on derailleur hangers. Given that the derailleur pivots around its mounting bolt, the B-tension screw allows us to change its resting angle. Dialing the B-tension in rotates the guide pulley back and away from the cogs, facilitating better access to the larger gear ranges; turning it back out refocuses the derailleur on smaller cogsets. Excepting the road bikes, in other words, as a default we usually dial the B-tension most of the way in. Doing so also helps prevent the guide pulley from rubbing on the larger cogs.

⚬⚬⚬⚬

The **indexing front derailleurs** are not the villains of this story—if anything, they're just kind of particular. They flew in alongside the triple-ring cranksets made popular by the 1980s mountain bike boom, an affiliation reflected most clearly in the profiles of their cages: it'll be more of a stepped vertical effect when seen from the side. More recently, what was old is now new again—double-ring mountain cranksets are once again more popular among some newer 10-, 11-, and 12-speed-equipped mountain bikes. It's a formula the industry knows well, of course; most road bikes have subsisted on double cranksets this whole time.

This distinction between two and three chainrings provides for a fine starting point. While most **triple-ring derailleurs** anticipate smaller mountain-range chainrings, some will favor larger road rings instead—the cage profile is less vertical with the latter. We'll compare a triple derailleur's outer cage plate against the largest chainring to suss out the difference here—when mounted, a good match will maintain the same 2 mm gap distance across the entire contact line.

It is the triples' inner cage plates that really set them apart from double-ring derailleurs, however—they'll drop down far deeper than the outer plates, creating a distinct stepped effect. And we must mind the fence here. A double-ring derailleur set up on a triple crank would downshift poorly to the smallest ring. And if it worked at all, a triple-ring derailleur on a double crank would keep dumping the chain onto the frame's bottom bracket shell.

Mountain and gravel bikes with 1×9 drivetrains—one chainring, nine cogs—were the first to challenge front derailleurs' hegemony, relying on chunky first-generation chain guides in place of front derailleurs. On new bikes, 2×9 was never that big. (Many "2×9" setups are just 3×9 in disguise—they sub a bash guard for the outer chainring.) Of course, 1×10 is exactly one cog richer than 1×9.

In addition to the aforementioned road and 2×10/11/12 systems, compact road cranks will also favor the **double-ring derailleurs**. The 2×10 standard has been developed further than 2×9 ever was, with some new bikes even enlisting dedicated 2×10 front derailleurs. Both the 1×11 and 1×12 formats have benefited from the broader shift away from front derailleurs; we'll find more parts options for both.

Braze-on indexed front derailleurs are not uncommon among those higher-end road bikes still bearing double cranksets, but as with their friction kin, the great majority we'll ever see are **clamp-on front derailleurs**. The indexing era overlapped with the introduction of wider aluminum frame tubes, which in turn required wider clamp sizes—while steel frames often abide by the original 28.6 mm clamps, aluminum and carbon fiber frames will require front derailleurs with 31.8 mm or 35.0 mm clamps. (All three measurements describe the seat tube's exterior diameter; the corresponding seatpost sizes will vary.) Cheaper new derailleurs are sometimes cast in one of the larger sizes, with standardized **front derailleur shims** filling in the remaining distance on frames with narrow seat tubes.

The clamp's vertical position on the seatpost has also come under challenge. Those on the original friction front derailleurs sat above the parallelogram, a format now known as **high mount** or **traditional**. By contrast, the clamp ducks below the pivot on more modern **low mount** (also called **top swing**) front derailleurs. A given frame's water bottle mounts might anticipate one style or the other here; don't clamp a front derailleur over these.

Positioning the indexed front derailleur such that it works at its best can take a minute, as we'll see, but Shimano's **E-type front derailleur** assumes we're all simply incapable, offering only a large steel plate in place of the clamp. The bottom bracket shoots through an appropriately sized hole in the plate's base, securing the derailleur and physically preventing us from dumping the chain on the inside, but it eliminates any possibility of using different-sized chainrings as well. The **E-2 direct mount front derailleur** improved on this by bolting onto a couple newly standardized threaded fittings on the seat tube. E-2 derailleurs featured elongated windows, allowing some up-down motion to accommodate different-sized chainrings. SRAM

**Traditional bottom pull road derailleur.**

has units to fit these same E-2 frame mounts, which they call S3. Note that their S2 and S1 mounts are distinct—the former flattens out the E-2/S3 mounting holes, which are offset 5 mm; the latter repositions them.

Finally, the **front derailleur cable routing** provides for one further distinction. The cables may arrive from above or below, contingent on how the frame's cable housing stops are set up, and the derailleurs themselves must anticipate this. The traditional **bottom pull derailleurs** look down to find their cables; the **top pull derailleurs** learnt to look up instead.

Older mountain bikes sometimes featured a grooved brass pulley mounted behind the bottom bracket shell, allowing frames with top-run cables to work with bottom-pull derailleurs, at least until the pulley drowned in all the mud down there. Some more recent Shimano derailleurs provide ambidextrous grooves, accepting cable runs from above or below. SRAM's approach here is more intuitive, fixing two cable binder positions to opposing sides of the pivot.

Catch all that? It's almost like the front derailleurs *want* to go extinct sometimes. Make no mistake, though: they were pushed.

**Top pull front derailleur.**

As with friction front derailleurs, as outlined on page 148, before beginning any **indexed front derailleur adjustments** we'll need to attend to the derailleur's positioning and limit screws. There may be one additional caveat here—while friction front derailleurs anticipate an even 2 mm clearance distance between outer cage plate and top chainring, from 9-speed on up this distance may shrink yet further. The best way to know is to set it up and take a test ride. The chain should drop down to the smallest ring without hesitation, but it shouldn't end up on the bottom bracket shell. The front derailleur's positioning sets the baseline for this result.

The insertion of additional cogs along the rear axle required a reconfiguration of front derailleur cage profiles, especially among those paired with triple cranksets. Looking down from above, what began as more of a simple box has become a blunt-nosed wedge with stepped laterals. The new rule is that the longest edge of the cage's outer plate should be made parallel with the chainrings—this is usually, but not always, at the front. Front derailleur cages are rarely bent; these days especially, it's more likely that they're simply born crooked.

Cross-gearing was thought to be more of a threat when first the indexing front derailleurs appeared, and for this reason their cages will typically rub noisily against the chain in the most extreme cross-geared combinations. The middle rings on triple cranks should allow unfettered access to all or almost all cogs out back, dependent on their number. Cable tensioning adjustments can optimize shifting performance within this narrower spectrum, but they will not be able to expand its parameters.

Here it bears mentioning that the front friction shift levers have never so much as entertained this problem; we can simply trim it away. Some Campagnolo Ergopower levers approximate this ease with a series of micro-clicks, but the Shimano and SRAM dual control levers have more typically offered but a position or two for each chainring in their care.

**Indexed shift levers** have appeared in a few different formats over the years. Suntour and Shimano presented the original **indexed thumbshifters** in 7-speed and 8-speed versions. The various trigger shifters later began nudging the thumbies to the margins, where they became quite scarce until smaller, newer companies including Paul Components, microSHIFT, and Interloc Racing Design brought them back, recognizing opportunities where the majors refused to see any and offering indexed thumbshifters compatible with Shimano and SRAM wares up to 11-speed. Shimano Deore thumbies look about right on my 1990s Trek 970, but they're also some of the most reliable shift levers I've ever used.

**Indexed down tube levers** have not fared as well: microSHIFT offers these up through 10-speed, but that's as far as these go anymore. **Indexing bar-end levers** are more popular; Shimano and SRAM have both kept them current through 11-speed. The left (front) bar-end traditionally works as a micro-ratchet rather than indexing to particular positions as the right (front) lever will, making it universally compatible with front derailleurs.

**Bar-end shift levers.**

    The bar-end shifters' mounting arrangements are unique. The lever always mounts laterally to a down-tube-style shifter boss, which in turn slides into place from the back side. As the bar-end shifter mount enters the handlebar, a bolt head fitting our 6 mm Allen wrench threads into a radially expanding wedge inside the bar. We can't see what happens inside the handlebar, but the detail to recall about the bar-end levers' secret handshake is that it effectively works in reverse—we turn the bolt *clockwise* to loosen the mount and *counterclockwise* to tighten it in place.

    Bar-end shift levers only fit into road handlebars; mountain bars are too narrow. The mounting hardware also requires at least an inch of straight handlebar, meaning that they won't fit with flipped-and-clipped drop bars either.

    **Trigger shifters** are indexed by definition. These bear distinct push buttons set above or below the handlebar, which we'll use to shift up and down the front and rear gear ranges. Some trigger shifters can tear through multiple gears on a single push; others cannot. Our same basic rules regarding indexing compatibility apply here as well—each system works best (and sometimes only) with its own kin, at each successive gradient in the parts hierarchy. What legitimate cross-compatibility we find exists on the Shimano side, across the 7-speed, 8-speed, and 9-speed shifters and derailleurs.

When trigger shifters fuse to brake levers on flat mountain bars, we may call them **integrated levers**. (This term is often applied to road bike levers as well, but for our purposes here we'll call *those* "dual control levers" or "brifters," both being common labels. Stay tuned.)

As with the other control levers, trigger shifters should be tightened in place only to the point where they cannot move around. Trigger shifters are neither adjustable nor repairable. We're sometimes able to unbolt trigger shifters from the brake levers on integrated levers, but when this isn't possible we'd be looking at replacing the entire Happy Meal at once should one or the other fail.

The trigger shifters' original factory lubrication tends to dry out over time, and some light lubrication with an oil dropper bottle often helps their performance. It's generally possible to unbolt the trigger shifters' top plates, exposing their inner workings—drop just a bit of Tri-Flow or other penetrating oil over the mechanism and gently work this into the shifters' pawls with a pick or 3 mm flat-tip screwdriver. Old, dried-out grease can hinder the springs' movement; the lighter oil breaks this down.

A majority of survey respondents prescribed similar recommendations for getting older Shimano Rapidfire or other trigger shifters unstuck, so we know this is definitely a thing. Most involved injecting lightweight oils such as WD-40 to loosen the shifter pawls before gradually beginning to work the inner parts back and forth. Ryan Harris of Recyclistas Bike Shop in Victoria, British Columbia, offers what may be an even simpler solution: "We find pouring boiling water will fix an index shifter. Will often melt the sticky grease and get it working again."

Before **replacing a trigger shifter cable**, shift to the derailleur's resting position—this will be the smallest cog out back, unless you're working on a Rapid Rise/Low Normal derailleur, in which case it'd be the largest. Release the cable's binder bolt. Use cable cutters to snip off the cable's ferrule—or the frayed length, if there wasn't any

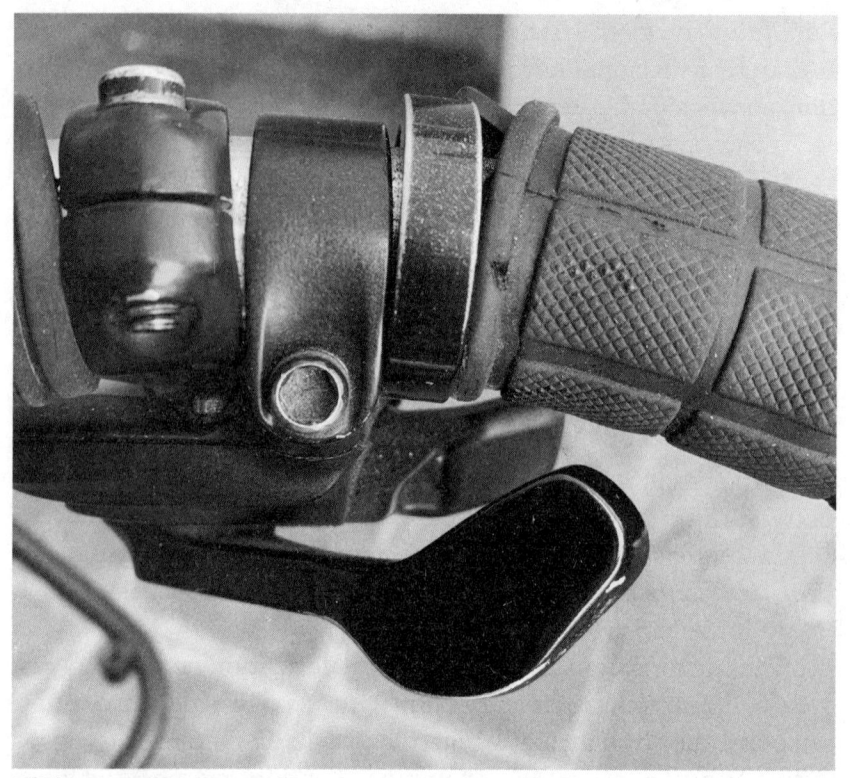

**SRAM 10-speed trigger shifter.**

ferrule—and then use a box pliers to flatten out any serious bends left by the binder bolt. This should allow you to pull the cable free of its housing segments. Use your fourth hand tool to pull it free if needed.

The particular exit strategies used with trigger shifter cables have evolved over time. Shimano's original Rapidfire pods allowed for telling cable-head-sized holes, but they let the mud right in, so these were later sealed over with bigger threaded plastic plugs. More recently we see distinct contoured top plates secured by pairs of tiny screws, which we'll attack with a #1 or #2 Phillips screwdriver. Cup your hand under the shifter to catch them—they can be hard to find if dropped. Stow both screws and the top plate in a jar lid or something until you're ready for reassembly. Don't try to pry the lid off if it doesn't fall away and release immediately—some Shimano lids release by sliding sideways, out toward the handlebar ends. Once the top is off, pushing the cable length into the trigger shifter should cause the cable head to back out in the opposite direction.

Cable extraction for SRAM trigger shifters follows a similar pattern, with variations over time and model ranges. Look for a cable hole, a removable rubber button that may be covering a cable hole, or perhaps a couple tiny screws holding down a top plate. And as we'll see with the twist shifters, some SRAM levers also cover their cable heads with small **cable set bolts**, answering to 2.5 or 3 mm Allen wrenches.

Whatever their other attributes, servicing the **twist shifters** is not always so intuitive. Some of the oldest Grip Shift levers went out into the world with nothing more than small plastic linear springs, which over time proved no match for the furious derailleur springs. At one point we were able to replace these with proper metal springs—a detail that reminds us that they were literally making it up as they went along. Which, of course, is fine; it just provides a useful context here.

The twist shifters' formatting has changed considerably over time, to put this another way, before and since SRAM bought Grip Shift. The derailleur cable's head, for example, has rested in various different places. Cable replacement for SRAM/Grip Shift twist shifters often involves partially disassembling the lever, which in turn requires removing the grips and any bar-end extensions beforehand. While the cable routing used with some levers allows for cable replacement without disassembly, this is usually only possible with new (uncut) replacement cables. You'll most likely need to disassemble the lever when reusing cables.

Some twist levers require that we make a kind of figure eight with the cable just before it goes in; others do not. Pay close attention to how the cable is routed through the lever when taking it apart—take pictures, even, or make a quick sketch if it helps. SRAM/Grip Shift twist shifters, on the whole still the best ones made, have used at least five distinct methods:

1. With some older models, the cable head may be just visible up a shallow hole on the fixed (inboard) part of the lever. No disassembly required!
2. The lever's fixed and rotating parts may be held together by a molded triangular U-shaped bracket, situated directly beneath the lever's barrel adjuster or cable housing stop. In such cases, one side of the triangle's seam will feature a telling screwdriver-sized slot: stick your 6 mm flat tip into this and

rotate to widen the gap. The triangular bracket will slide out laterally, allowing the lever's two sides to separate.
3. If no triangular clamp is visible, it's also possible that the lever simply snaps together. Remove it from the handlebar and see if you can pull the fixed and rotating sides apart. Go easy; this should not require much force at all.
4. The rotating grip sections provided with some SRAM MRX levers allow for exactly one corner apiece: prying this up with a 3 mm flat-tip screwdriver would reveal the cable's head.
5. Other SRAM twist shifters adopt a similar strategy, hiding the cable head beneath a discrete rubber flap. As with MRX, pry up the rubber with a small screwdriver for access.

At some point, SRAM thought it best to deny the cable heads any backward movement—in efforts to improve the consistency of shifting performance, presumably—and this they did by a couple different means. For twist shifters employing methods 4 or 5 above, the cable head may be secured by (a) a small plastic lip, which we'll push aside with our 3 mm flat-tip screwdriver, or (b) a cable set screw, removed with a 2.5 or 3 mm Allen wrench.

While the cable routing within SRAM/Grip Shift levers can vary as well, in each case a distinct cable-sized pathway should be plainly visible once the lever is taken apart. Each cable's journey through the lever will end with an abrupt 90-degree turn just before the cable exits the shift lever. Threading used cables through such sharp bends is difficult; taking the lever apart makes it easier to do so. Not all SRAM/Grip Shift levers allow for disassembly, however, and when reusing cables in such circumstances it's important to *really* twist them as they are installed. This approach is always useful in preventing frays, of course, but here we need to really max it out—you're vigorously rolling the cable across your fingertips while almost incidentally nudging it forward into the shift lever.

Higher-end SRAM twist shifters of a certain vintage sometimes incorporate extra springs, entirely redundant to the shifting process, meant to soften or modulate the feel of the action. These same levers may also feature gear indicator windows; disassembly disrupts both these processes. You may face a choice, in other words, between reusing a previously cut cable and maintaining a lever's modulation and gear indicator window. Going with used cables, we can reassemble these fruits with both features intact, but it may take a few tries—you'd want to remove the lever and hold it steady in a vise.

Within SRAM's parts hierarchy, the MRX label has been applied across a range of quality standards. While some better MRX twist shifters perform well enough, older or cheaper versions often share a more basic problem: they come apart. The basic plastic clips holding the levers' stationary and rotating sides together wear down over extended use, even as the cable's particular routing tends to push the two sides apart. The shorter, stationary grip segments almost invariably lack the purchase to remain in place, unfortunately—our hands inevitably push them away from the levers under the slightest exertion, and thus do the more basic MRX levers unravel. There's nothing to do for the levers here, so we must convince the shortened grip sections to stay put.

It is never a good idea to glue handlebar grips in place. Besides, we have other options here—installing bar-end extensions, for example. Alternately, the more durable threaded BMX-style handlebar plugs will also do the job—those with bolt heads at their ends, threaded into expanding segments inside the handlebars. (The more common push-in handlebar plugs are not useful here.)

Shimano called their twist shifter the Revo Shift. Some of the original versions used odd little cable segments to delegate their gear indicator windows to what they called a Central Information Deck, an odd plastic box hovering over the stem, and these things were not designed to last. They're entirely superfluous to the shifting process, however, and are relatively easily removed. We'll need to unbolt the shift levers' top plates to fully remove the CI Deck's odd little cables.

The 24" Specialized I bought for my son at Phoenix Bikes in Arlington, Virginia, last fall came with a more recent Shimano Revo Shifter, and six months in it has held up fine—save for the stationary grip, which pulled an MRX and escaped. Cable extraction is pretty basic. Look for a solitary #0 Phillips bolt atop one end of the cover on the stationary part of the lever—unscrew this, then use your 3 mm flat-tip screwdriver to nudge the cover's other end free of its catch on the lever.

The **dual control levers**, also sometimes called **brifters**, combine road brake and shift levers. We mount and position these just as we would with any other drop bar brake levers, as described on page 108.

As with the aero brake levers, you'll want to get the cables and housing set up before fully tightening the lever to the handlebar—we always want to confirm the brake cable housing cap fully bottoms out against the lever before taping the housing down and wrapping the bar. The lever's mounting bolt head will be either behind the brake cable or hiding beneath the brake lever hood somewhere, depending on the manufacturer and vintage.

We'll push or pull different parts of the lever to downshift, upshift, and brake. Shimano combines these last two in the brake lever itself—push in to upshift; pull to brake. Pushing a second lever behind this one downshifts. SRAM's Double Tap keeps the braking and shifting distinct, with the smaller lever inside controlling both upshifting and downshifting. Push it laterally inward a short distance for an upshift, marked by a single click; push farther for a double click and the corresponding downshift.

The dual control lever's derailleur housing may travel alongside the brake housing under the grip tape, or it might sprout laterally from the inside of the lever. As with regular drop bar brake levers, we'll loosen the brake's quick release or pinch bolt and pull the lever to access the brake cable's head. Fold the brake lever hood forward from the bars to access the derailleur cable. Road dual control levers provide no accommodations for barrel adjusters. Indexed rear derailleurs do, but indexed front derailleurs do not. Down tube or **in-line barrel adjusters** are thus standard equipment with all those brifters overseeing front derailleurs.

---

Our bike chains are composed of pins, rollers, inner plates, and outer plates. Were we making sandwiches instead, the roller would be the filling, the two inner plates the sauce and lettuce respectively, and the outer plates the bread. The pins skewer it all together, press-fit into the outer plates' holes, and just slightly looser through the inner plates and rollers. Chain width comprises two elements: the distance across the rollers is known as the **inner width**, while the **outer width** describes the breadth across the two outer plates. Both dimensions inform which chains go where.

Chain width began with imperial measurements, but as chains have narrowed they've gone more and more metric. Both track and

BMX bikes traditionally use ⅛" chains, but the latter are more common, so the wide ⅛" size, referring here to the chain's inner width, is often simply called a **BMX chain**. We also see extra-wide ³⁄₁₆" BMX chains, stronger and heavier than ⅛" chains and meant for use with cogs, chainrings, and singlespeed chainrings in the same ³⁄₁₆" dimensions.

Chains with a ³⁄₃₂" inner width have been used for decades, across multispeed gear ranges from 5 to 8 cogs; ³⁄₃₂" 7- and 8-speed chains are thus broadly cross-compatible. Nine-speed chains mark the first real point of departure: the outer width may stay the same or shrink to ¼", dependent on vintage and manufacturer. The inner width narrows to ¹¹⁄₁₂₈".

This same ¹¹⁄₁₂₈" inner width dimension carries over to 10-, 11-, and 12-speed chains, but the 10-speed chains' outer width narrows to between 6.5 and 7 mm. KMC also makes a yet narrower 10-speed chain, with a ⁷⁄₃₂" (5.88 mm) inner width. Some 11-speed chains adopt the ⁷⁄₃₂" width; others narrow to 5.5 to 5.62 mm. Twelve-speed chains have an outer width of 5.15 to 5.30 mm.

Mixing and matching chain segments of different brands or widths is always a bad idea. Doing so greatly increases the odds of sudden chain failure. However, 9-speed chains are broadly cross-compatible with other 9-speed systems. The wider versions of 10-speed and 11-speed chains will also work with 9-speed drivetrain parts, by virtue of their shared ¹¹⁄₁₂₈" inner width; they won't last as long as the wider 9-speed chains, however. Shimano and SRAM cogsets and chains are cross-compatible at each successive level, 9-speed through 11-speed—SRAM 10-speed chains work fine with Shimano 10-speed cassettes, for example, and vice versa. KMC and Wippermann chains marked as "Campagnolo compatible" likewise align with the corresponding Campagnolo drivetrains at each step.

The narrowest chains are not easily discerned from each other—we may need a chain's original packaging or a set of digital calipers to really know for sure. Lacking such, the best way to actually confirm a chain's compatibility is to see it in action. A good match will be capable of shifting fluently through its full gear range, up in the stand at a minimum but preferably out on a test ride.

The **half-link chains**, available in ⅛" and ³⁄₃₂" sizes, merge the inner and outer chain plates into one—each identical link is thinner in front before broadening to the wider outer plate width out back. These are

**BMX master link.**

heavier than regular chains, but their format allows us to adjust the chain tension with twice the precision, which can be really useful for frames with shorter or semivertical dropouts.

When **removing a chain,** first look for a master link—this will always be the quickest and safest way to proceed. Suspend the rear wheel and pedal backward, looking for that one link that looks a bit different than the others. The **BMX master links** are easiest to spot: both pins stick out a bit farther than all the others, and we'll see a thin lateral clip holding the two in place. This clip should be on the outside, facing away from the bike's centerline. To release, grip the clip's two flat fingers and the chain pin behind them with pliers and squeeze. The clip slides off sideways, revealing the tiny slots atop the chain pins that hold it in place. These are the connectors to use with track bike chains; we can safely reuse them for the life of a chain.

Chain manufacturers also produce distinct derailleur-compatible master links meant for use with multispeed bikes. Both sides are symmetrical—each features both a pin and an elongated hole. Pulling sharply on the chain's ends snaps the pair into place; we open them again with pliers. The **master link pliers** are designed for this task in

DRIVETRAINS

**Removing a master link with Channellock pliers.**

particular. Lacking such, we can also use our big Channellock pliers to open some of these—set it up at angles across the chain, with the jaws pressing the master link's openings together, and squeeze. This works best with the stouter 7-, 8-, or 9-speed chain connectors, less so with the thinner 10-, 11-, or 12-speed versions.

SRAM's 9-speed PowerLinks may be reused for the lives of their chains, but their 10-, 11-, and 12-speed PowerLock connectors are meant to be used only once. The same holds true for Shimano's 11/12-speed Quick-Link, as well as KMC's MissingLink11 and MissingLink12. The 7-, 8-, 9-, and 10-speed KMC master links may be reused for the life of their chains. KMC's MissingLink10R is reusable, and it also works with Shimano 10-speed chains. Their single-use MissingLink11 fits Campagnolo and Shimano 11-speed chains.

Wippermann's **Connex links**, by contrast, arrive with a simpler mandate: we may open and close them as needed. Their useful ambivalence here owes to their presciently carved chain pin holes, which enlist small nubs to keep the opposing pins in place. Connex links, like the others, can be found both individually and with complete chains, 8-speed through 12-speed in their case.

**Wippermann Connex link, 8-speed.**

Lacking a master link, our chains may be reassembled in one of two ways: with a chain tool, as we'll discuss shortly, or with a **chain pin**. Shimano chains 7-speed through 10-speed are meant to be joined with **Hyperglide chain pins**, which are twice as long as the others. We push their pointed noses through first, until the slightly wider permanent chain pin behind it is almost centered between the two outer plates. Snap off the extended nose cone with your box pliers—far easier than it looks; it'll break cleanly—and then loosen the resulting tight link, as described on page 175. Campagnolo offers distinct chain pins for their 11-speed and 12-speed chains, but we're only allowed to use the same $200 Campagnolo chain tool to install them both. (An even *more* special $200 chain tool is also available for the 12-speed chains specifically.)

Always select a fresh target when using any of these replacement chain pins—they widen the targeted chain plates just a bit, barging through, and thus should not be sent through the same place twice. The replacement pin always looks a bit different; wipe the chain clean and you should be able to spot it. The other chain pins are probably identical; pick any one of them.

DRIVETRAINS

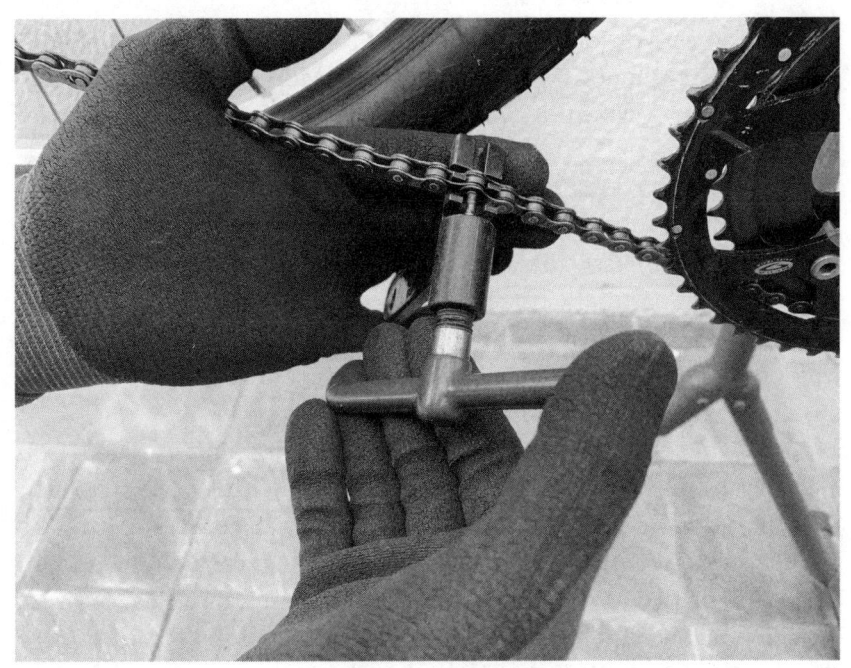

**Breaking a chain.**

Chains lacking master links or replacement pins are broken with chain tools. The chain should be as slack as possible to start—shift to the smallest chainring and cog, front and back. Even better, drop the chain onto the frame's bottom bracket shell while you work. We attack the middle of the chain's lower run, as it passes between the derailleur's tension pulley and the smallest chainring.

When **breaking a chain**, we'll be threading the chain tool's pin directly down atop a chain pin. Move slowly, to help ensure that the tool's pin remains perfectly centered atop its target. Chain tool pins break all the time, especially the cheap ones, precisely when they're driven down off-center. (Replacement pins are available for better chain tools.)

If you'll be using a master link or a new chain pin, go ahead and push the pin all the way through. We'll stop short of that otherwise: 0.5 to 1 mm of the pin's trailing end should still remain on the *inside* of that second outer plate. Bend the chain sideways just a bit, and it should come right apart. Even better, we'll have a very useful toehold when it comes time to reassemble the chain.

Most **chain tools** provide for two positions. The lower saddle is braced by the bulk of the tool's base, which can absorb the force required to shove a chain pin back in place. The tool's upper saddle, closer to the threaded handle, is only meant for loosening tight links. Reassembling a chain in the upper saddle will probably break the chain tool.

You'll want to confirm the **chain length** is correct when replacing chains. The default is usually overlong; we typically cut new chains to fit. The line formed by the derailleur cage's pulley bolts should never be more than parallel with the chain run extending below it. When shifted to the smallest gear combinations, the chain's lower chain run should not sag—we don't want the chain doubling back and riding along the cage.

At the far end, the chain should still have just a bit of slack when shifted into the largest gear combinations: it should not be stretched flat-out between cogs and pulleys. Riding a rear derailleur like this truly wrecks it. Our solution would be to replace the chain, add an extra link or two of the *exact* same kind of chain, or adjust the rear derailleur's low limit screw to prevent access to any cogs too large for the chain to accommodate. Or, in especially extreme cases, we may even dial in the front derailleur's high limit screw. Either of these two last emergency measures would of course limit your gearing options, which is likely still preferable to pulling the rear derailleur apart.

Both worn-out springs and a lack of lubrication can cause the chain runs exiting especially old and crusty rear derailleurs to sag, suggesting they may be too long, but we have a simple test: can you pull the derailleur's lower, tensioned pulley backward? Said derailleur would need oil at a minimum, if so, and possibly replacement.

The **chain orientation** also bears mentioning. Some of Shimano's 10-speed and 11-speed chains are labeled as **asymmetrical** or **directional**, a designation that signals that their plates were engineered to better climb the cogset gears on one side while reaching for the larger chainrings on the other. The chain's Shimano-logoed plates will face to the outside, in such cases, with the blank plates faced inward. Get in the habit of doing this for Shimano chains more generally, and you won't have to worry about it. Campagnolo does something similar—chain plates stamped with their production batch numbers should face the outside.

Make yourself a **chain hook** before reassembling a chain with a chain tool. Broken spokes are great for this: put a 90-degree bend in the middle and then the same again closer to each end. Passing the ends through the chain links immediately to either side of the break dissipates the rear derailleur's spring tension, which would otherwise pull from both sides—an effect the chain tools find truly annoying. These are also useful when installing the replacement chain pins mentioned above, or working with master links.

When **reassembling bike chains** with a chain tool, the pin we'll be pushing back through always needs to extend about 1 mm through the outer plate, toward its interior. Bend the chain laterally to snap this place-keeper nub in place. Line up your sandwich-to-be in the chain tool's lower saddle and continue turning the tool's handle to press the pin in until its length is *almost* centered between the two outer plates—one side should stick out *just* a hair farther. The link will emerge too tight, and this is where the chain tool's upper saddle rides in to do its magic.

Line up the tool's pin on whichever end of the chain pin protrudes more, this time in the tool's upper saddle. Lower the chain tool's pin to make contact, and then turn its handle a quarter turn—just enough to center the chain pin between its outer plates, with each end protruding by the same measure. The upper saddle is designed to have just enough give to allow this transaction to happen.

Neglecting this last step will leave us with a **tight link**. These are easily seen on derailleur-equipped bikes—just pedal backward. Does the chain bump around, passing between the pulleys? Confirm by touch: any links not demonstrating their usual range of motion should be loosened in a chain tool's upper saddle. (Rust can do something similar, but typically to whole sequences of chain links rather than individual ones.)

The cogs, the chain, and to a lesser extent the chainrings all wear together, as detailed from page 228. The causes of **chain failure** are more anecdotal than documented, but on the rare occasions when it does happen we may suspect improper installation, excessive wear, external impacts, or even shifting under load. This last can also bend chain links, so just stop, okay? (Under duress we can straighten bent chain links with a couple big crescent wrenches or pliers, but in any other circumstance it'd be safer to replace the chain.)

Some manufacturers claim their drivetrains are *so* special that you can actually shift under load—and maybe you can for a minute, but they also have something to sell you. Shifting under load inevitably wears parts out faster, and it may damage them as well; that's just what happens. It's a rich consumer fetish.

I've worked in shops where the chains' original packing grease is preserved in place as a kind of "super lubricant." At other shops, management has encouraged me to disperse the packing grease with actual chain lubricant whenever building a new bike or installing a chain. So you'll hear different things. As a rule, **chain lubrication** should be kept as minimal as possible—wet chains attract dirt and grit, which gets all over everything. The grime also acts as a kind of liquid sandpaper, wearing down drivetrains before their time is due.

Personally? I like alcohol-based **gel lubricants** such as Rock "N" Roll, which suspend oil within alcohol. Shake up the bottle, get the chain turning, and drop a bead on the chain for a few seconds. Shift through the gears and then wipe off the excess. The gel lubricants get down in the rollers, in theory, while the alcohol evaporates. Leaves everything reasonably nice and neat. Spray oils such as WD-40, by contrast, tend to have the opposite effect.

**Belt drive** has always been pretty rare. It is lighter, cleaner, quieter, and pretty much maintenance-free. It also cannot work with any derailleur systems, limiting users to singlespeeds, internally geared hubs, or fixed gears. Belt drives run at higher tension as well, which in their case means that they have a very low tolerance for the mud and debris regularly thrown up in the course of riding.

Frames requesting belt drive once needed special cutouts near their dropouts—the original belts didn't ever disconnect; we'd literally pass them through a break in the stay—but this is no longer the case. Any bike with horizontal dropouts or an eccentric bottom bracket is now eligible.

○○○○

The **cranks**, like every other major component, have gone through numerous iterations. Each one must always fit correctly with the bottom bracket, the chain, and any front derailleur in use, and here especially everything needs to be nice and tight. The cranks' rotations must also remain perfectly flat, in plane with the frame, without trending off to the slightest degree—a responsibility they share with the bottom brackets, as we'll discuss from page 191.

The ancient **cottered cranks** are almost extinct—no new bike has been built with them for at least fifty years. While the cotter project surely thrilled enthusiasts at its inception, the brutality of time has revealed certain inherent deficiencies: the crank arms must be made of heavier steel rather than aluminum; replacement parts are hard to find; gearing options are limited.

We'll recognize cottered cranks by their cotter pins, both set laterally at either end of the BB spindle. The pins are made of softer metal—they're meant to deform slightly, going in, such that their profiles align with channels set across the spindle. This very softness also makes it very difficult to remove cotter pins with a hammer—an approach the design seems perhaps to suggest. And for the same reason, we'll always want to use a new cotter pin when reinstalling cottered cranks.

Cottered cranks are best installed and removed with a proper crank cotter press, such as Park Tool's CR-2; alas, this tool went out of production years ago. Bikesmith Design continues to offer a crank cotter press, alongside cotter pins in various dimensions. As with our chain tools, we'll center its pin atop the cotter to be removed and start threading the handle down, delivering the slow and even pressure recalcitrant fifty-year-old cotter pins are more likely to appreciate.

Alternately? Brace the crank arm from below, such that your hammer blows won't bend the bottom bracket spindle. Transmit your hammer's message through a block of wood rather than directly. And when reinstalling cotter pins with a hammer, first fit the nut loosely atop its threads to shield them from direct impact.

The two cotter pins should always be replaced together and installed from opposite sides. Only tighten the cotter pin's nut once it has been fully pressed or hammered back into place—the threads may strip otherwise. Also be sure to reaffirm the nut's tightness after riding a few miles.

The cottered cranks' threaded three-piece bottom bracket format went on to host various other projects, as we'll see, but the steel arms also found expression in the **one-piece cranksets**. These were used on various older bikes, as well as children's bikes—look for the wider "American" bottom bracket shells. The one-piecers were the BMX standard for years, so a few decent examples were produced. There are no crank bolts: as the name implies, a single steel rod bends just enough to pass through the BB shell, emerging with pedal threads set at right angles. For disassembly, we remove the neutral-side pedal, undo the lockring and cone, and pull the crank out the drive side—note that these parts are all reverse-threaded. Similar but regular-threaded kit on the drive side will hold a replaceable chainring in place. For each side, be sure to keep track of the keyed washer between cone and locknut.

Most bikes awheel today use what we call **three-piece cranks**, which update the format first advanced by cottered cranks. The bottom bracket shell returns to the smaller, threaded "Euro" dimensions, with the crank arms and bottom bracket again rendered as separate pieces. We'll dive into bottom brackets shortly, beginning on page 191. Suffice it here to say that our BBs' dimensions and other characteristics can vary considerably.

The traditional **spider crank** originally supported its chainrings across five sturdy shelves. The **neutral crank arm**, opposite, observed. Tandem cranksets include pairs of neutral-side spider cranks to support the stoker chain, the rearmost of which—using a bolt-on or splined cog—could conceivably be set up as a fixed gear, if yours wanted to switch sides. (Simply switching sides with the regular parts would be asking your pedals and cog to unthread.)

We'll use steel **crank bolts** to tighten our three-piece crank arms to their intended BB spindles. Check their tightness periodically if you ride a lot—before long rides, for example. Riding loose three-piece cranks will destroy them: the harder steel spindles wear down the aluminum cranks' fittings, widening them out until they literally fall off the bike. The crank bolts are always on the out-the-door checklist for bikes sold at independent shops. I've never met a crank tightened so much it couldn't be removed, but I've seen several left loose and destroyed.

Our various crank manufacturers provide exact torque recommendations for their wares, in technical documentation we'll find at their websites or in little booklets folded into the packaging. Similar advice is available online for historic examples. Speaking more generally, crank bolts should be made as tight as possible. The same holds true with regard to pedals and bottom bracket cups.

Older crank bolts are mostly removed with 14 mm sockets. (You may need a 15 mm socket to draw out those associated with old Stronglight or TA cranks, whose inner dimensions are slightly wider.)

**Spider crank.**

These are all meant to hide beneath dust caps, whose primary role is to protect the crank arms' fragile **extraction threads**, which ring the crank bolts. The oldest dust caps threaded in all by themselves—we'll use a flat-tip screwdriver, a 5 mm Allen key, or a tiny spanner to thread them out. (A small needle-nose pliers can usually fill in for the spanner here.) Newer dust caps are plastic; we'll remove these by sticking a 3 mm flathead screwdriver into the small slot we'll see on one side. The most current three-piece crank bolts incorporate their own dust caps, built around a socket for an 8 mm Allen wrench.

**Three-piece crank bolts and nuts.**   **Three-piece crank dust caps.**

Crank bolts are traditionally threaded to M8, though some more modern systems will anticipate M12 or M15 crank bolts. Aluminum crank bolts exist as silly costumes—the torque required to tighten our cranks in place would erase their fragile threads. You'd install the cranks with steel crank bolts, remove them, and sub the lightweight alloy ones, in other words. Crank bolts sometimes loosen, of course—the manufacturers here seem to anticipate that you (or "someone") will repeat this same procedure each time you do a bolt check. (And just imagine how fun it'd be to drill these things out, if "someone" forgets!)

The **self-extracting (SE) crank bolts** effectively pack their own crank extractors, allowing us to simply bolt and unbolt our cranks. These can be really nice to have, used correctly. As a rule, always confirm that an SE bolt's **retaining ring** is fully tightened before removing the crank—it'll be the threaded metal disc around the bolt itself. The original retaining rings featured pairs of small holes, tightened with a small spanner such as Park's SPA-2 or a small needle-nose pliers. (More modern SE bolts used with two-piece cranksets may be tightened by other methods; see the discussion of One-Key-Release [OKR] systems on page 182.)

You should definitely remove at least one of the SE bolts before installing a three-piece crankset on a splined BB. You'd be wrenching blind otherwise—unable to actually see whether or not the spindle's hungry steel splines are devouring their softer aluminum counterparts on the crank arms. (With practice, lining up one crank arm this way will provide a sufficient reference point for aligning the opposite arm.)

More generally it's wise to take your time when installing any cranks atop splined bottom brackets. There may be a little lateral play as the splines connect, but you should never feel as if you're suddenly trying to crush metal together. Get one of the bolts all the way out, press the crank onto the BB spindle's splines, and continue holding it just like that until the bolt is tight enough to prevent the crank arm from moving; follow this with the torque needed to secure it.

Contingent on the SE bolt's vintage and manufacturer, you'll use a 6, 7, or 8 mm Allen wrench to tighten or release the cranks. SE crank bolts are tightened just like any others, but their extractive function also makes them more difficult to release—you may even ask a burlier comrade for assistance. Alternately, set Vise-Grip pliers or a pipe over your Allen key and push against the opposite crank arm for extra leverage. A toe strap may be useful when removing the remaining crank arm, so long as you're working on a nice old steel frame—just wrap it tightly around the crank arm and the nearest chainstay, hold the frame, and push your wrench. (Do not try this with any ultralight frames, especially those made with carbon fiber, which may lack the strength to accommodate torque applied from unexpected angles.)

**Removing three-piece cranks** involves pulling the arms off individually. They both come off the same way. Now stop: make sure you can see the end of the bottom bracket spindle inside. Look for a squared end, for tapered spindles, or a circle of splines. The oldest crank bolts (for tapered spindles) used thick steel washers inserted between bolt head and spindle end—remove anything such before proceeding.

Tool choice is equally crucial. Two factors make them distinct. The wide and wispy threading surrounding the bolt head provides for the *first* distinction among the **crank extractors**—while 22 mm eventually became standard for these threads, the wider 23.35 mm (Stronglight) and 23 mm (TA) threadings still make occasional appearances. The fit should feel exact—not loose at all. Stein Tool makes extractors for both Stronglight and TA.

The crank extractors' *second* and more modern distinction splits those intended for the traditional 11 mm square bottom bracket spindles from those meant for the modern 16 mm splined spindles. The pin threading down to push off square spindles is narrow; the one meant for splined spindles is much wider. (We can also find small metal buttons known as ISIS adapters, which allow the 11 mm extractors to pull the 16 mm ISIS or Octalink cranks.) Once the crank bolt and any washer are removed, we'll confirm which extractor we need.

The crank extractor should thread in smoothly: back it out and clean up the threads if it doesn't. Also be careful not to cross-thread it when starting out—finger-tighten the extractor all the way down to the crank arm's base, then use a wrench to snug it down until its threads bottom out. Next, begin applying even pressure to the extractor's handle (or the wrench holding it), always in plane with the crank arm. It'll start out pretty tight before gradually loosening.

Damaging the extraction threads will cement your three-piece cranks in place, pending either Stein Tool's Crank Extractor System or serious destructive force. (It will also trap any demons lurking in your bottom bracket.)

The **two-piece cranks** are more recent. Shimano's 2004 Dura-Ace Hollowtech II was marginally lighter than previous examples, as the new ones must always be, but it also displayed a whole new design concept. A wider steel pipe rises securely from the spider crank's midpoint, charging straight through a lightweight sleeve spanning between a pair of new external bearings set just outside a standard threaded BB shell. Emerging on the neutral side, the splines atop this pipe are delighted to discover a set of matching counterparts nestled within the neutral-side crank arm. Always keep track of any washers installed between the neutral-side crank and bearings whenever removing or installing two-piece cranks.

Many two-piece cranksets use a headset-style preload bolt to draw the two arms together, with a pair of pinch bolts at the neutral-side crank's base tightening it all together. Various people make the eight-splined sockets needed to remove Shimano's FC series crank arm fixing bolts; Park's BBT-10.2 also includes a special tooth to snag the safety plate Shimano uses with their Hollowtech II cranks.

Other manufacturers such as FSA and Race Face have brought the self-extracting crank bolts to two-piece cranks, this time calling them One-Key-Release (OKR). These work the same way, as outlined on page 180, though some enlist novel approaches for securing the retainer rings—we'd need a 16 mm Allen wrench to tighten or

DRIVETRAINS

**Two-piece cranks with bottom bracket.**

release some OKR retainer rings deployed by Race Face, SRAM, and Truvativ. Alternately, go find a standard 7/16" bolt at your local hardware store and use its 5/8" head as a kind of reverse socket for these. (Your bog-standard 16 mm box wrench will be happy to turn it.)

Note that SRAM's aluminum DUB retainer rings are reverse-threaded, as are the steel versions they issue with their Eagle cranks. Yet while the latter surrender to a regular Allen wrench for removal, the DUB retainer rings offer a circle of four small holes instead—you may actually need their socket if your needle-nose pliers don't do the trick.

Despite all the aforementioned developments, the **riveted crank** remains the most common in terms of production and actual use, having long ago leapt over from the budget bikes to colonize various cheaper models sold at independent bike shops. The riveted crank's steel chainrings will last longer, but they're also heavier, and you will not be able to modify their gearing. The crank arms may be plastic-coated steel or aluminum, dependent on vintage and manufacturer.

We'll discuss pedal threading a bit farther ahead, beginning on page 203, but it bears mentioning here that it's almost always going to be the same 9/16" size used for adult bike pedals for decades now. The one-piece cranks, traditionally threaded for ½" pedals, represent our only major exceptions. The two sizes are visually distinct.

There may also be some small chance you'd encounter a crankset old enough to bear 14 × 1.25 mm French pedal threads; you may even find a not-quite-dead set of 1960s French pedals to match. Alternately, we can also use a set of pedal taps, a tap handle, and some cutting oil to retap the French cranks to accept regular 9⁄16" pedals. But retapping threads is a topic more at home within the chapter on rust, beginning on page 231.

The **chainline**—the chain's distance from a bike frame's centerline—is a function of the bottom bracket spindle length, the rear cog or cogset, and the **crank profile**, which describes the spider's lateral positioning in relation to the frame's centerline. Having a good chainline is critical to drivetrain health. It's not something we need to worry about with new or stock bikes—this is low-hanging fruit for manufacturers, so all their various steeds are born with decent chainlines. It's just something to keep in mind when setting up a bike or making major drivetrain changes. Also bear in mind that a spider crank may inch toward the frame's centerline as we tighten its hardware—wait until everything's tight before evaluating the chainline.

A healthy 1× chainline exhibits two characteristics: the chainring should line up at the midpoint on its rear wheel's gear range, and it should also sit as close to the chainstay as possible. With triple cranks, we'll use the middle chainring as our reference point with relation to the cogs. The gap between the rings on a double crank should also line up centered in relation to its cogs.

With some exceptions, the cranks' profiles have broadly narrowed over time—the trend is clear, comparing the broadly flat old road cranks to the more wedge-shaped modern mountain cranks. The pedal axes' distance from each other, known as the **Q factor**, is a function of the crank profile, the BB shell width, and the BB spindle length, all of which should be in agreement. Drivetrains with narrower Q factors are more efficient—or, to put it another way, we rarely win races while running bowlegged. When pushing fixed gears, bikes with lower Q factors are also less prone to catching pedals.

The different **crank arm lengths** exist to better accommodate shorter and taller people. Alongside narrower pedals, they're also useful in allowing our fixed gear conversions to avoid catching their pedals. The crank arms are measured center-to-center, from pedal threads to spindle hole. This length should be noted in small script somewhere along each arm's inside surface, facing the frame. The shortest common size is 165 mm; 170 mm and 175 mm are more common. A few manufacturers produce 152 mm cranks for kids' bikes. Lengths of 172.5 mm and 180 mm are both rare.

Those **chainrings** not riveted in place are usually bolted to their spider cranks. We can find heavier but longer-lasting steel rings up to 34 teeth—the largest size used with modern 1× mountain drivetrains, typically—as well as various larger titanium rings, but our nonriveted chainrings will otherwise be made of aluminum. We replace them when they wear down, as described in greater detail beginning on page 228, or to modify a bike's gearing.

All older and most newer chainrings are joined to their respective spider cranks with bolts. The **bolt circle diameter (BCD)** describes their pattern. This number may be noted on the chainrings somewhere, but it won't feature on the crank arms themselves. The riddle is easily solved, however—spoke rulers often feature BCD gauges along their lengths, and we can also use tools such as Park's CDG-2 Chainring Diameter Gauge. And if you have access to a computer, printer, and internet connection, manufacturers including Wolf Tooth Components offer printable BCD templates.

The 110 mm and 130 mm **five-bolt BCD** patterns were once the most common, used historically for mountain and road bikes respectively. Five-bolt 110 mm BCD rings have been cut from 34 teeth to 62 teeth, meeting needs from the middle rings on mountain cranksets to the outer rings on small-wheeled recumbents. Most 110 cranks bear a second 74 mm BCD sequence for the smallest chainring, down nearer the bottom bracket. We've seen 130 rings from 39 teeth to 53 teeth; the triples among them often include the smaller 74 mm BCD as well. Campagnolo did similar, substituting their own 135 mm BCD for the larger rings but keeping the 74 mm BCD for the smaller ones on triple cranks. These are the most common five-bolt BCD patterns, but it bears mentioning that at least a dozen others have also existed. Most are old, obscure, and kind of surprising to find at this point.

Surveying these options, the original **compact road cranks** sagely hopped aboard the well-established five-bolt 110 mm BCD pattern. Their typical 34-tooth/50-tooth range represented a lighter, happier midpoint between the traditional 42-tooth/52-tooth road cranksets and the more generous triple crankset range, a compromise that has proven popular. We can find (or assemble) compact road cranks for three-piece cranks, but their introduction coincided more with the two-piece cranks, so that tends to be their format.

Shimano's five-bolt compact 58 mm/94 mm BCD caters to rings a few teeth smaller than those the old 110 mm BCD supported—which, for mountain bikes, often reached 46 or 48 teeth. Shimano's compact cassettes duly shrank in compensation, going from 13 to 11 teeth for the smallest cog, reprising the pattern Suntour's MicroDrive first established in the 1980s.

The world moved on again with the **four-bolt BCD**, which saved a bit more weight. The mountain chainrings were game, being small enough to rest comfortably across a mere four shelves, but the broader road cranksets stayed with their five-bolt patterns. With this, 64 mm/104 mm emerged as the most common four-bolt mountain standard, but there are a few other ones.

**Spiderless cranks** were also a thing for a while, in the 2010s—splines were cut to the drive crank and a short stack of threads was set atop them, with a proprietary spider and lockring sealing the deal. These new spiders arrived with various different BCD patterns, potentially allowing greater flexibility in our gearing, but the main thing was that they could be replaced independently of the crank arms. The benefit here has always eluded me, however—crank spiders are rarely bent, and even when it happens, almost all can be straightened in a vise. Remove the rings first; work slowly. (And yet more recently, One Component's Switch spiders have brought this same spiderless "benefit" to the direct mount chainrings described below.)

◦◦◦◦

The **oval chainrings** may or may not improve our riding experiences, depending on whom you speak with. It's quite an old debate, actually—Shimano originally called theirs Biopace; for Sugino it was OvalTech; others preceded both. **Asymmetric chainrings** are something different: their absence of symmetry refers to the bolt pattern, which becomes a rectangle rather than a circle, which allows manufacturers to better accommodate wider jumps between two chainrings. Alas, they cannibalized the world-standard 110 mm BCD in their supreme haste, forcing us now to specify between the five-bolt 110 mm BCD and four-bolt *asymmetric* 110 mm BCD. A smaller 96 mm asymmetric BCD exists as well.

The **narrow-wide chainrings** are meant for the 1× systems—alongside the clutch derailleurs and chain guides, they are critical to keeping our chains safely atop their chainrings in the absence of front derailleurs. Their name is usefully descriptive: every other tooth is rendered extra wide, in perfect alignment with the pattern our standard chains already provide between their inner and outer plates. Not a good match for front derailleurs, of course.

We'll use standardized **chainring bolts** when attaching our chainrings to all but the oldest crank arms, which may hold out for narrower antique versions. Shorter and taller stacks of the standard chainring bolts will otherwise skewer single- or double-chainring sandwiches. Depending on the circumstances—the chainline, the width of the spider crank's shelves, the distances between successive chainrings—we may be moved to install equally standardized spacers at points along the chainring bolts' lengths or beneath their wider nuts. We'll install a full round of these, fitting the same allotment to each bolt in our four-bolt or five-bolt BCD patterns. Chainring bolts are traditionally made of steel—lighter aluminum variants are also available, but these are not safe for use with fixed gears.

The distance between chainrings is critical—friction derailleurs will happily dump chains between chainrings, given the opportunity. The indexed front derailleurs will also struggle to perform when lined up atop unfamiliar patterns. The above-mentioned chainring spacers can provide useful remedies here, distributed in equal measures across all four or five crank bolts. Find a good template to use for comparison when resolving such issues—an equivalent new bike's crankset, perhaps, or at least one you know to work well. Line up this example directly in line with your own project, comparing how their chainrings sit.

Cranks with removable chainrings allow us some choice with regard to **chainring size**—larger rings allow for greater speed; smaller ones may make it easier to climb hills. Beyond aligning with the crank's BCD and the front derailleur's cage profile, any replacement chainring will also need to present an appropriate **chainring profile**: how far forward or backward it leans in relation to the chainline. Older

**Chainring bolts.**

and singlespeed chainrings are all pretty flat, but the chainring profile often renders modern cranksets distinct.

Finally, chainrings also have front and rear sides. The countersunk halos we see around the bolt holes should always face away from the spider crank's shelves, whether that finds them oriented toward or away from the bike's centerline—while those on inner road or middle mountain rings face inward, the ones on the outer rings face outward. The holes' halos are just wide enough to accept the broader tops and bases of our chainring bolts. The steady vibrations inherent to riding perpetually threaten to loosen our chainring bolts; lining things up as designed, and nice and tight, can greatly hinder their unraveling.

The more current your multispeed chainrings, the more likely they will bear various pins and ramps around their edges. These are designed to help facilitate the shifting process, and as such they will also share particular orientations in relation to matching features on the other rings. We call this synchronicity **chainring timing**.

Were the chainrings clocks, midnight would strike at the crank arm—its largest chainring marks this with an outward-facing squat metal post, meant to prevent the chain from falling between chainring

DRIVETRAINS

and crank arm. The post also provides our starting point for the chainring timing: exactly one orientation across the crank's shelves will find this post centered beneath the crank arm, as it is always meant to be. The other rings in turn will then provide more subtle cues to indicate their own timing—a single inward-pointing tooth may be positioned to fall right behind the post and crank arm as well, or perhaps the chainrings will share matching etchings, which a specific orientation across the crank arms' shelves will allow to form into a line.

Recall the indexed drivetrains' storyline around parallel and redundant subscription models? I can't wait to tell you about the **direct mount chainrings**, which join to their spider cranks in exciting new ways. Forget all those dusty old BCD patterns cyclists worldwide have relied on for decades, because new options! Guess how many? At last count, Cane Creek, Cannondale, Easton, e*thirteen, FSA, Race Face, Shimano, and SRAM have each offered direct mount rings. SRAM and Cane Creek direct mount rings are cross-compatible, and Cannondale and FSA have reached a separate agreement of their own, but that's it. Happy hunting!

We'll use a T25 Torx wrench to remove the three bolts anchoring SRAM or Cane Creek direct mount rings; e*thirteen has their own tool for removing their direct mount rings and BBs. FSA has another unique tool for what they term their Modular Cranks, to which Cannondale direct mount chainrings will also submit. Park's 20-tooth BBT-22 extractor, long familiar from its work with the Shimano and ISIS Drive BBs, will also grip the lockrings on Race Face direct mount chainrings; their LRT-4 will dispatch those from Shimano.

The crank arms come off the same way other two-piece cranks do. Their chainrings are best replaced with the crank arm cradled in a vise—throw a rag in there first if the crank's finish is important to you. (Carbon cranks are afraid of vises. Best to just pull them off and use independent leverage instead—you might ask a comrade for their assistance here.)

Clean the crank's flat interface with the chainring, as well as the chainring itself. Grease the lockring threads prior to reassembly, being sure to use carbon-safe cleaners and grease instead when working with carbon cranks.

Crank arms break very rarely, usually across the pedal threads or spindle hole. **Bent cranks** are marginally more common. Spinning the spider crank and using the front derailleur cage or chainstay as a reference point, we'd see it bow out of round at some point. This might simply be a bent chainring, if the other rings are straight, but any multiples here would suggest a bent shelf. The bent spider shelves we must straighten in vises, gripping their broad surfaces and levering with a large crescent wrench, using a slow and even pressure.

Bent chainrings are most easily straightened by means of a vise—just rotate the chainring through, using a pliers or a large crescent wrench to lever out any deviations. It may also be possible to do this while the chainrings are still mounted to the cranks, using large screwdrivers and pliers. First, confirm that all the rings' attachment hardware is fully tightened. Be careful about levering against the other chainrings, lest you bend them as well.

Both the crank arms' pedal threads and those on the pedals themselves should be clean and free of excessive rust prior to their joining. Crusty pedal axles can be cleaned up with light oil and a rag, but indistinct crank threads should really be retapped at a bike shop. Dab a half jellybean's worth of grease on each pedal axle prior to installation. Your pedal axles might actually be wider than your crank arms, and this is fine, so long as they clear the chainstays without issue. The important thing is that we always get the pedals nice and tight.

Our cranks may also face the specter of **cross-threaded pedals**, in the event we're trying to rush through things—or maybe not really paying attention. The pedal axles must always go in perfectly straight, on the correct side, and to at least 11 mm worth of thread engagement, as described in greater detail on pages 209–10. The steel pedal threads will eagerly erase their softer aluminum counterparts, given the opportunity! If only the first few threads get erased, *stop*—we can often limit the damage by reinstalling the pedal from the back side of the crank arm before spinning it out and trying it again up front, nice and even. This won't repair the damaged threads so much as arrange their rubble in useful rows, but I've seen it endure over time.

You might also just obtain a new-to-you crank arm, given the means and the opportunity, but there may be a further remedy as well. Unior still makes the steel thread replacement inserts known as Helicoils, last I checked—the silver-colored one goes on the left, with the brass-colored one on the right. A complete Helicoil kit will include the oversized Helicoil ⅝" × 20 TPI left- and right-handed tap set needed to install these, together with a tap handle. We send them in bathed in a strong thread-locking compound, which we'll let fully cure before installing any pedals—that'd be a full twenty-four hours, for the Loctite at least.

○○○○

A bike's **bottom bracket (BB)** must be strong enough to efficiently transfer our pedaling force to the drivetrain without flexing or otherwise displacing our energy. The technology used has evolved quite a bit over time, often in insightful ways, but this process is increasingly guided—or blindered, perhaps—by the increasingly desperate braying of declining neoliberal capitalism, which is to say that sterile competition increasingly undermines what positive cooperation had existed. While bicycle and component manufacturers were once able to glimpse common interests in abiding by a mere handful of BB formats, we now see an almost whimsical scattering of noncompatible BB designs. Which, if you're just trying to fix your bike, can get pretty tedious.

The **bottom bracket shell size** refers to the diameter. (BB widths, as we'll see, have also expanded in recent years.) Within the North American market, many older bikes and kids' bikes have 51.5 mm **American BB** shells, which in the original design use press-fit bearing cups. Most other *bicicletas Norteamericanas* awheel today have been designed around the ubiquitous 1.37" × 24 TPI **ISO** or **English BB** standard. *The drive-side cup is reverse-threaded on English/ISO bottom brackets.* The original English/ISO BBs have also expanded laterally to 73 mm, 83 mm, and 100 mm, to accommodate mountain, downhill, and the wide-tired fat bikes, respectively.

A small number of high-end road bikes use 36 mm × 24 TPI **Italian BB**s. These shells alone measure *70 mm* wide. Italian BBs, being conventionally threaded on both sides, are also vulnerable to what is called precession—the drive-side cup may gradually thread itself out over time, by virtue of the threads' alignment with the pedaling axis. The old 35 mm × 1 mm **French BB**s are all but extinct. Two press-fit (nonthreaded) BMX-specific BB shells have also been used—the 36.5 mm **Spanish BB** and the 41.2 mm **Mid BB**.

The **one-piece bottom brackets** were the first to occupy American BB shells. The name comes from their crankset, a single metal beam bent to 90 degrees, with shoulders just round enough to pass through. The drive-side bearing cone is in a fixed position; we'll make our bearing adjustments using a threaded cone and locknut over on the neutral side. Note that there should be a thin keyed washer between the two—our adjustments will be difficult in its absence. We'll grip the locknut with a 30 mm headset wrench or a large crescent wrench, but within the North American market Park's HCW-11 wrench may be our best option for the cone.

One-piecers famously arrive aboard old or cheap bikes, both traditionally underserviced categories, and thus will often merit overhauls when first we encounter them. Remove the neutral-side pedal, then both the cone and locknut, and pull the crank out from the drive side. You should see a pair of caged bearings, each hosting nine or ten huge 5/16" bearings. Two formats are in use with the one-piece internals, each with a distinct threading. The bearing count provide for a useful shorthand here, projecting a like-with-like simplicity—a cone and bearing cup from a nine-bearing BB would not work with a ten-bearing crank arm, for example.

Lacking solvent tank access, the caged bearings may be cleaned by soaking them overnight in undiluted citrus solvent. (We'll discuss drivetrain cleaning more beginning on page 225.) The one-piecers' relatively massive bearing cones are rarely pitted, their races even less so. At worst, replacements should be cheap.

Prior to reassembly, first confirm both bearing cups are evenly pressed into the two sides. Our bearing adjustments also follow the pattern established by the hubs and headsets—get the cone just *slightly* too tight, hold it there while firming the locknut down atop it, and then back the cone out hard against the locknut. As with any other bearing system, the range of movement should be strictly two-dimensional, and it should not bind at any point in the crank's rotation. Double-check the bearing cups' installation if it does bind.

The domain of **three-piece bottom brackets**, also called **ball-and-cup sets**, technically includes the cottered cranks—three pieces, after all—but in general conversation the phrase describes our cotterless options. Prying one open, we'll be able to pull out its spindle, neutral-side cup, and drive-side cup with lockring. Each side will host either

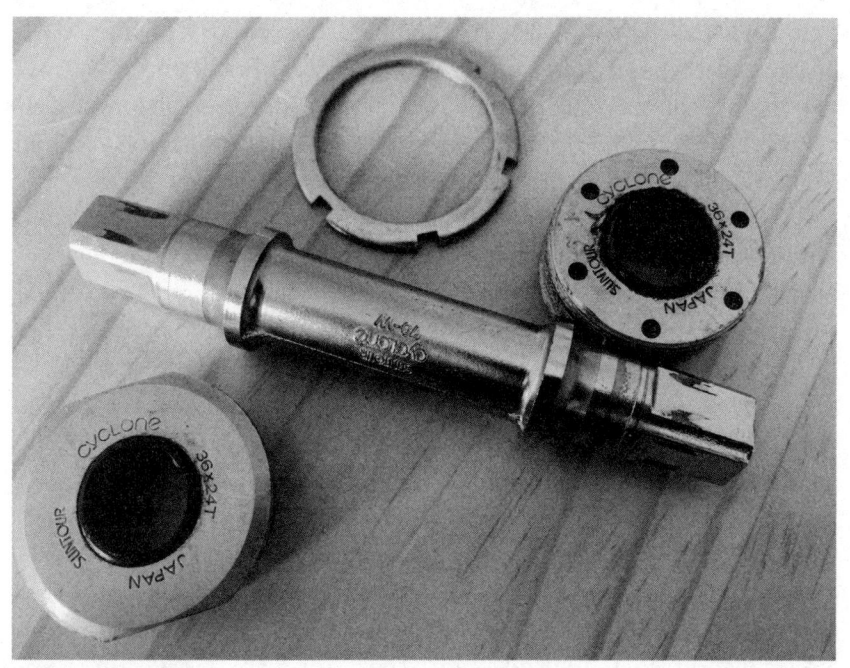

**Ball-and-cup set.**

ten loose or eight caged ¼" bearings, depending on its vintage and manufacturer.

By definition, three-piece bottom brackets enlist spindles with square tapers—the splined spindles came years later, after sealed (nonadjustable) bearing cartridges had become the norm for three-piece cranksets. The square spindles' tapers are split between the Japanese Industrial Standard (JIS) and the International Organization for Standardization (ISO) versions. The great majority of square-tapered spindles within the North American market are on the JIS standard, owing to Shimano's monopoly. European manufacturers such as Campagnolo went with the ISO standard instead. This is often the simplest way to separate out the ISO spindles, actually—look for a European manufacturer's name engraved to the spindle's midsection.

The bearings and bearing cups are broadly cross-compatible; it's only some cranksets and spindles that aren't meant to work together. While both JIS and ISO use the same angle for the taper, ISO spindles are slightly longer, meaning that their square ends become slightly narrower. In practice, a JIS crank would sit about 4 mm closer to the bike's centerline when installed on an ISO spindle, while an ISO crank paired with a JIS spindle would sit 4 mm farther out. It'd be more than enough to torpedo your chainline, either way. But if you must mix and match, the second option would be the safer one: the longer and smaller ISO spindle might bottom out on the crank bolt. No installing Shimano cranks on Campagnolo BB spindles, in other words.

The square-tapered spindle lengths have also varied over time, but we're talking decades here; 108, 113, 118, 122.5, and 127 mm have all been common sizes, and we'll occasionally see others as well. The spindle lengths went through a long and gradual period of narrowing prior to the rise of two-piece cranks—while older, flatter cranks sat relatively far out from their bikes' centerlines, more modern cranksets gradually migrated inward, in coordination with their respective BB spindle lengths.

As we saw with the hubs and the headsets, nicer three-piece BBs will have polished bearing races as well as distinct rubber dust seals. And while the original cotterless BB spindle ends were threaded for M8 crank nuts, in recent decades they've been drilled and tapped to accept M8 crank bolts instead. And as with the crank arms, we'll want to use a lot of torque when installing the BB cups as well. Manufacturers' recommendations here once again vary, but the shorthand would be "as tight as you can make it," unless you're a machine or something.

The three-piecer's fixed cup should have a couple wrench flats cut to its sides; these are meant for a fixed cup wrench such as Birzman's BM17 or Park's HCW-4. A 36 mm headset wrench, failing one of those. The wrenches we use for removing historical fixed BB cups are all curiously thin—such was the mechanical imagination back then. In practice, these thinner tools tend to disengage pretty easily if ever they fall away from right angles. Stein's Fixed Cup Wrench Clamp is unique in its dedication to retaining a focus here—you might seek one out if you're seeing a lot of older BBs.

Over on the neutral side, we first remove the lockring. Numerous tools approach this old problem, but here again Stein's Locking Lockring Wrench has no rival. Like the track lockrings, the old BB lockrings are *very* easy to strip: when using one of the more common single-toothed lockring removal tools, always keep a firm pressure atop the tool whenever making adjustments.

Some older adjustable cups will feature only a pair of unlikely raised 16 mm wrench flats—Birzman's clever BM17 will grab these

DRIVETRAINS

**Adjustable bottom bracket tool, sharing the bench with a chain hook at Bike Saviours, Tempe, Arizona.**

**Bottom bracket cup remover used at Back2Bikes, Port Melbourne, Australia.**

**Old bottom bracket removers at Back2Bikes.**

too, as will Park's HCW-11. More often we'll see a circle of six pinholes, requiring a pin spanner such as Birzman's BM15 or Park's SPA-1.

Lacking better tools, people also make their own. At Bike Saviours Bicycle Collective in Tempe, Arizona, volunteers assembled "a bolt, nut, and shaped washer assembly to remove stuck adjustable bottom bracket cups for cup-and-cone-style BBs," explains shop manager

Nicole Muratore. Geoff Smart, volunteer operations director at Back2Bikes in Port Melbourne, Australia, reported similar homemade BB tools in use there.

Clean up the cups and spindle and any loose ball bearings with an oily rag. Toss any caged bearings in a solvent tank if possible, or at least in some degreaser overnight. Clean and regrease the frame threads before reassembling.

Squirt a nice fat donut of grease into each cup to hold the bearings in place during reassembly, be they caged or loose. Note that the cages' rims should face the cups rather than the spindle. The bearings just hang out in the cups while we thread them in, waiting for their spindle.

Reinstall the fixed (drive-side) cup first, tightening it fully. The spindle's orientation is key to the chainline. Most will be stamped with either the manufacturer's logo or a long-forgotten letter code referencing the length—were the frame invisible, anything such would be legible if we were sitting in the saddle, with the tops of the letters nearest to the fork. The drive side is usually the longer side.

Thread the adjustable cup in finger-tight once the spindle's in, and then run a rag back and forth across the spindle end to spin it and help the bearings settle into the grease. It's the same thing we do with the axle when finishing hub overhauls, but this step is especially useful with three-piece BBs.

Our adjustment here mimics that we'd seek with the hubs, as described on page 75—neither loose nor binding. Get the adjustable cup just *slightly* overtightened, and then use the tool to hold it still while tightening the lockring around it. Ultimately, the crank should spin freely, without binding, and only in plane with the frame's centerline. It might take a couple attempts to get this right, just like with the other bearing adjustments, and as with those it's worth your time to do so.

Our final exam for the ball-and-cup BB adjustments swings a crank arm back to the chainstay, where we see if we can pull it back and forth laterally at all. You should not be able to—if you are, redo the adjustment just a bit tighter.

Most mechanics, myself included, would encourage you to lightly grease the bottom bracket spindle ends before reinstalling the cranks, but it bears mentioning that debate exists on this point. While Shimano recommended greasing their three-piece BB spindles,

DRIVETRAINS

Campagnolo asked adherents to degrease them before reassembly. Truvativ asked us to "install cranks onto a clean, grease-free surface" for their square-tapered BBs while encouraging us to grease their splined BB spindles. Greasing spindles will allow the cranks to slide on a bit tighter, and it's been my experience that grease tends to minimize any creaking generated by three-piece cranks, but that's really all I can tell you.

○○○○

The **sealed-cartridge bottom brackets** update the original three-piece design by encasing the spindle and both bearing sets within a single impervious tube, *usually* joined to the drive-side bottom bracket cup, with a hollow threaded cup bracing the cartridge's edge on the far side. Shimano's 1992 UN series were the first of these, proudly hosting the then-current square-tapered spindles. No real bearing adjustment is possible, beyond fine-tuning the adjustable cup's positioning, as described below. We'll use them until they begin to feel grainy or loose and then replace them as whole units.

We install and remove sealed-cartridge BBs for three-piece cranks with an extractor such as Park's ubiquitous BBT-2, which fits Shimano cartridge BBs as well as those from manufacturers including SunRace and Sunlite, among others. Like other cartridge BB extractors, we'll drive the BBT-2 with a ⅜" ratchet or torque wrench.

For Campagnolo sealed cartridges, we'll use either their six-pinned UT-BB100 extractor—meant for Xenon, Mirage, and Veloce ACH, ACS, or SCS BBs—or a tool such as Pedro's aptly named Campagnolo BB and Cassette Socket, which fits Record, Chorus, Centaur, and Athena cartridge BBs in addition to the company's cassette lockrings.

Grease both the frame threadings and the interior of the hollow BB cup prior to reassembly. It's comparatively easy to cross-thread these heavier drive-side cartridges, so we'll thread the hollow cup halfway in first—its inner edge becomes a kind of shelf, helping the blind cartridge head in straight and find its threading. You should be able to get both sides started by hand; back everything out and clean up or better yet chase the threads if this is not the case.

As noted, the cartridge itself is *usually* integral to the drive-side cup, but this has not always been the case—there was a period in the mid-1990s when Shimano and other manufacturers anchored the cartridge to the neutral side instead. We have a couple ways to sort this out, though. Simplest is seeing what there is to read: as with the spindles on ball-and-cup sets, any manufacturer stickers or etchings on the BB cartridge would be legible when sitting on the saddle, were the frame invisible. Also recall that the drive-side BB cup is reverse-threaded on ISO BBs—they'd be angling in the opposite direction compared to the threads on anything else you'd pull out of your bike—excepting, of course, the neutral-side pedal. The two cups' threads form an arrow, putting it another way: this will point to the rear of the bike when it is right side up, or toward the front when it is upside down.

Once the cartridge is lined up with its threads, turn it in as far as it will go. Again, nice and tight for BB cups. We may be moved to grant the sealed-cartridge BBs' hollow cups a bit more discretion, however. Spin the spindle in your fingers before tightening it down, noting how freely it turns. Continue tightening, and as you finish, stop every quarter turn to check how the spindle is turning—if you start to feel more friction, loosen it just until the action is smooth again. Tolerances can vary slightly across manufacturers, leaving some BBs a bit too narrow for their certain frames, and rather than crush the bearings we'll do this to compensate. This said, any lip extending over the hollow cup's threads should end up flush against the frame's BB shell—should it fail to do so, back the cup out and add a 1 or 1.5 mm spacer under the hollow cup's lip.

In addition to the square-tapered spindles, the cartridge BB format also hosts various **splined bottom brackets**. These, unlike the old square tapers, are wide enough to be hollow, and this makes them stronger and lighter both. Common standards include the ten-spline ISIS Drive (International Spline Interface Standard), as well as Shimano's shallower, narrower-splined Octalink V1 and their deeper, broader-splined Octalink V2, none of which are cross-compatible.

At their inception, wider spindles sometimes implied smaller bearings—within regular-sized BB shells, at least—which, unfortunately, the bottom brackets churn through like snacks. Needle bearings will also struggle in such environs, as Shimano's Dura-Ace 7700 BB once arguably demonstrated. Thus were born the **external bottom brackets**, which set larger bearings just outside the BB shells, expanding the possibilities for wide and hollow spindles.

**Inserting a BB/cassette spacer beneath a hollow cup's lip.**

Like the cartridge BBs, the external BBs have also taken important lessons from their predecessors' shortcomings around the installation hardware—as a group, they favor sturdier methods. Some Shimano and ISIS Drive external BBs carry over the cartridge BBs' internal spline standards, answering to Park's BBT-22 extractor. Others bear rings of nice and wide splines all the way around the outside—it'll be twelve or sixteen splines most often. Common Outer Diameter (OD) sizes include 39, 41, 44, 46, and 49 mm. Some tools will answer to more than one of these—Bike Hand's 4 in 1 Removal Tool, for example, hosts extractor sockets to remove Shimano, Campagnolo, FSA, SRAM, and Truvativ external BBs.

We must also discuss the **press-fit bottom brackets**. Cannondale's BB30 standard famously kicked things off in the early 2000s, deploying a new bottom bracket shell with an internal diameter (ID) of 42 mm. The BMX bikes may have provided an inspiration here—the Spanish and Mid BB formats pressed sealed bearings directly into threadless shells. BB30 also eschewed both threads and bearing cups, trusting pairs of circlips, or retaining rings, to brace bearing cartridges wide enough to admit a hollow 30 mm spindle.

**Park's BBT-22 extractor.**

Other designers stretched BBs in different ways, in service of concurrent advances underway with aluminum and carbon fiber frame design—properly executed, press-fit bottom brackets can allow for lighter and stiffer designs. (Press-fit BBs only feature on various BMX and some recent high-end bikes; none of this means anything to the vast majority of those awheel today.) Not cutting threads also lowered production costs, as did skipping the bearing cups, so the investors may have been marginally more keen as well. The neoliberal turn continued with the naming process, with which manufacturers deployed a whole new jargon of signifiers, referencing the shell's inner diameter, its width, or the spindle width, among other details.

The catch? Press-fit bottom brackets quickly became famous for creaking—far more so than threaded BBs, at least. Some traced this back to subpar manufacturing techniques. Others offered new BB cups, a few of them threaded, for use between the bearing cartridges and BB shells. Whatever the cause, in recent years some of the manufacturers concerned have even welcomed threaded BB shells back into their circle of light.

Investments were made, however, so others instead dug in. The 68 mm (road) and 73 mm (mountain) BB shell widths continued, as a kind of neutral ground. Adding external-bearing BBs to either, we reach new widths in the range of 86 mm and 92 mm, respectively—dimensions many new road and mountain cranks will anticipate. (Downhill and fat bikes may demand wider shells yet.) The new BB shell ID dimensions provide for the most useful organizing framework, so here we'll go from smallest to largest, beginning with the threaded shells.

Before we begin, it also bears mentioning that the original names have grown less descriptive—more malleable, at least. Recent adaptations have allowed BB30 shells to accept 22/24, 24, and 29 mm spindles, for example. Rather than focusing on the manufacturers' original design intentions, in other words, at this point it probably makes more sense to just verify what you're working on and determine what needs to happen. Someone, somewhere might produce hardware that would allow otherwise incompatible systems to work together.

The 1.37" × 24 TPI threaded ISO shell is smallest. The 68 mm road/73 mm mountain shell width begins here as well; 83 mm and 100/120 mm versions are also used for downhill and fat bikes, respectively. The ISO external BB shoves the bearings outside in favor of 22/24, 24, 29, and 30 mm spindles—I've had a Deore two-piecer on my Wisconsin-made lugged-steel Trek commuter for a decade, actually.

The best way to identify a 36 mm × 24 TPI Italian BB shell is by its 70 mm width. Nobody else uses that dimension. Both cups are threaded regularly—right to tighten, left to loosen. Not all Italian bikes have Italian BB threads.

Colnago has a new ThreadFit 82.5 BB standard, speaking of Italy: M45 × 1 mm, with a 68 or 73 mm shell width. Spindles of 24, 20, and 30 mm may be convinced to fit, using adapters.

Chris King and Argonaut Cycles presented the ThreadFit 30i BB, also known as T47, with M47 × 1 threads in a 68 or 73 mm shell. This one only works with 30 mm spindles, as far as I know.

The 37 mm ID Spanish BMX standard is the smallest press-fit BB shell. It has a 68 mm shell width, like most BMX bikes, but no BB cups. Versions with 19, 22, and 24 mm spindles are available.

Trek's BB90 and BB95 standards effectively apply the Spanish BMX standard to road and mountain bikes, with 90.5 and 95.5 mm shells respectively. Both share the same 37 mm ID, using a 24 mm spindle without BB cups.

Lots of names have accumulated around the 41 mm ID size: PF41, BB86, BB89.5, BB92, BB107, BB132, Shimano Press-Fit, and PF24. Most of these reference BB shell width: 86.5, 89.5, 91.5, 104.5, 107, 121, and 132 mm are options here, all of which use BB cups. Spindle widths include 22/24, 24, 29, and 30 mm.

Continuing up the size ladder, we make a quick return to BMX with the 41.2 mm ID Mid press-fit standard. No cups; 68 mm shell; 22 mm spindle.

The 42 mm ID provides an assembly point for PF42, BB30, BB30A, BB30AI, BBRight Direct Fit, and Specialized's OSBB (road). No cups; four circlips. Shell widths should be 68 or 73 mm. Spindles of 22/24, 24, 29, and 30 mm are all accepted in different iterations, using step-down spacers for the smaller sizes.

Landing on the 46 mm ID we are greeted by PF46, PF30, PF30A, PF30AI, BB386EVO, OSBB (mountain), and BBRight Press Fit. We'll install 42 mm bearings in composite cups with these, a convenience that allows us to use the same range of spindle options as well.

Rounding off our list, we return to the original 51.5 mm ID American BB shell, as discussed on page 191.

Some 42 and 46 mm ID press-fit setups are **asymmetrical bottom brackets**, adding a few millimeters' worth of width on the neutral side. These are used in support of the wider, lighter chainstays said to provide for the most efficient energy transmission. Examples include Cannondale's BB30A and BB30A-83, as well as Cervelo's BBRight Direct Fit and BBRight Press Fit. Asymmetric BBs denied their intended cranksets will require adapters before accepting any substitutions.

The press-fit bottom brackets go in with a press—think headset installation, but sideways. Park's BBT-30.4 set includes a removal tool to punch out the old bearings, as well as drifts to line up their headset press when reinstalling bearings. Some BBs will be too narrow to accept the BBT-30.4's removal tool; revert to a narrower headset cup removal tool such as their RT-1 in such cases. Some frames use removable C-clips mounted within the BB shell to brace the bearing cartridges' inner edges—make sure you're not accidentally pounding on these when punching the bearings out.

DRIVETRAINS

Lightly grease the metal sides of the bearing cartridges, as well as their hollows in the BB shell, prior to reassembly. The correct set of drifts will line right up with your bearings and help keep the press centered, which is key for installing the bearings evenly. Lacking such, the bins at your local hardware store may host washers or nuts of dimensions appropriate for your project. Absent proper tools such as those noted above, use a hammer and wood block to install each bearing individually.

The **press-fit threaded bottom bracket**, another foot soldier in the war on creaks, arguably carries greater significance for frames with damaged BB threads. The name is less contradictory than it may sound: the smooth cups' inner edges are elongated enough to overlap and are then cut with matching threads, such that they screw together *inside* a frame's BB shell. The **30mm bottom brackets** are also available with ISO threads, in both 68 mm and 73 mm ISO shell widths.

Tandems, finally, often rely on **elliptical BB**s to manage the stoker chain tension. An ISO threading is drilled at an offset into a thick aluminum plug sized to fit an American BB shell. Pinch bolts and a corresponding seam are then added to this last, allowing us to simply rotate the big aluminum plug as needed to set the chain tension. (Single-cog bikes sometimes use these as well, as a way to incorporate vertical dropouts into their frame designs.)

◦◦◦◦

The **pedals** are traditionally sold by the pair. For all the harms that may befall them, their axles themselves are rarely to blame—each must be burly enough to support our weight and match our strength. We can always anticipate at least two sets of bearings to mediate between the axles and the **pedal bodies**, which we'll examine shortly.

The beleaguered and misdirected bottom bracket fittings might even envy the 9/16" × 20 TPI **pedal threads**, which—among imperial fittings, at least—are notable for their staying power. The long-ago 14 × 1.25 mm French pedal threading is all but extinct, and in recent years the ½" × 20 TPI size, associated with steel one-piece cranksets, has been fading away as well. The 9/16" and ½" sizes are visually distinct, and in both cases our eternal war against precession dictates that the *left pedal* (neutral side) is reverse-threaded. Note that this is the opposite of our ISO-threaded BBs, on which the right (drive-side) cup is reverse-threaded.

Older pedal wrenches such as Park's PW-3 bear sets of 9/16" flats, opposite the obligatory 15 mm flats: perhaps counterintuitively, the former are meant for ½" pedals and the *latter* will address our 9/16" pedals. Yet any ½" pedals we may encounter will have flats wide enough to be gripped by standard 9/16" box wrenches, so the modern **pedal wrench** typically replaces the 9/16" flats with a second pair of 15 mm flats, faced off to useful angles. (Various adapters allowing 9/16" pedals to be retrofit to ½" cranks can be had. Anything such would widen the Q factor by a pedal axle's width on each side, but if you're working with one-piece cranks that's probably not a top concern.)

Installing pedals correctly involves a lot of torque, as we'll see, and for this reason we shouldn't ever be using the slender 15 mm cone wrenches for pedal installation or removal. Some especially modern pedals—including whole categories of the clipless pedals, described below—will eschew the pedal wrench's boring old 15 mm wrench flats entirely, favoring 6 or 8 mm Allen sockets in the axle ends instead.

I've never seen a bent pedal axle, but the pedal bodies get roughed up all the time. This is especially true of the budget bikes' pedals, most of which are made of cheap black plastic. (Some manufacturers inject other colors, in hopes of confusing our sensors.) Both ½" and 9/16" versions are still common. Cheap plastic pedals crack, which makes them creak, at least until the cracks expand enough to free the worn plastic husks from their ever-shinier axles. This was a standout memory of Mauritania for me—people riding ancient bikes with only shiny and rusty axle pegs in place of pedals. It can be done, and for better or worse it is done.

Various resins, nylon fibers, and composites have more recently rehabilitated this plastics approach, as we'll see, but in the aggregate these more durable sorts of plastic pedals remain far less common than they could be.

The old steel **rat trap pedals** presented one of the first identifiable pedal genres—boxy steel constructions assembled around built-in orange reflectors, with rows of pointy crenelations for traction. They first appeared on one-piece cranksets before later bridging the gap from ½" to 9/16" axles. These later begat the smoother-profiled **road pedals**, the narrower **track pedals**, and eventually the various extra-grippy iterations of **mountain pedals** as well. Among each, the better versions bolted aluminum **pedal cages** around distinct aluminum pedal bodies.

Most of these older pedals have top and bottom sides, and thus fronts and rears as well—we might only find the two holes needed to attach toe clips on the front side, for example. The cage's rear may feature a single prominent tooth midway along the bottom edge: we'll press this down with our toes in order to flip the toe clip up into position.

Here as well, shadowy "market forces" are *alleged* to have demanded that yet further shortcuts be exploited. Beware any pedals with plastic bodies and steel cages: these tend to come apart, to my experience, as a simple function of riding the bike. I was responsible for maintaining dozens of Specialized Crossroads rental bikes in the dark years before the rise of proper bikeshare systems, all of which arrived with steel-caged plastic pedals: over our busy summers, I quickly found myself needing to tighten all the pedal cages, of all the ridiculous things, over and over again. (A metal-to-plastic thread-locking compound might have helped, in retrospect—something to try, at least, should your bike be so cursed.)

In recent years the **platform pedals**, also known as **flat pedals**, have become the go-to option for new bikes and replacement pedals alike. Their bodies may be plastic or aluminum. Better examples will feature sealed bearings, as well as replaceable threaded pins for increased traction. **Fixed gear pedals** derive from the platform pedals, but they're narrower, so as to avoid catching on the turns.

Fixed gear pedals are almost definitionally compatible with **toe clips**, the metal or plastic baskets that keep our feet atop the pedals. Almost all toe clips are designed to work with integral **toe straps**, which function as the enforcers—we tighten these around our footwear, leaving just enough grace to back out safely. The clips and straps enable us to better capture pedaling force on the upswing, in addition to the pushdown, thereby channeling more of our pedaling energy into momentum. Pairing toe clips with stiff-soled cycling shoes can improve our pedaling efficiency further still.

For all their potential benefits, the toe clips can take some getting used to—you'll need to yank a foot straight back to release it, and this can take a second. The various stubby and strapless toe clips offer some compromises in this respect, but the **clipless pedals** have always been more popular. Their catch-and-release mechanisms snag **pedal cleats**, which in most cases are affixed to **clipless cycling shoes**, and

**Platform pedal.**

suddenly we only need to rotate our heels outward to free the feet. Counterintuitive though it may be, it's actually easier and quicker to get out of properly deployed clipless pedals than toe clips.

Different cleats work with different pedals. Shimano's SPD, their distinct SPD-SL, Look, Time ATAC, and Speedplay are all common cleat standards. Each anticipates one of two common bolt patterns on the shoes' soles. These in turn incorporate adjustment windows, allowing us some discretion to establish the cleats' optimal positioning in terms of our comfort.

Be sure to grease the cleat bolts! Cleats do wear out—steel SPD cleats will last longer than brass ones, which in turn may long outlive the big plastic Look cleats—and given the opportunity, any of their bolts will quite happily rust in place regardless. Cleat lifespan varies, but it's definitely something to keep in mind. SPD cleats become

DRIVETRAINS

**Clipless pedals and SPD cleats.**

progressively more difficult to release as they wear, for example, with all the attendant risks that implies.

The two-bolt SPD cleats are the smallest and most common. Time's ATAC pedals also use this pattern; Look calls their two-bolt version the X-Track. Look's road pedals and Shimano's SPD-SL both use the same three-bolt mounting pattern, but as they meet the pedals the two cleat standards are not cross-compatible. Speedplay pedals rely on a distinct four-bolt pattern; their new sets include adaptors for using them with the three-bolt cleat pattern associated with road clipless shoes. The various generic or off-brand versions may mimic any of the above standards, save for Speedplay.

Different pedal cleats offer greater and lesser degrees of **float**, a measure of how far the cleats can rotate laterally while still being clipped in. Limiting the float can make your pedal stroke more efficient, assuming your fit to the bike is super dialed in and everything lines up just perfectly; your knees might not like it so much, otherwise. Having some float is just more comfortable. Some clipless pedals offer **adjustable float**, but the standard allotment—six degrees or so—is usually enough for most knees to scoot around as needed. The **tension**

**adjustment** is more critical—how easy it is to release, basically. It'll be a small bolt with a +/– on the side. Note that double-sided clipless pedals will have a pair of these each.

Speedplay pedals delegate the catch-and-release mechanisms to their cleats, in the process rendering them more expensive. The pedals, in turn, become more spoonlike. They do win the flotation championships, however, with a generous 7.5 degrees allotment. As with Look and SPD-SL cleats, the walking is going to be more toes-up.

The two-bolt mountain clipless shoes, in contrast, carve minor valleys for the SPD cleats to settle into. This makes it much easier to walk around in them. These **recessed cleats** don't completely shroud the metal cleats, however—the pedals wouldn't stand for it—and this limited overlap allows the various metal two-bolt cleats to scratch hell from any hardwood floors they may encounter. So just take your shoes off at the door like everyone else, okay?

As with the fixed gears, given the opportunity it's always best to begin practicing with your new clipless pedals in some quiet, car-free flat area before charging into traffic. Line up the cleat's nose atop the pedal and push down; the cleat should click into place. You might do this while holding a branch or a railing until you get used to it. We can't actually see what we're doing here, obviously, but this is more intuitive than it sounds.

◘◘◘◘

At minimum, **pedal removal** requires a wrench and a plan. First, see to it that the bike is positioned securely—in a stand, or upside down on the floor. The pedals will be tight, so with each we'll grab the opposite crank arm for leverage, pushing off against it as we pull the wrench. Make sure you're actually pushing the wrench in the correct direction: excepting the ancient French-threaded pedals, only the *left pedal* (neutral side) is reverse-threaded. Each one will likely release quite suddenly, so you'll also want to set things up such that the chainring is not going to gouge your knuckles. In the event the bike has only one crank arm, wrap a toe strap around the crank arm and chainstay a couple times, flip the bike upside down on the ground, and arrange it so that you're pushing downward on the wrench.

Absent encouragement bars or other force multipliers, we'll always get the best leverage by clasping our hands over a pair of

DRIVETRAINS

**Using leverage to remove a pedal.**

wrenches and squeezing them together. Applying this concept to pedal removal, you'll maximize your leverage by positioning the wrench such that it's almost parallel to the opposite crank arm, where pushing on it will draw them more parallel.

Still no dice? If you're focused on a one-piece crank's neutral-side pedal, you might be stuck. There may be something for you in the chapter on rust; check page 231. Otherwise, go ahead and remove the offending crank arm, as described in the treatment on cranks beginning on page 176, and set it up nice and tight between some rags in a vise. A pedal wrench and encouragement bar should take it off, assuming your bench and vise are both well secured.

**Pedal installation** is usually simpler. Many pedals have an *R* or *L* stamped to their axle ends so we'll know what goes where. Use a lightweight oil to clean up any rusty or dirty pedal threads before installation, and always dab a pea's worth of grease on the threads before installing them. While we're often able to thread new pedals most of the way into new cranks with our fingers, we'll probably need the wrench to get the oldsters started. Never should we need much force, save for the final torque at the very end.

If a pedal won't go in straight, it is best to retap the crank arm's threads. Failing that, chase an angled pick down the crank arm's threads to dig out as much gunk as possible.

Just lately, some manufacturers send thin washers between the pedal threads and the crank arms—I suspect these are crucial indeed for the carbon cranks. All the pedal threads should engage their counterparts in the crank arms not less than 11 mm. And while the manufacturers' specific torque recommendations will vary, as with the bottom brackets and crank arms, as a rule the pedals should be installed nice and tight. I have read of pedals being tightened enough to strip the crank threads, but I've never seen it happen.

There is unfortunately not much to discuss regarding **pedal repair**. Keep an eye on your pedals' dust caps—these get knocked off in battle sometimes, which itself can start a downward spiral: the grease seeps out, the grit gets in, the bearing adjustments fade, and pretty soon your pedal's all creaky and loose. I've never seen the sockets-within-sockets that the pedal bearings would seem to require for any adjustments—I imagine they're mere digits of big machines, bolted to factory floors. Given this lack of serviceability, I'd sooner glue or even duct-tape a dust cap in place than lose another pedal. Another reason why sealed-bearing pedals are preferable, should those be an option for you.

⦁⦁⦁⦁

Our journey through the drivetrains leaves us better positioned to appreciate the **singlespeed** bikes. Manufacturers offer purpose-built singlespeeds at all points along the quality spectrum. Setting aside the full-suspension mountain bikes, it is also possible to convert most other multispeed bikes to singlespeed.

Singlespeeds are famously less complicated, but that doesn't make them stupid. In fact, their fair treatment requires numerous references to topics detailed in previous chapters, especially when it comes to the singlespeed conversions. Everything will make more sense if you, the reader, are first familiar with the topics discussed so far.

Purpose-built singlespeeds are similar to track or fixed gear bikes, in that we'll see horizontal dropouts out back, but the spacing is more fungible. While dedicated **singlespeed cassette hubs** are often spaced to 135 mm, some 120 mm flip-flop hubs will bear singlespeed-capable

BMX freewheel threads on the flange opposite their track threadings. Purpose-built singlespeed frames also make provisions to accommodate a rear brake in addition to the front brake.

The singlespeed wave has crested already, in places. "Singlespeed demand is still there, but has dropped in the past years," observes the Hub's Jody Chandler. "The $350 online single speed is one factor in this. Perception of singlespeeds has also changed as they have become mass-market."

Like track bikes, the singlespeeds carry a potential to be somewhat lighter than their multispeed kin. The ride qualities, however, are quite distinct—singlespeed bikes lack the fixies' hill-climbing prowess, but they'll do better on the descents. Some find singlespeed easier on the knees.

The best singlespeed chain tension adjustment is looser than what a fixed gear bike would need. We need to provide the freewheel or freehub with a bit more room to do its work—we'll still walk the hub back in the frame to minimize chain slack, just as we'd do with the fixed gear chains, but not to the same degree. Turning the pedals backward, the coasting mechanism should not bind or tighten at any point in its rotation. And as with the fixies, the chainline is also critical: a purpose-built singlespeed hub's wider body pushes the cog out toward the axle end. This favors a proper chainline, and—by diminishing the dish—a stronger wheel as well.

**Singlespeed conversions** do not necessarily turn bikes into unicorns—better multispeed bikes become better singlespeeds, generally speaking. Rather, the gearing-down can sometimes mitigate certain other exigent problems, such as nonfunctional shifting. Singlespeed bikes may likewise better tolerate worn cogs, chains, and chainrings, depending on how they're set up.

A few thoughts on finding a good candidate among the multispeed bikes. As noted, full-suspension frames are rarely singlespeed-convertible—the chain may be asked to stretch more than it should, bouncing around like that. And while it's possible to reuse riveted cranksets and multispeed freewheels with singlespeed conversions, in either case the bike wouldn't lose much weight. There might be reasons to proceed regardless—while some bikes lose their gears to become lighter or more rockabilly or whatever, others may undertake the transformation more from a lack of options. This treatment will cover both.

The default gear ratio for a 26" singlespeed bike is 2:1—we'd pair a 32-tooth ring to a 16-tooth cog, for example. Yet the gearing is also subjective, contingent on both your terrain and how you like to ride. You might even import your favorite cog and chainring combination directly from the multispeed bike—or perhaps something like it, at least. Working with mountain frames, we're often limited to using the middle chainring—the outer ring's teeth might encounter the chainstay before reaching a good chainline. Substituting a longer BB or BB spindle may allow us to proceed with the big ring so long as the commensurate chainline revisions are undertaken out back as well.

The leap from fixed gear to singlespeed can be pretty basic if your bike has a flip-flop hub—you'd just flip the wheel around backward to engage the freewheel, reassemble with the chain tension just a bit lower, and set up the brakes. (Cog and freewheel would need to be of roughly similar sizes in order to share the same chain length.) In general conversation, however, "singlespeed conversion" usually means we're coming from a bike with multispeed origins.

Any chain run through derailleurs will lose a few links going singlespeed, so go ahead and break the chain first. Clip off the shifter cable ferrules and pull the cables out of their housing. The rear cable and the housing might be spooled and set aside for later use, but your singlespeed conversion may actually require the shorter front derailleur cable, so hang on to that one for now. Remove all derailleurs and shift levers, as well as any extra chainrings, if possible. Just throw it all in a box for the next swap meet.

If you are able to ditch the extra rings, the original chainring bolts will suddenly be too long. You might be able to get them going again with sufficient spacers or washers, but it may be simpler to track down a set of single-ring chainring bolts. These are fairly common; their thread depth is 7 mm.

So long as you've got the tools out, take a minute to make sure the brakes are working as well as you'd like them to.

The chainline is easy enough to measure: hold a ruler or similar flush against the chainring; see how it lines up out back. Your chainring might need to move from the outside of the crank arm's shelves to the inside, depending.

Using multispeed hubs, we'll have a couple options for the chainline. The freehubs are simplest. Older 7-speed Shimano HG cassettes

DRIVETRAINS

**Setting a chainring on the inside of the crank arm's shelves.**

are often held together with trios of especially tall and narrow bolts, the heads of which would answer to a 4 mm socket—not likely anything we'd have in the toolbox, but we can make our own using an M5 bolt with a 4 mm bolt head. Countertighten a couple nuts along the threads, and suddenly you've got your own custom 4 mm socket! Use it to disassemble older cassettes to salvage their spacers and cogs. These last might be worn down already, but they might still fill in as spacers in a pinch.

Newer cassettes deny us any such salvage rights, but dedicated freehub singlespeed conversion kits with cogs, splined top cogs, spacers, and cassette lockrings are also now available. Cassette spacer sets can be had as well.

Whichever of the above you're working with, press your ruler against the chainring, with the target wheel installed, to see where the cog should sit. Arrange the spacers accordingly. Finish the stack with a top cassette cog—it'll be the one with the splines matching those we'll see in the locknut. Get it all nice and tight, and go for a test ride.

We have a pair of options when converting threaded freewheel hubs to singlespeed. The simpler route involves convincing the original rear derailleur (or some other sort of chain tensioner, as described below) to stack its pulleys directly beneath the cog of your choice on the original multispeed freewheel. We'll return to this approach momentarily.

The long-division method requires a BMX freewheel as well as hub and wheel dish adjustments. It's also best to begin with a double-walled rim, to better accommodate our wheel dish adjustments, but you'll also get a lighter and stronger wheel as a result.

Begin by moving all the drive-side axle spacers to the neutral side and moving any axle washers on the neutral side over to the drive side. Note that the hub cones may be specific to the drive or neutral side and should thus stay put through such an operation—you'll just be moving the spacers. (If necessary, this would also make for an ideal moment to overhaul the hub.) We simply thread the axle across both cones over toward the neutral side and set it back up again, making sure the same length of axle extends beyond both locknuts as you finish your hub adjustment.

Next, redish the wheel to compensate for the axle-spacing changes. Apply the same adjustments to every other spoke all the way around the wheel, loosening the drive side all the way around before tightening the neutral side, again all the way around. Begin with larger adjustments—something in the range of three or so complete turns of the spoke wrench. You'll finish with rounds of half a turn, or maybe a full turn, dialing in the centering. Our goal is to line up the frame and rim's centerlines—we'll flip the wheel around in the rear triangle to confirm the rim appears centered from either orientation. (See pages 50 and 48 for more on wheel dish and wheel truing, respectively.)

Redishing a wheel to this extent can cause the neutral-side spokes to thread beyond their spoke nipples, a development the inner tube would not likely appreciate. This is precisely why you should begin with a double-walled rim. One can file down every other spoke end instead, if absolutely necessary, but this is a truly tedious task.

We'll always need to make certain accommodations when singularizing frames with vertical drops. This is what a **chain tensioner** is for—we'll thread one into a derailleur hanger, from which vantage it'll do nothing more than keep the chain taut around the chainring. (Not to be confused with chain tension *adjusters*, which merely pull the axle backward in track dropouts.)

Various lightweight and brightly anodized chain tensioners have been available for years now, sometimes alongside the singlespeed cassette hub conversion kits mentioned previously, but the for-free approach simply repurposes the bike's original rear derailleur. You'll first need to convince its pulleys to settle directly beneath your choice of cog, when viewed from the rear. First, check and see if you're able to achieve this result by dialing in the H limit screw. You probably won't be able to—unless you're able to substitute a longer screw of the same threading, perhaps—but it's worth a shot. If that's not happening, thread an old derailleur cable directly into the barrel adjuster, pulling it right through the binder bolt. Hold the derailleur such that its pulleys line up under the cog, and then cinch down the pinch bolt right there. You'll then be able to fine-tune the pulleys' resting position with the barrel adjuster.

Setting up the chain is the last thing before the test ride. It should end up as tight as you can make it without the chain tensioner (or rear derailleur) getting fully stretched out—the tension pulley should rest well forward of the cog, at about a 45-degree angle.

*○○○○*

**Planetary gearing** moves the shifting indoors. Gears arrayed inside a tellingly wide hub shell facilitate our reductions, often in the absence of any derailleurs. The old steel Sturmey-Archer (SA) 3-speed hubs may provide the most familiar examples of this technology, but progress has been truly relentless—modern planetary hubs accommodate up to 14 speeds, alongside fittings for disc brake rotors or freehub bodies. Sometimes even both.

**Brompton antirotational washer and locknut.**

 Most planetary hubs continue to sport a solitary **sprocket**, however, so their respective gearing ranges are thus best described in terms of percentages. These will reflect the total difference between the lowest and highest gears—ranges that roughly overlap, hub to hub. Increasing the number of speeds within a given hub does not necessarily add extra-high or extra-low gears, in other words—rather, it provides a greater spread of options within what we may call a general range of human potential. We are able to shift this window up or down a bit as well, using different-sized cogs or chainrings to better favor easier hill-climbing at one end or increased speed at the other.

 A planetary hub's sprocket is often held in place by means of a **circlip**, which we'll nudge out of the way with a 3 mm flat-tip screwdriver: poke it in near the circlip's gap and lever upward. Reinstalling these, we do something similar in reverse, levering the same small screwdriver around the clip from its split until the whole thing sits nice and level.

 Pedaling encourages the planetary-geared hub axles to rotate, for reasons I lack the training to explain, and this tendency can become their undoing. Thus do we see the all-important **antirotational**

**washers**, splendidly planetary-specific hub ornaments made further distinct by their manufacturers' proprietary inclinations. While most look similar—tabbed near-rectangular washers, with the shorter sides rounded—you should use those intended for your particular hub. They should fit well, but easily too. The planetary axles, in turn, anticipate their arrival with axle ends ground flat on parallel sides to meet them. Most, but not all, will do this on both sides. The antirotational washers' tabs slot into the frame dropouts.

The original 3-speed SA cables bore two opposing heads, with a specified length of cable housing measured out between them. Their antique approach to cable tensioning was unique: rather than relying entirely on a barrel adjuster, we'll first get it in the ballpark by loosening and moving the cable housing stop up and down the tube until the cable approaches an appropriate tension. We attach the cable at both points first, then slide the housing clamp as needed until the slack mostly disappears, finishing with the barrel adjuster.

Full-length cable housing has since become standard on modern planetary-geared bikes, as a fitting complement to their intrinsic weatherproofing. A friend once showed me a 3-speed (Shimano?) trigger shifter paired to a recent Brompton's 3-speed hub—this worked, apparently—but officially the internally geared hubs are best paired with their designated shift levers.

The planets' transactions take place through an **indicator chain**. A rod threads into the hub axle and sprouts a chain, which in turn lolls like a tongue off a long and beveled axle nut. The shifter cable, looking down, pinches a threaded fitting to its tail, into which the wee chain's end segment eagerly disappears. The global standard for decades, it was.

Indicator chains are none too sturdy, alas; they perish quite easily. Observing this, some newer planetary hubs have adopted other methods. Many Shimano planetary hubs eschew the indicator chains entirely, replacing them with diminutive steel bus shelters—which, like so much of the company's other shifting hardware, are held together with tiny Phillips screws. Inside we'll find only a pinch bolt mounted to a pivot, nudging a simple **push rod** into the hub. A marked window on the back side provides the reference points needed to line up our cable adjustments.

SRAM stopped producing internally geared hubs in 2017, but many of their most recent planets kept the indicator chains, plugging them

**Indicator chain.**

into small wedge-shaped plastic boxes known as **adjustment sleeves**. We'll see a linear brass spring running up one side, the tail of which catches on the indicator chain's threaded end segment—pressing on the brass spring releases the indicator chain. Once the flat tire is fixed, it'll then slide right back in place. The shifter cable passes through a nostril in the sleeve's narrower end, gets clamped beneath a pinch bolt, and finally streams out an exit to the rear.

Supplementing planetary gears with conventional derailleurs and cassettes is known as **hybrid gearing**, a strategy that finds its best expression aboard those bikes less amenable to front derailleurs. My Brompton S6L, to take one immediate example, pairs a 3-speed hub

DRIVETRAINS

gear with Brompton's 2-speed rear derailleur. SA has produced hybrid-geared hubs to accommodate both freewheels and cassettes. Dual Drive paired SRAM's 3-speed planetary hub to an 8/9-speed freehub body, updating their previous 3×7 hub—a single lever on the right controlled both the hub gears and rear derailleur. The Dual Drive's hub/cable interface, known as a **Clickbox**, allows for quick-release removal, although you may need to jiggle things around a bit to get it all back in place.

Come time to replace the cable, we shouldn't feel compelled to clip and cap it inside the Clickbox—just spool it out the big hole on the back side instead. While clipping a cable immediately adjacent to a pinch bolt invites fraying, sending it out back—as was likely intended here—neatly sidesteps this minor dilemma. Better to look a bit quirky than to accidentally pop a fingertip on the spiky cable bouquet.

The planets, like the derailleurs, rely on their shifter cables' tension for guidance. Most incorporate barrel adjusters in their cable runs for this reason. The planetary hubs' adjustment parameters are sometimes looser, however—a few, such as SRAM's Monsoon TS200, seem to manage without barrel adjusters. A too-loose cable may balk and jump around when trying to drop into gear; one too tight might refuse to reach its final gear.

The reference points we'll use to confirm the correct cable tension are typically found on or near the drive-side axle locknut. SA's old steel 3-speeds drilled a lateral hole into the side of the elongated axle nut, through which we may glimpse the indicator chain—markings on each are meant to line up when the hub is shifted to second gear, leaving us to dial the barrel adjuster as needed to achieve this goal.

Both SRAM's Clickbox and the Shimano bus stop update this approach. We'll see a bright yellow bar through a tiny window in either case, and for each we'll dial the cable's barrel adjuster until this lines up between a pair of thinner lines on the window itself while in second gear. The Shimano cable shelter, like SRAM's Clickbox, also incorporates a quick-release mechanism. So you won't need to take apart the indicator chain—and with it your cable adjustment—to change a flat tire.

Opinions on proper lubrication have varied—the planetary geared hubs have embraced both oils and grease at different times. Here again, you'll do best to research the manufacturer's recommendations for your particular model and vintage. Note that planetary hubs work best with planetary hub grease—regular bearing grease can cause the pawls to stick. Heavier-weight machine oils such as SAE 20 reliably do better than lighter oils such as penetrants or chain lube, but the structural issue here is that some planetary hubs are sealed far better than others—oil will find ways to seep right out the gaps, given the opportunity, and without enough lubrication the planets begin to break down.

Many users neglect to oil their planetary hubs, unfortunately, even after they start making noise. Grease thus became a solution for some manufacturers, in part because it simply stays in place better than oil—minimizing, in theory, the planetary users' potential for self-inflicted damages. The planetary gears are made a bit less efficient, however, swimming through grease. The custom approach thus involves using an appropriate oil for the internals and then a waterproof marine grease for the bearings: keeping the water out but the oil in. The sad truth is that planetary geared hubs too often arrive underlubricated from their factories—as a precaution, it's a good idea to top up with an appropriate lubricant before beginning regular use.

While the hubs' planetary gears are better protected from the outside world, they channel the same torque external drivetrains do. Over extended use, their lubricants may become shinier, reflecting tiny chips of suspended metal—there to stay, slowly wearing away, until the grease or oil is purged and replaced.

The most livable planets provide for ports on their hub shells, meant for injections of oil or grease. Lacking such, remove the indicator chain, lay the bike on its neutral side, and shoot fresh machine oil directly into the hollow axle. The process will ideally flush older, dirtier, perhaps shinier oil out the far side, so don't be doing this over Grandma's favorite rug—get a pan under there, in the basement maybe. Give it some time; leave the wheel on its side overnight. The discharge might otherwise centrifuge down, when out riding, to the spokes and rims, where it could cause problems with any rim brakes.

We can of course disassemble, clean, and relubricate the planetary geared hubs, given time and incentive, but you'll always want to have a proper schematic or instructions for the particular hub in question. Nothing to rush through.

The planets continue to evolve—a German manufacturer, Schlumpf Drive, produces a series of planetary-geared bottom brackets meant to facilitate either hill-climbing or higher speeds. The sun

DRIVETRAINS

gear straddles a rod shot through the spindle; heel-activated buttons atop each crank bolt shuttle it back and forth between low and high positions. Rohloff has been making their 14-speed Speedhub since 1998.

⚬⚬⚬⚬

The **electric bikes** further expand the bicycle's range of possibilities. They don't do it for free, of course—any new horizons they might offer are only functions of their increased complexity, weight, and cost. Yet as with the recumbent bikes, they are also plainly instrumental in empowering all kinds of cyclists to continue riding, when otherwise they may not have.

The industry's deft marketing teams lacked the creative vigor or strategic depth to do much of anything with the 'bents, for the most part—just too damned weird, apparently—yet the physics of increased power are more plainly seen, and whole piles of manufacturers have thus sought to realize their own individualized e-bike dreams. This makes it difficult to quantify any "average" electric bike, let alone their ailments; it'd be a whole other book, really. But we can provide the outlines here.

Electrification essentially drapes a supplementary layer of technology over an existing bike, which otherwise remains vulnerable to the same range of mechanical issues detailed previously. The e-bikes' increased weight and speed bear heavily on their brakes—their pads are famously short-lived. You'll want to keep a close eye on the wear lines, especially if you begin to notice any screeching or reduced braking performance. The same factors can even cause disc brake rotors to crack—if ever you see cracks in a rotor, get off and walk until you can replace it.

Manufacturers including Kool-Stop and Tektro make thicker, more durable V-brake pads meant for use with e-bikes. There are also a few basic things you can do to help your brake pads last longer. Should your riding circumstances accommodate it, allowing more time to stop can potentially extend your brake pads' lifespans—coast toward a stop when possible, or apply the brakes more gently and from greater distances. And to whatever extent you can keep the braking surfaces clean and dry, this will surely help as well. Keeping a bike neater can be a chore, especially in the elements, but it's also a good way to defer certain expenses.

I haven't yet seen sociable e-bikes, or even regular tandem e-bikes, but the more usual formats are already amply covered—mountain bikes, cargo bikes, folding bikes, what have you. The e-bikes' nascent classification system straddles across these existing categories, rolling out new combinations wherever they might seem to fit. Within the North American market, the motors on both class 1 and class 2 e-bikes are set up to cut out at 20 miles per hour. The former are pedal-assist, meaning that you turn them on by pedaling; the latter have throttles on the handlebars. Class 3 e-bikes may use throttles or pedal-assist; their motors stay engaged up to 28 miles per hour. Different categories are legal in different places; you should probably check.

When it comes to diagnosing and repairing problems with an e-bike's electrical systems, the first hurdle might simply be in finding a good and current map. As one anonymous source puts it, "The main problem is there's no true standard." With each iteration of the e-bike, we'll see some variation of a motor, battery, wiring, display, and controller. This last element functions as the brains of the system; better e-bikes sometimes incorporate it alongside a battery management system inside the battery casing itself.

"Mechanics will need to learn some trial and error, plus some process of elimination in performing diagnostics," our source continues—a task, they note, made more difficult by the lack of coherent standards across the sector. "Trying to come up with a standard diagnosis procedure is a mission, though it's all basically the same stuff." Patterns do emerge, with practice: "When diagnosing an issue, the first thing to do is to check connections. Sometimes just unplugging certain things can fix the issue."

Within the context of the e-bikes' rapidly growing and changing market, having the necessary support is key. While some manufacturers are more committed to supporting their products, not all are nearly so broad-minded. "Between safe battery handling, the cost of components, and the complexity of each bike involved," our source says, "low-cost and nonprofit setups with an e-bike focus is a big-time lift, [one] I'm not sure anyone is ready *or* willing to tackle."

Such skepticism is perhaps understandable, if not always accurate. Among survey respondents, eighteen (60 percent) indicated that they do not currently service e-bikes, while twelve do so. "We see the need in the community for resources for e-bikes," notes one community bike shop mechanic. "I'm sure we'll update our stands and train our staff if funding becomes available to do so."

Others are less interested. "Nothing against them," says Recyclistas Bike Shop's Ryan Harris. "We just decided to stick with what we're good at." Manufacturers' choices can inform such decisions as well. "We don't plan on servicing electric bikes until our vendors start offering parts and support," notes West Town Bikes' Alex Wilson.

"There are certain limitations on what we can even work on based on our insurance provider," explains the Hub's Jody Chandler. "No high-powered or throttled bikes. We see a fair amount of problems with internet brands that give no customer support. Brick-and-mortar brands are much better at providing support to the bike shop."

The tools useful for repairing electric bikes can include the spare parts themselves. "It's hard to lock down what component is failing if you don't have good ones to test against," our source explains. "Having, say, an extra motor controller you can easily plug everything into and fire up removes a *ton* of guesswork in the process."

For better or worse, this snapshot seems set to change yet further as e-bikes continue their rapid ascent. "The industry on the whole is undergoing a massive amount of growing pains right now," our source observes. "Shops that don't want to learn how to work on these things are going to go the way of the dodo. Shops that are willing to learn, though, with a focus on service, repair, and relationship-building—instead of sales—will do well."

Opinions differ on the best approach to electrifying bikes. "It would be great if consumers went for modular aftermarket e-bike systems like the Bafang mid-drive that can be swapped between bikes and for which different battery arrangements can be used, rather than proprietary frame-specific designs that inevitably create more waste," says Glen Mason of the Community Bike Hub. Pending design improvements, however, others question the project's very feasibility. "They require more attention to maintenance across the board, wear out chains, unscrew fasteners, and rattle themselves to death," notes Jack Kelleher of the Clonakilty Bike Circus. "Brakes wear out quickly. Basically, a bicycle wasn't engineered with power in mind."

Concerns around the e-bikes' quality present more of a consensus. "We see lots of cheap aftermarket bolt-on kits, which are often dangerous with exposed wiring, etc.," notes Isaac of Troy Bike Rescue. "I would never recommend anyone spend less than $1,600 to $2,000 on an e-bike." All too often, electrification involves cutting corners elsewhere: "Most popular electric bikes have really poor component groupings, very low quality, and so we see failures in almost every basic component," says Jesse Cooper of Vancouver's Bike Kitchen.

Taking in the emerging topography, the e-bikes' development arguably trends in a more cynical direction already—as in, *go on, take the money and run*. "The industry is moving more and more to direct-to-consumer products," our source explains, "which means shops need to be prepared to handle a growing influx of folks that may not have bought the bike through them but want to cultivate that relationship."

Needless to say, the budget bike "manufacturers" are keenly interested here—which, given the e-bikes' greater speed and power, arguably trends more hazardous than democratic. "Google 'e-bikes' right now and you'll see a slew of off-brand companies that are trying to snag a piece of the pie," our source points out. "They use substandard electrical and lack the large customer support structure" needed to adequately support e-bike users. "Think Walmart bikes, except you have an unknown, with the battery between your legs." The brands sold through independent bike shops, in our source's assessment, are at least better at "ensuring that [the] customer is not getting a ticking time bomb sent to them."

Within our current economic system, the e-bikes' growth projections merely incentivize manufacturers to push their own products and standards, some of which are far more useful than others. At the same time, our short-changed and impoverished political context works to imply that any efforts to seek cooperation and compromise between divergent interests could only represent some kind of backward, totalitarian, communistic fascism. Nobody is coming to our rescue, though. It's on us to figure this out. Now is the time for enforceable standards around safety and quality.

As one important component of this, we clearly need more and wider bike lanes throughout our cities and suburbs, to better accommodate the new and accelerating discrepancies between cyclists' velocities. Just as electricity will be near the core of the coming struggle—truly *public* power being our only guarantee for decarbonization and affordable energy, for all those who need it—so, too, will the e-bikes' development either advance or undermine the potential for human-scale assisted transportation. We need a *genuinely* public e-bike enterprise, alongside the commensurate infrastructure improvements this will require.

◦▭◦▭◦

The previous treatments of all the various drivetrain bits leave us better prepared to talk about **drivetrain cleaning**. The grit that so naturally accumulates on your chain and other drivetrain parts threatens more than your pants' cuffs—think of it as liquid sandpaper, masquerading as lubrication, wearing your cogs and chainrings down to nubs.

Shops rely on all manner of solvent tanks to take care of this. The **ultrasonic parts cleaners** are among the newest—to clean things, they send high-frequency sound waves through solvent-free degreasers. Their white noise agitates the solution, shaking our parts clean.

Older approaches are still common, however. Some community bike shops have parts cleaners; others do not. "We do make our own degreaser out of vinegar, baking soda, and lemon juice, and it's effective for most drivetrains," says Gateway Bicycle Hub's Ed Mark. Alternatively, Dave Falini at the Newark Bike Project sees mineral spirits as "the most affordable option." At the furthest extreme, "rusted antique chains that are irreplaceable go through the wire wheel," says the Bike Kitchen's Jesse Cooper.

What to use? What's at hand; what's available. I recently finished up a gallon jug of Finish Line citrus degreaser, which I'd been slowly draining for years. Five survey respondents recommended Simple Green, a common and inexpensive general degreaser. Mac Liman of Denver's Bikes Together also suggests dish soap and water as an option for home mechanics.

Those lucky trophy bikes that only get out for a few nice summertime rides might be spared this procedure for a time, but working bikes will often benefit from an annual drivetrain cleaning. The winters are the worst, in terms of picking up grit, making spring the most natural season for this to happen. I tend to remove the individual drivetrain parts and drop them in a bath, which I'll agitate occasionally. You'd need a large water-tight container for this method—an old plastic jar, perhaps, or a Tupperware. Something you're able to sacrifice, as this will foul it for good.

Our bikes accumulate all kinds of detritus when completing their rounds. I tend to let this dry in place before cleaning up, because it actually makes the job easier—counterintuitive, but true. Begin with a *dry* rag when cleaning up a truly dirty bike. Rub it down convincingly, flossing back and forth to get at the tight spots—the dry, caked-on mud and grit falls harmlessly to the floor once you shake out the rag.

Following this beginning, a spray bottle with degreaser diluted in four or five parts water makes for a fine secondary treatment—wiping down with a second, cleaner rag now. For the drivetrains themselves, I use undiluted citrus solvent. It'll darken quickly, but that's fine; you can keep reusing it. Many of the solvent tanks at the shops are doing this already. Just keep the lid on tight to prevent evaporation.

That first dirt rag might only last for a bike or two before surrendering to the dead rag box. The rags of course can always get washed, eventually—here again, what the shops' rag services are already doing. You may need to run a second empty cycle afterward, also on high heat and with enough soap, depending on what you've been cleaning up. I'd recommend you spare the dryer though, as the rags' scent tends to linger there. Just let 'em air-dry. I've been cycling through the same slowly evolving batch of bike rags for years, to be refreshed occasionally as I get more new-to-me clothes from the nearest Goodwill store. But you get the idea.

An important caveat before proceeding further: we must avoid dunking any sealed bearings in the solvent, which would wick the grease right out of them. This comes up most often with the derailleur pulleys, the best of which are built around sealed bearings. Some manufacturers, including Shimano, set small dust caps over their sealed-bearing pulleys, making them indistinguishable from regular bushing pulleys—you'd have to take them out of their derailleur cages to know for sure. But we should probably be doing this anyway, with the home method described below, which is not as efficient as the proper shop solvent tanks.

We should also avoid submerging the freewheels in solvents, for similar reasons. (These can usually be relubricated with machine oil, which is sent through the seam on their backsides, so it's less of a big deal.) Usually, it's enough to floss between the freewheel's cogs, using lightweight oil and a rag. You may need to get in there with a pick or your 3 mm flat-tip screwdriver first to dislodge any dried debris. The cassettes can go in the solvent bath, however—run a ball tie or similar loosely through them first, to keep track of any loose cog-and-spacer sequences. Chainrings are easiest cleaned when removed from their spider cranks; the pedals have no business in the solvent.

So take off all the dirty parts and toss 'em in their bath. Brakes can go in too, if they need to; just remove the pads first. Shaking the container periodically helps the degreaser dislodge grit—double-check the lid's seal before doing so. After a while, you'll see this accumulating as goopy black silt on the base of the container.

Let this sit overnight if possible. Give it another good shake in the morning. Put on some rubber gloves, pull your parts out, and rinse them off with dish soap, hot water, and a nice firm nonmetallic brush—sounds rough, I know, but the parts really like it. Straighten and then fold the chain down flat, sort of how it looked coming out of the box, scouring each side's plates in turn.

We'll sometimes dry the parts with an air gun at the shops, but at home you can just lay them out on a box or a rag to air-dry. Once they do, hit the derailleurs' pivot points with drops of penetrating oil, wiping off any excess as you go.

Go ahead and put your bike back together after that—unless you suspect its drivetrain parts may be worn, in which case you'd want to check out the treatment of drivetrain wear and replacement on page 228. And there could be no better time, obviously, to switch to a cleaner gel-based lube or similar for the chain, if you haven't done so already—the drier your chain stays, the less you really need to do this.

The derailleur pulleys rarely loosen on their own, but they just might if not tightened sufficiently. Even better, dab a speck of mild thread-locking compound on the threads prior to reassembly.

Do you have a spare container, though? This second one doesn't need a lid. Let your solvent sit a couple days, then pour it into this surrogate. Looking inside the original one, you'll likely see a thick layer of sediment left at the bottom, along with any washers or chain link parts you may have forgotten about. Rub, scrape, or blast this crap out before replacing your solvent in its original tank for next time. Stow it somewhere out of the way, where small children won't be tempted to look inside.

As with the singlespeeds and the e-bikes, a workable understanding of drivetrains provides a useful basis for discussing **drivetrain wear and replacement**. The chains, cogsets, and chainrings all wear together, but we'll notice it first with the chains. Assuming we take care of them—just enough oil; the occasional cleaning; not shifting under load—a chain may endure for 3,000 miles or more. Solidarity forms the rule among the cogs and chainrings: the more teeth translating our pedaling force into momentum, the slower each wears. This is why the smallest cogs out back wear out first—the 11-, 12-, or 13-tooth, for most of us.

The significant cumulative wear that concerns us here is most visible on the cogsets and chainrings. It takes slightly different forms with each. Out back, the valleys between cog teeth expand with wear— we see this sometimes when comparing the smaller cogs' profiles against the larger ones. The teeth on worn chainrings will exhibit more of a shark-toothed profile: their tops become less flat, more pointed. A worn-out chainring will also feel sandy or grainy when pedaling. The smallest chainrings on triple cranksets are typically used the least and thus last the longest. The middle rings on triple cranks typically wear the fastest; it's usually the small rings on double cranks.

A toasted chain may point to a worn-out cogset, and perhaps worn chainrings as well, as we'll see. We yet lack any specific instrumentation to quantify either cog or chainring wear, however—our best test remains cranking the bike up a hill and seeing if the chain skips out of gear. (You'd want to confirm all the relevant derailleur adjustments are correct before doing so, of course.)

As it reaches our bike chains, we typically describe this entropy as **chain stretch**. This labeling is not strictly accurate—our chains' pins and rollers gradually wear with use, effectively widening the distances between links under tension, a process that merely makes the chains *appear* slightly longer. The idiom remains common, however.

The chain pins' center points are each an even half-inch apart, so the classic approach to measuring chain wear requires nothing more than an imperial ruler: over 12 inches, a viable chain will have stretched less than $1/16$ or perhaps $1/8$ of an inch, depending on what kind of chain it is—11/12-speed versus 8/9/10-speed—and on whom you talk to.

Quite a few manufacturers now produce **chain wear indicators**, which are what shops use. Most incorporate two or three markers or

**Using a chain wear indicator.**

pins, which we'll insert between the links. Other features on the tool will indicate chain wear at quarterly intervals, with 0 marking a new chain and 1.0 standing in for a chain's official death certificate. (The rollers on SRAM AXS 12-speed chains are slightly wider than average, making them tougher to measure accurately with most chain wear indicators. Park's CC-4 knows the difference, however.)

Fixed gear bikes, singlespeeds, and to a lesser extent clutch-equipped rear derailleurs are each better able to continue functioning with worn drivetrain parts—the more consistent a given chain's tension, the less it will be able to skip out of gear. Most manufacturers recommend that 11-speed and 12-speed chains be replaced once they demonstrate wear to the 0.5 mark. Simpler derailleur drivetrains might keep their chains until they're worn to 0.75. Fixed chains, single-speed chains, and the like may be considered viable until they actually reach 1.0.

We can further anticipate that the cogsets used with chains worn to 0.75 or more will also require replacement. For this reason, many bike shop types recommend replacing derailleur chains once they wear to the 0.50 mark—doing so typically allows the same cogset to be used across three chains. Whether or not this argument holds for you may be a function of your drivetrain's quality and vintage: while 7- or 8-speed cassettes are usually pretty cheap, the same is not true of their 11- and 12-speed kin. It also bears mentioning that a new chain will not breathe any new life into a worn-out cassette—rather, the decrepit old cogs will corrupt the new chain until it's equally burnt and cynical: *I mean, who gives a shit, skipping out of gear or whatever?*

While the demographic imaginary our industry terms "performance riders" may be expected to indulge discrete expectations with regard to maintaining or improving their own subjective experiences, for many other riders—"performance" or otherwise—the cost and frequency of replacement drivetrain parts may be a more immediate concern. It is with this in mind that I mention one final option. Should you happen onto a bike with a SRAM or Shimano 1×12 drivetrain, but you're not sure when you might be able to afford the $150 or $200 *minimum* required to replace just the chain and cassette, one preemptive step you could take to forestall drivetrain wear would be dialing in the high limit screw—enough to close off the smallest few cogs. You'd need to make commensurate adjustments with regard to the cable tension as well, of course. The smallest cogs wear out the fastest; interacting with worn cogs also wears the chains more quickly. So you skip that, instead, and increase your pedaling cadence as needed. This would completely defeat the purpose of having those two or three extra gears, I do realize, but if your mission is just getting from A to B—as opposed to performing—it may be something to consider.

## XIII
# RUST

Corrosion may be more or less of a problem for you, depending where you live. It can be bad anywhere there's snowy winters, owing to road salt, but it may be worse in humid areas near the ocean—rust kept me from locking my bike outdoors overnight when living across the Public Road from the ocean in Guyana. Nobody's truly safe, though. The tide may even have turned by the time your chain begins to squeak: your seatpost or bottom bracket might be seized in place already.

It is not my purpose to alarm you. I merely wish to present a context for the fine art of **rust prevention**. As a starting point, any decent steel frames existing near salt water or other rusty regions might usefully be stripped down for an application of Frame Saver spray. Done correctly, as described in the can's instructions, this treatment can protect a frame's interior from rust.

Unless you're working with a carbon fiber frame or parts, in which case you'd want to substitute a substance such as carbon fiber assembly compound for any direct contact points, you should always grease seat tubes, bottom bracket shells, head tubes, steerer tubes, stem/handlebar interfaces, Q/R skewer threads, seat rails, seatpost hardware, seat tube clamps, rear derailleur pivot bolts, and pedal threads before putting things together.

Sometimes you'll just smear on a bit with a fingertip, as with the stem/handlebar contact points, but most often—seat tubes, BB shells, head and steerer tubes, and so on—we just collect a couple peas' worth of grease on a segment of cable housing and then twirl that around inside. I like grease guns for our frames' various M5-threaded water bottle and fender fittings, as well as for shooting into Q/R axles to get their skewer threads.

There are only a couple exceptions here. Spoke compounds are discussed on page 46. Those fixing bolts charged with securing brakes or brake rotors also get a pass: manufacturers have been treating these with thread-locking compound in place of grease for decades now. Such substances help maintain the bonds, but they also prevent corrosion. (Some also treat BB cups with the same compounds, but this is less common.)

We shop rats typically employ an escalating sequence of steps when it comes to **freeing rusted parts**. Time is an important ally here—the deep, parts-seizing rust we're most concerned with does not set in overnight, and most often it requires patience to resolve. The creative application of leverage might itself be sufficient to get the goods, as we'll see, but just how we set things up is also important. Misdirected leverage can make for problems of its own.

As a starting point, rust is best attacked with our sharpest or newest tools—the small M5 Allen bolts in particular are vulnerable to stripping out when handled incorrectly. Lacking new Allen wrenches, you can add new edges on the oldsters with a bench grinder.

The **seized bottom brackets** begin by stalking us silently, biding their time, counting on our distraction. Any bike denied service for long enough becomes their target—think older bikes, budget bikes, those roaming rural hinterlands far from bike shops. There's no easy tell, but you'll know one when you try to remove it.

Unless you're working in a sturdy shop-grade repair stand—bolted to a big metal plate underfoot—go ahead and flip the bike upside down on the floor. The lightweight so-called consumer repair stands can absorb and displace some of the force we'll need to apply here.

Remove both crank arms and pedals, if that hasn't happened already. See the treatment on bottom brackets, beginning on page 191, to confirm that you have all the tools needed for your particular BB.

We'll begin by securing the BB removal tools as best as possible, in ways that can allow for additional leverage as needed. Stein's Locking Lockring Wrench and Fixed Cup Wrench Clamp are particularly useful for bracing the tools needed to remove old ball-and-cup sets. We can do something similar for the various splined bottom bracket extractors, using just a crank bolt and a nice thick washer or two—something wide enough inside to admit the crank bolt, and broad enough on the outside to hold the tool in place over the bottom bracket cup.

Unless you have access to Unior's BB shell installation tool, or Hozan's C-358 fixed cup tool—both of which require the adjustable cup's evacuation to do their work—I recommend removing the drive-side fixed cup first when working with the old ball-and-cup sets. Lacking one of these two, or the Stein tool mentioned above, use a fixed cup wrench or a 36 mm headset wrench to thread it out. You might enlist a comrade here, with one pair of hands holding the wrench on target and the second pushing on the tool's encouragement bar.

Over on the adjustable side, our second best option would be to use a multitooth BB lockring tool such as Park's HCW-5. And if your lockring tool only features a single tooth, keep your fingers pressed firmly atop it to help prevent the lockring's notch from stripping out. Sometimes rust works to our advantage—the BB lockring and adjustable cup might even spin out together, with luck.

The adjustable cups themselves will answer to tools such as Park's HCW-11, or perhaps their SPA-1 pin spanner. Neither tool is particularly stout, you'll notice, nor do the old-fashioned BB cups provide much purchase for them. Given this, it's often useful to enlist a pair of door hinges and a quick-grip-style clamp to hold your BB tool in place—the hinges become the sandwich bread in this scenario, firmly pressing the tool into the neutral BB cup, while also serving as a platform for the clamp's opposite foot over on the drive side. Once it's set up nice and tight, you might even slip an encouragement bar over the tool's handle. (This is why I'd suggested removing the drive-side cup first—the broad wrench flats allow for far more leverage than these old-style adjustable cups will, and pulling the spindle out from the drive side allows us to lay the second door hinge flush atop the BB shell.)

For seized cartridge BBs, begin with the side anchoring the cartridge. As mentioned previously, this is usually—but not always—the drive-side cup. It won't be plastic, though.

However it is you're securing your BB removal tool in place, keep in mind that we only want to get the bolt holding it in place finger-tight, with the idea that you'll gradually loosen the bolt as the BB cup loosens. Slip the encouragement bar over your wrench, double-checking to ensure you'll be pushing it in the correct direction—recall that only the drive-side cup is reverse-threaded with standard ISO BBs. You'll gain the most leverage by setting things up such that you're pushing the very end of the encouragement bar downward—from a point just better than waist level, ideally. You may want to ask a comrade to hold the bike while you push—standing on the handlebars, maybe. The going becomes progressively easier once the initial rust bond is broken, until the damned cup finally spins free.

If you're lucky, this combination of compression and leverage will do the trick. The BB cups typically prevent penetrating oil from being too useful here—it would face quite a journey, seeping down the long BB threads. The seized BB cups themselves might provide us one last option, however. Do you have access to a die grinder? Use it to carve out an elongated box from the cup's face—something just broad and tall enough to admit the open end of your 15 mm box wrench. Clamp your Vise-Grip pliers or a large crescent wrench across its head, right up next to the seized BB cup. Slip an encouragement bar over the end of this, and push.

It is only when this last approach fails that I would reach for a torch. (Carbon fiber is flammable, so this is not for that.) Heating expands metal, momentarily creating openings we might exploit. Propane is fine; oxyacetylene is overkill. A hair dryer, if nothing else, right up next to the BB shell. Set up all the appropriate tools and leverage before lighting the torch. Also be sure to slide any rubber gums off of your quick-grip clamp's jaws, as these may burn. Just clamp down with the tool's metal skeleton; the door hinges won't mind. Heat up the frame's BB shell right around the seized cup for a minute or two, slowly back and forth around the circle, and then as soon as you turn the torch off, get in there with your leverage again and see if you can't break the rust bond.

A torch may melt or burn a cartridge BB's bearing seals, leaving the spindle loose—this makes heating one up a final sort of commitment, with respect to the frame's prospects. The other complication here comes with the plastic placeholder BB cups Shimano and others have used to support cartridge BBs over on the hollow side. I'm not sure how the rust is able to seize these, not being a plastics engineer, but it happens—I've seen these plastic BB cups both melt and burn, at different times.

The cup is not going to survive either way, so if nothing else is working, you might get in there with a 6 mm flat-tip screwdriver and a hammer to physically break it out. (We're not really supposed to hammer on the screwdrivers, I realize, but this would be a special occasion.)

Maybe you're halfway lucky, though, and the cartridge side cup survives intact and you only need to destroy the doomed plastic cup over on the neutral side. Might that cartridge earn another life elsewhere, if it still works? Allow me to introduce the Up-Cup #54, another brilliant innovation from Problem Solvers. It is a metal neutral-side cup designed to work with the ubiquitous Shimano UN54 bottom brackets, threaded to ISO dimensions, for either 68 mm or 73 mm bottom bracket shells. (I'm not sure if it is compatible with more generic BBs, a few of which have also used plastic cups if memory serves.)

This would be a good place to mention **chasing threads**, which is the only way to bring them back to life. This is always a good idea after freeing rusted parts, the bottom brackets especially. Smaller metric taps like the M5 and M6 are fairly common, as are the tap handles that hold them; better-equipped shops will have the heavier and more elaborate sets needed to retap BB shells. Always use copious cutting oil whenever you do this. Send the tap in slowly, half a turn at a time, and after each back it out by a quarter turn to help the tap clear any accumulating debris.

I've yet to encounter a seized threadless stem, but **seized quill stems** are not entirely uncommon. Here again, we'll need to be creative with our leverage, but it's also important that we don't damage the fork. The Community Bike Hub uses "wooden blocks secured in C-section steel that can safely clamp the fork crown in a vise and allow a seized quill stem to be loosened without bending the fork," as Glen Mason describes it.

A **seized seatpost** can present especially vexing challenges. "Our first step in refurbishment is seeing if the seatpost/stem is seized," says Ed Mark of the Gateway Bicycle Hub. Sometimes we're lucky, and a seemingly frozen post can be moved with reasonable efforts. The Laprade posts almost anticipate this eventuality, providing us with a pair of broad, flat parallel surfaces up top—these are easily gripped with a big old crescent wrench once the seatpost hardware is removed.

Ask a comrade to brace the bike up front; get an encouragement bar involved if you need to.

Alternately, do you have access to a vise? Is it mounted securely to a heavy and well-built workbench? If so, strip or mostly strip the frame, turn it upside down, and clamp the seatpost flats in the vise. Grab the frame and see if you can rotate it around the frozen post. (This is about where lesser benches may topple.) Don't try to pull yet; focus on rotation.

The straight seatposts are much more difficult to remove, especially when we're not able to destroy them, which is often what it takes. Strip the frame, put the post in the vise, and then slip an encouragement bar over its handle—our goal here is to squeeze a pair of flat surfaces into the post, which we might be able to use for leverage. This'd be making a commitment, obviously.

The immediate landscape right around a frame's seat tube interface typically prevents us from setting up a reservoir for the penetrating oil to soak in, but this isn't always the case—as when the seat tube rises above the down tube, for example. So we drip penetrants around the edges, coming back every few hours to do it again. Among those survey respondents who offered solutions to this problem, most provided variations on this approach—giving penetrants time to work before inverting the frame and clamping the post in a bench vise.

One key tip I learnt through the survey: when working on an aluminum post stuck in a steel frame, use *ammonia* in place of penetrating oil. "Just drops of ammonia in the seat tube does wonders in breaking the oxidation bond," Mark explains. "The rest is time and effort. More stubborn posts take about a week to free, with constant dripping of ammonia." And once the rust bond is broken, it's time to really push. "It's so rewarding," Mark says, "to get a seized post free."

Such a result, however, is far from guaranteed. Freeing seized posts has proven "almost always to be extremely time consuming, with poor results," notes Jesse Cooper at the Bike Kitchen. "I think that we could be more effective tackling this if we had a homemade post-pulling jig that I've seen on some mechanic forums." Enter Danni Limonez of Chicago's Bikes N' Roses: "We also have a seatpost remover tool from our friend Max Astell, and he calls it the King Arthur tool, or the Seat Post Shimmy!"

The frames themselves provide us one further option here. Remove the bottom bracket and clamp the frame upside down in a

**King Arthur tool for removing seatposts at Bikes N' Roses, Chicago.**

stand, with the seat tube at a slight angle from vertical. Snake an oil straw in there from your dropper bottle or spray can and feed it. (Here again, substitute ammonia when working on an aluminum post in a steel frame.) Aim for the tube's walls rather than the post's empty core, and turn the frame through a few rotations to help ensure the whole interior of the tube gets coated. Give it some days or a week before applying leverage.

Removing a seized post with a torch is challenging, because we won't be able to see how deeply down the seat tube the rust bond may extend. Aluminum also expands faster than either steel or titanium when heated, so this would not be the way to remove a seized

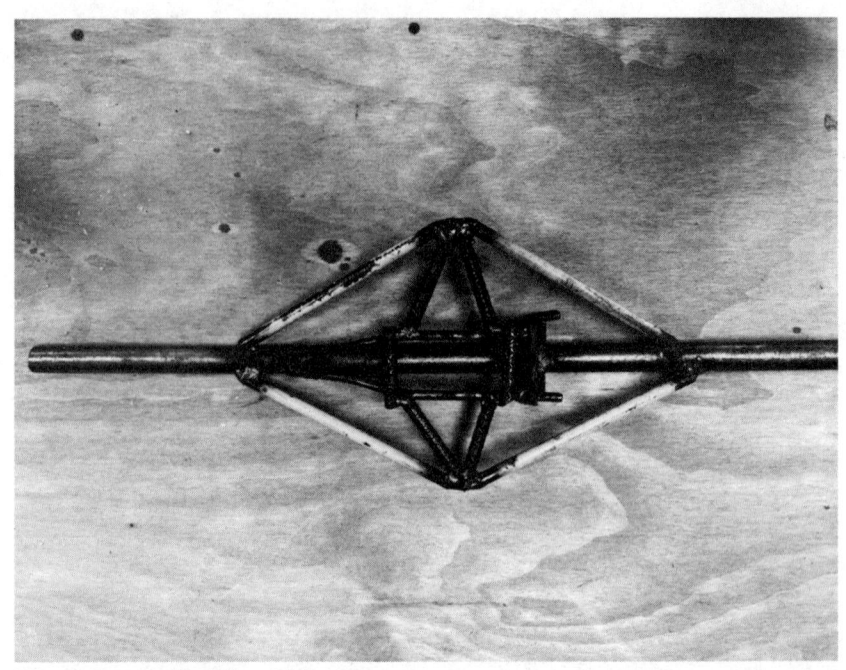

**King Arthur tool at Bikes N' Roses.**

aluminum post from a steel or titanium frame. Nor do we want to ignite the penetrating oil, if that has been used—try this with a hair dryer instead if you've previously been feeding the post with oil.

Cutting the post out would be the last resort. If the post is on the wider side, with relatively thin walls—higher-end posts, typically—it may be possible to just leave it in place, cut a second slot in back for the binder bolt, and insert a new, smaller post inside. This would mean cutting it down to the seat clamp, then measuring the interior diameter with a seatpost gauge to find the new size.

If that's not happening, your last shot would be cutting the post out with a hacksaw. This is a truly time-consuming process, through which you'd need to be careful not to cut into the seat tube—when possible, moving on to a more amenable frame might prove the more attractive option here.

The **rusted bolts** are often smaller problems, in that they rarely prevent us from sitting on or pedaling the bike, but they're also our Cassandra figures—if rust prevents you from loosening the M5 bolt needed to attach your rack, fender, or water bottle cage to your steel frame, a preemptive application of Frame Saver treatment would be a solid idea. A coating of grease across the BB threads and down the seat tube, even more so.

Back to the bolt, though. First, confirm it is actually seized. Use your best Allen wrenches for this—those with the sharpest edges. Duller tools are more likely to strip the bolt head. Go find someone with a grinder wheel and scrape a sharp new face onto your Allen key. Failing that, see if you can track down a new tool.

Using a slow and even pressure, hold the key's short end firmly in place over the bolt head. (If the bolt head fits a screwdriver head instead, use the longest one you can find—more leverage.) Turn the tool only as forcefully as you normally might when tightening an M5 bolt; ease up if it doesn't move. Drop a bit of Blaster PB, Boeshield T-9, or similar into the threads, let it sit for half an hour, and then try the same thing again.

No dice? Such situations are textbook candidates for the penetrating oils. These can take some time to work, so it's often useful to devise ways to keep the rust we're concerned with submerged in oil. First, find a way for the rusted threads to sit more or less level and facing upward, such that gravity might assist the oil in its descent. You can even set up a kind of miniature oil reservoir, using duct tape and segments of a durable plastic bag, right around the problem. If possible, it's best to leave the bike just like that for a few days, or even a week. And, if applicable—as with some rack or fender mount bolts brazed to the stays, for example—flip the bike over and do this same thing on the back side of the threads as well.

Maybe that'll do it, with luck, but it's also possible the bolt head will at least be starting to strip out at this point. Depending on how it looks, you may earn yourself a second chance by filing a pair of parallel wrench flats on the side of the bolt head or cutting its face in half with a hacksaw or wonder wheel to make room for a 6 mm flat-tip screwdriver.

The bonds of rust may have already outstripped the strength of the bolt, unfortunately, so at any point it's also possible that the bolt head will simply snap off. Amazingly enough, however, this need not be the end either—given the proper tools, ample lighting, and patience, we might remove the rest of the bolt as well.

See to it that the frame is firmly secured, in a stand or within frame blocks in a vise, then grab a drill. Do you have a bolt extractor

**Rusted bolts, author's bench, Capital Bikeshare, 2016–18.**

set? Select an appropriately sized drill bit—one small enough to run a hole down the middle of the rusted bolt. Drilling into the head of an existing bolt head is fairly straightforward, but getting the bit started after the bolt head has snapped off may take more concentration. You're barely pushing on the drill, only enough to keep it on target, playing with the angle as needed to keep it centered—you aim for the center, the drill trends off-center, and you compensate by changing the drill's angle. It's as if you're carving out a tiny bowl, scraping its sides only when you need to, always aiming back to the deepening pit.

The purpose of this exercise is merely to blaze a trail for one of the various easy-out bolt extractors, the splines of which burrow into the seized bolt as a means to corkscrew it back out. But it's also possible that the act of drilling will itself yield the desired results.

# XIV
# A FUTURE FOR BIKE REPAIR

"All bike repair organizations have a personality or ethos," says Jack Kelleher of the Clonakilty Bike Circus. "Ours is to keep bikes rolling, upgrading them when we can." At Recycle Bicycle Harrisburg, Ross Willard explains, "Our general policy is the parts are free, tool use is free, knowledge is free. Let's get your bike fixed and back to riding. But if we have high-grade parts, they go to major swap meets to help with bills."

"There are many approaches to the community bike shop," says Paul Laudeman of the KickStand Community Bike Shop in Knoxville, Tennessee. "There are four different models in Knoxville." Many incorporate bike repair classes and open shop hours; both often become popular features. Returning to the survey, fully 100 percent of responding community bike shops provide public education on bike repair, with 94 percent making tools available as well. "I always try to impart the difference between repairs and maintenance," notes Jody Chandler at the Hub in Minneapolis. "Maintenance helps minimize the cost and frequency of repairs! Pump up your tires, lube your chain, clean your bike! If you can do those three things at a minimum, you are ahead of the curve."

Community bike shops saw a range of impacts during the COVID pandemic. Many began by cutting or reducing open hours and public programs. Later, some implemented physical distancing policies as a means to continue operations—shifting repair work outdoors, trading the weighty certainty of professional repair stands for the more portable expedience of "consumer" models. "Lonely people came to our yard to hang out and talk," Kelleher relays. "Since bike repair is exempt from lockdown, we thrived. The Bike Circus became a kind of social center."

Others expanded virtually. "We opened an online store to sell bikes and accessories, which has been relatively lucrative and quite helpful for selling bikes," notes Second Chance Bikes' Sylvie Baele. Supply chains tightened across the board—the Newark Bike Project began "running out of everything," Dave Falini recalls—but in the context of the pandemic, many bike shops thrived regardless. The Newark Bike Project went from $156,000 sales in 2019 to $232,000 in 2020, Falini says.

Despite broader similarities across programming, opinions on mass-market or so-called budget bikes—those sold by big-box stores—can vary considerably across community bike shops. Of those who responded to the question, twenty-five (89 percent) service budget bikes, and three do not.

"We love them," Willard says. "It's how we start everyone out for free." The sheer scale of their market share can make them difficult to avoid. Budget bikes account for "the vast majority of the bicycles that are donated to us, or brought in for repair," explains Durham Bicycle Cooperative's Greg Garneau. "If they will work," notes Simon Batterbury of WeCycle, "we fix them up."

This openness can reflect other considerations as well. "We are not bike snobs," say Montreal's Flat Bike Collective. "If it's your bike and you want to learn to fix it, we can help you do that! A lot of people in the bike scene are elitist about bicycles and look down their noses at mass-market bikes. But for many people, they go to a big-box store and that's what they can afford, so that's what they buy." Yet others recognize the inherent technical challenges at play. "The mark of a talented mechanic is getting a department store bike to run and feel decent," observes Isaac at Troy Bike Rescue. "It takes lots of experience to understand whether to repair or replace any individual component."

The budget bikes' market dominance can also remove the element of choice. The Newark Bike Project fixes up budget bikes because "unfortunately, we have to," Falini says. Tom Costello adds, "We're going to work with what we're given." Squaring such facts with the omnipresent reality of liability concerns can require additional focus. "We write ABAP on the repair tag, meaning 'as best as possible,'" says Ryan Harris of the Recyclistas Bike Shop.

Filtering represents another solution to the same problem. "We only accept [budget bikes] as donations if they are in like-new or very good condition," Baele explains. Yet the root problem remains. "Perhaps it's not the case for many bike sheds," explains Glen Mason of the Community Bike Hub, "but I feel like consumer throwaway culture is creating a surge in secondhand items that should be repaired but aren't, because of time constraints and the value of that time, combined with the fact that these repaired goods need to compete with the diminishing costs of producing and importing new goods. I feel like this is the main challenge for modern bike-recycling sheds (at least in wealthy nations), rather than niche repairs, however artful and skillful."

Among other projects, this tendency toward disposability must also be convincingly disincentivized. Pending sincere efforts in that direction, the educational component becomes an important tool for community bike shops seeking to change the equation—albeit on a smaller, more atomized scale. "Individuals who ride mass-market bikes become quickly familiar with the amount of repairs they need, and the conversation inevitably occurs where we encourage them to consider a more efficient and affordable option," says the Bike Saviours Bicycle Collective's Nicole Muratore. "Our shop allows folks to do work trade in exchange for what they need, so we try to remove money as an impediment to securing a safe, quality bike. We have no policy other than helping people fix their bikes, no matter the variety, so long as it can be done safely."

Views around selling used parts become more cohesive given this broader context. Feedback I'd received on my first bike repair manual, *How to Rock and Roll*, suggested that its emphasis on reuse cut against bike shops' business model, yet for Baele this line of critique fails to resonate. "That's silly and capitalist poison," she says. "We [sell used parts] more for convenience and mission achievement than the money." For other community bike shops, however, the additional income can also be crucial. "Used parts are a massive revenue generator," says Jesse Cooper of the Bike Kitchen. For Bike Saviours, notes Muratore, "The sale of used parts makes up most of our revenue each month." Per the survey, twenty-six respondents (81 percent) indicated that they regularly sell used parts, while six do not.

Anticipating local needs, many community bike shops sell both new and used parts. "While the past months have been unusual due to COVID, over the last seven months, 17 percent of sales have been for new parts and 12 percent have been for used parts," notes the Vélocity Bicycle Cooperative. "In our FY 2020 (June 2019 to May 2020), new parts were 21 percent and used parts were 10 percent of FY sales." At the Community Bike Hub, notes Mason, "about half of parts sold are used."

Beyond any exchange value, used parts are also, quite simply, useful. "Probably 80 to 85 percent of the parts we use are 'used,'" notes Dave Somerford of Vancouver's Kickstand Community Bike Shop. "We have a recycling program where we collect parts, wheels, and tires from a number of shops. We glean those to determine what we can reuse and what is to be recycled." Freeride Montpelier takes a similar view: "We think that a major part of our work is assessing/storing/reusing used parts/bikes. In many ways, we are more of a recycling center than a typical bike shop."

"We can service the era of bike technologies that other bike shops find too time-consuming to repair," Cooper explains, "only because of our roster of salvaged bike parts that can be supplemented into the repair." The alternative to novelty-for-turnover business models, in other words, may simply be a kind of continuity. "We sell a large number of used parts to folks who are keeping old bikes running, or need a low/no-cost solution to get rolling again," notes another community bike shop mechanic. "Rough estimate is 10 percent of our annual revenue comes from selling used components."

Safety concerns can also inform decisions to stock used parts. "For people in need, who may have a dangerous MacGyver setup," notes Bikes N' Roses' Danni Limonez, "we give away gently used parts so they can ride safer."

Ironically, selling used parts can itself invite speculation. "Our standard policy is that used parts are used on project bikes in workshops/classes, on refurbished bikes for sale, and on occasion for repairs if a used part is a better fit for the repair. We don't sell used parts out the door, to avoid cherry pickers and those who flip parts online," explains West Town Bikes' Alex Wilson. Alternatively, other community bike shops lean into this tendency. "We sell some higher-end or vintage parts on eBay," notes another mechanic. "I am guessing that it accounts for 8 percent of our overall income. We don't sell used parts in the shop. We offer the parts freely, and people are able to make donations to the program."

Despite their differences, community bike shops tend to coexist well with other neighborhood bike sellers. "We refer customers back and forth with local full-service shops for sales or service depending on the customer's needs," the Vélocity Bicycle Cooperative explains. "Our goal is to best meet customer needs and have people be able to ride safe, comfortable bikes that meet their budget limitations." Ross Willard of Recycle Bicycle Harrisburg describes a similar dynamic: "They know that we are not their competition, but we make future customers for them. Plus they collect bikes for us, and during COVID, we gave them free parts since the worldwide supply chain was broken."

As with so many other segments of the "service sector," mainline and community bike shops both face certain especially familiar challenges. "Usually, it's interactions with tough customers and clients that are the most bedeviling," notes one mechanic. Chandler observes, "When customers come in frustrated by another shop, I do everything I can to keep from fueling the flames. Keeping it positive is always the best course of action."

"The biggest barriers to riding bikes are capitalism, classism, sexism, and racism," observes Mac Liman of Bikes Together. Amidst our society's burgeoning schismogenesis, the community bike shops' emphasis on social solidarity can be distinct. "We include everyone: old white guys, gay, transgender, halfway house residents, homeless, challenged, Republicans, Democrats, college students, internationals, etc.," says Willard. "I miss our Chinese volunteer since she went home." Crucially, this embrace often includes the realistic consideration of people's material needs. "We love the old kid carriers that are donated with broken plastic, because the metal frame will universally clamp to seatstays, and we recycle the plastic seat and replace it with a milk crate," Willard continues. "Kid trailers with torn canvas become property carriers for the homeless."

"Santa Cruz is an extremely hostile environment for unsheltered folks," notes the Bike Church collective. "A lot of places and the city itself [have] used the pandemic as an excuse for austerity."

Yet "at the Bike Church, everyone gets a chance, and usually people get many chances. They may be belligerent one day, but if they come back sober and/or not belligerent they get another chance. With limits and boundaries, of course, but either way, we try to meet people where they're at. Let's just say, it's a process, and there's a lot of things we're doing/trying to make it work."

Says Kelleher, "In good weather, people come to sit and chat in our forecourt, which feels like a public park."

At their best, community bike shops provide us with powerful examples of how things can be—we can take what's useful from the past, and leave what is destructive behind. However things may have been before, what we do now is up to all of us.

# ACKNOWLEDGMENTS

This book would not have been possible without input provided by the following:

Geoffrey Smart, Back2Bikes, Melbourne, Australia
Bike Church Santa Cruz, Santa Cruz, California
Jesse Cooper, The Bike Kitchen, Vancouver, British Columbia
Nicole Muratore, Bike Saviours Bicycle Collective, Tempe, Arizona
Matthew A. Pendergraft, Bikes del Pueblo, San Diego, California
Andrew Shaw-Kitch, Bikes for Humanity, Portland, Oregon
Danni Limonez, Bikes N' Roses, Chicago, Illinois
Mac Liman, Bikes Together, Denver, Colorado
Jack Kelleher, Clonakilty Bike Circus, Clonakilty, Ireland
Glen Mason, Community Bike Hub, Melbourne, Australia
Jeremy White, Community Cruisers, Canmore, Alberta
Greg Garneau, The Durham Bicycle Cooperative, Durham, North Carolina
The Flat Bike Collective, Montreal, Quebec
Freeride Montpelier, Montpelier, Vermont
Jody Chandler, The Hub Bike Co-op, Minneapolis, Minnesota
Paul Laudeman, KickStand Community Bike Shop, Knoxville, Tennessee
Dave Somerford, Kickstand Community Bike Shop, Vancouver, British Columbia
Dave Falini & Tom Costello, Newark Bike Project, Inc., Newark, Delaware
Ross Willard, Recycle Bicycle Harrisburg, Harrisburg, Pennsylvania
Ryan Harris, Recyclistas Bike Shop, Victoria, British Columbia
Marvin Macaraig, Scarborough Cycles, Toronto, Ontario
Sylvie Baele, Second Chance Bikes, North Charleston, South Carolina
Isaac, Troy Bike Rescue, Troy, New York
Velocipede Bike Project, Baltimore, Maryland
Vélocity Bicycle Cooperative, Alexandria, Virginia
Simon Batterbury, WeCycle, Melbourne, Australia
Dan Terkla, West Bloomington Revitalization Project Bike Co-op, Bloomington, Illinois
Alex Wilson, West Town Bikes, Chicago, Illinois
Richard Castelnuovo, Wheels for Winners, Madison, Wisconsin
Anonymous 1
Anonymous 2
Anonymous 3

I would also like to thank Angel York and Darin Wick at the Bike Collectives Network; Craig O'Hara, Wade Ostrowski, Jonathan Rowland, and all at PM Press; my lovely wife, Kerri; and of course our son, Atticus, for his patience while I was putting this together.

# IMAGE CREDITS

Sam Tracy: x, 24, 27, 42, 56, 69, 71, 74, 81, 82, 85, 100, 104, 110, 112, 114, 117, 119, 124, 136, 137, 160, 172, 180 (left & right), 188, 193, 199, 200, 240

Kerri Spindler-Ranta: 2, 3, 10, 15, 19, 20, 28, 30, 34, 36, 37, 38, 44, 48, 52, 58, 60, 62, 63, 65, 72, 75, 76, 79, 87, 90, 92, 97, 98, 106, 108, 123, 126, 142, 144, 156, 162, 164, 170, 171, 173, 206, 207, 209, 213, 216, 218, 229

Flat Bicycle Collective: 55

Ross Willard: 66

Velocipede Bike Project: 67

Richard Castelnuovo: 95

Nicole Muratore: 195 (top)

Geoffrey Smart: 195 (bottom left & right)

Danni Limonez: 237, 238

Vélocity Bicycle Cooperative: 242, 246

# INDEX OF SUBJECTS

Page numbers in *italic* refer to illustrations. "Passim" (literally "scattered") indicates intermittent discussion of a topic over a cluster of pages.

Allen wrenches, 4
    extensions, 5
axles, 11, 14, 61–77 passim
    bent, 74
    quick-release, 61
    spacing, 61, 62–63
    vises, 76

bearings, 226
    bottom bracket, 12, 191–203 passim, 234
    crankset, 203
    headset, 22–23
    hub, 64, 73, 75
    pedal, 210
belt drive bikes, 176
bike conversions. *See* conversions
bike repair stands. *See* repair stands
bolts, rusted, 238–40
bottom brackets (BBs), 12–13, 14, 191–203
    asymmetrical, 202–3
    bearings, 12, 191–203 passim, 234
    drop, 138
    elliptical, 203
    external, 198
    press-fit, 199, 203
    sealed-cartridge, 197–98
    seized, 232–35
    splined, 198
    three-piece (ball-and-cup), 192–97
brakes, 101–34
    cables, 84–96 passim, 113–16 passim
    cantilever, 112–20
    centerpull, 105, 107, 120–21
    fixed gear bikes, 140–41
    levers, 33, 34–35, 87–88, 94, 102, 107–8, 129
    noise, 102
    noodles, 93, 122, 123–24, 125
    pads, 103–6, 111, 118–20, 124–25, 129–32 passim
    sidepull (caliper), 109–12
    sidewalls and, 44, 106
    wrenches, 6.
    *See also* coaster brakes; disc brakes; drag brakes; drum brakes; hydraulic brakes; roller brakes; U-brakes; V-brakes
breaker bars, 66, *66*

cable cutters, 5, 84. *See also* cable housing cutters
cable housing, 88–92
    brake cable, 5, 84, 88, 89, 92, 94, 121, 131
    caps and stops, 89, 94, 98, 145, 168, 217
    creative use of, 29, 82, 231
    cutting, 5, 93
    disc brakes, 131
    full-length, 89, 91, 94, 96, 217
    guides, 89
    length, 90–91, 92
    reuse, 95
    seating/securing, 37, 88, 94, 96, *97*, 131, 144
    shifter cable, 88–89
cable housing cutters, 5, 84, 93, 99
cables. *See* cable housing; control cables
cantilever brakes. *See* brakes: cantilever

cantilever quick release, 115
cassette hubs, 46, 72, 128, 210, 215
cassettes (cogsets), 67–72 passim, 150, 151, 152, 228
    lockring tools, 70–71
    removal/replacement, 7, 67, 71–72
    spacers, 68, 69
    wear, 228–30 passim
chainline, 12–13, 140, 184, 194, 196
    singlespeed bikes, 211, 212
chainrings, 138, 139, 140, 178, 183–90 passim, *213*
    bent, 190
    bolts and bolting, 7, 140, 188, *188*, 212
    chain wrap and, 155, 187
    cleaning, 227
    derailleurs and, 148–49, 150, 157–61 passim
    direct mount, 189
    gear ratio and, 135
    guards, 154
    narrow-wide, 154, 187
    timing, 188–89
    wear, 228
chains, 168–76
    chain guides, 154, 157, 187
    cross-gearing, 146, 161
    failure, 175–76
    fixed gear, 138–39
    half-link, 169–70
    intentional breaking, 173–74
    length and orientation, 174
    lubrication, 176, 227
    master links, 170, *170*
    measurements, 168–69
    pins, 172
    tension, 140, 215
    tight link, 175
    wear, 228–29
chain tools, 7, 173–74, 175
chain whips, 7, 71, 72, *136*
cleats, 205–8
coaster brakes, 102, 126–27
cogsets. *See* cassettes (cogsets)
control cables, 84–100
    barrel adjusters, 98–99, *99*
    ferrules, 86, 99, *100*
    removal and installation, 86–92
    reuse, 95–96
    stops and guides, 89
    *See also* brakes: cables; cable housing; derailleur cables
control levers, 39, 97

brakes, 33, 34–35
brifters, 167–68
    *See also* shift levers
conversions
    fixed gear, 138, 139
    singlespeed, 210–15 passim
crank forward bikes, 83
cranks, 140, 176–86
    arm length, 184–85
    bent, 190
    cottered, 177
    crank profile, 184
    spider, 178, *179*, 184
    spiderless, 186
    two-piece, 182–83, *183*
    three-piece, 178–82
cranksets, 6
    bearings, 203
    bolts, 14
    crank backers, 7
    crank bolts, 178–81
    crank extractors, 6–7, 181–82
    one-piece, 177–78
creaks (noises), 13–14
cross-gearing, 146, 161
crown race tools, 18–19, 24, 25–26
cutters, 5, 84, 93, 99
cycling shoes, 205–8 passim

derailleur cables, 84, 88–89, 96–97
    cable pull, 150–51
    housing, 93
    routing, 159
    tension, 147, 155–57
    with trigger shifters, 163–68 passim
derailleurs, 141, 149–61
    adjustment, 45, 142–47 passim
    clutch derailleurs, 154
    double-ring, 157, 158
    front, 148–49, 153–54, 157–61
    hangers, 11, 12, 13, 141, *142*, 146–47, 153
    indexed, 149–57 passim
    limit screws, 97, 143–45, *144*, 147, 149, 174, 215, 230
    pulleys, 141–46 passim, 150–59 passim, 215, 226, 227
    rear, 11, 13, 45, 96, 141–47, 151–56 passim, 174–75, 214–15, 219
    triple-ring, 157–58
    *See also* derailleur cables
disc brakes, 44, 129–33
    cleaning, 103
    front, 62, 133

# INDEX

truing, 130–31
drag brakes, 127–28
drivetrains, 11, 135–230
    belt drive, 176
    cleaning, 225–27
    wear and replacement, 228–30
    *See also* cassettes (freehub bodies); chainrings; chains; crankset; cranks, derailleurs; pedals
dropouts, 10–11, 16, 62
drum brakes, 127

electric bikes, 221–25

fixed gear bikes, 109, 135, 138–41
flat tire repair, 57–59
fork, 14–16
    damage, 13, 16
    rake, 14–15
fourth hand tools, 5, 47, 97, 99, 164
frames, 9–16
    alignment, 13
    damage, 13
    lugs, 9
    tubing decals, 9
freehubs, 67–74 passim, 127, 211–15
    freehub bodies, 7, 67–70 passim, *69*, 127, 219
freewheels, 64, 150, 226
    disassembly, *67*
    hubs, 64, *65*, 214
    removal, 7, 64–67, *64*

gearing, cross. *See* cross-gearing
gearing, hybrid. *See* hybrid gearing
gearing, planetary. *See* planetary gearing
gear ratio, 135, 140, 212
greasing. *See* lubrication and greasing

handlebars, 33–39
    clamp diameter, 28, 33–34
    extension and shortening, 36–37
    grip tape, 37–39
hand tools. *See* tools
headset, 14, 17–26
    bearings, 22–23
    stack height, 16
    Standard Headset Information System (SHIS), 25
    tools, 6, 18–19, 24, 25–26
hubs, 44, 45, 46, 61–77
    bearings, 64, 73, 75

flip-flop, 139–40
loose, 17
planetary, 215–21 passim
spacing, 11–12, 14
track hubs, 64, 135, *137*, 138
wrenches, 6
*See also* cassette hubs; freehubs
hybrid gearing, 218–19
hydraulic brakes, 133–34

King Arthur tool, 236, *237*, *238*

levers. *See* control levers; quick-release (QR) levers; tire levers
lockring tools, 5
lubrication and greasing, 8, 14, 231
    bottom bracket, 196–97
    brake pad hardware, 103
    brake posts, 113
    cables, 85
    calipers, 110
    chains, 176, 227
    cleats, 206
    derailleurs, 147
    grease guns, 8, 231
    headset bearings, 22
    hub bearings, 75
    pedals, 209
    seatposts, 78, 82–83
    spokes, 46

noises. *See* brakes: noise; creaks (noises)
nyloc nuts, 8, 36, 110, 121, 127

oil droppers, 8, 86, 88, 147, 163

pedals, 138, 203–10
    bearings, 210
    removal and installation, 208–10
    threading, 183–84, 190–91, 203
    toe clips, 205–6
pedal wrenches, 6, 204, 208, 209
planetary gearing, 215–21 passim
pliers, 5, 170–71. *See also* Vise-Grip pliers

quick-release (QR) cantilever brakes. *See* cantilever quick release
quick-release (QR) levers
    hubs, 61, *62*, 77, 133
quill stems, 27, 29, 30–31, 37, 145, 235

recumbent bikes, 35, 83, 154, 185, 221
repair stands, 1–3, 232
roller brakes, 102, 122, 128–29
rust, 231–40
    cleats, 206
    prevention, 231

saddles and seatposts, 78–83
    seized posts, 235–39
    sizing, 82–83
shift cables. *See* derailleur cables
shifters, twist. *See* twist shifters
shifting under load, 146, 175–76
shift levers, 34, 35, 141, 145–46, 150, 161–68
    bar-end, 128, 145, 154, 161–62, *162*
    brifters, 167–68
    thumbshifters, 34, 128, 145, 161
    trigger shifters, 162–63, *164*
shoes. *See* cycling shoes
singlespeed bikes, 141, 210–15
slide hammer bearing extractors, 73
spanners, 5, 179, 180
    pin spanners, 195, 233
spokes, 42–52 passim
    broken, creative use of, 45, 174–75
    broken or damaged, 45
    compound, 46–47
    holders for spares, 48
    lacing, 43
    nipples, 7, 41–43, 46, 47, *48*, 51–52
    rulers, 46
    tensiometers, 8, 49, 51
spoke wrenches, 7, 43, 46, 47, 49, 214
steerer tubes, 14, 16
stems, 27–32
    seized, 21, 235
    *See also* quill stems

tandem bikes
    axles and hubs, 63, *65*
    bottom brackets, 12, 203
    brake cables, 84
    brakes, 127–28
    cranksets, 178
    wheels, 45
thread-locking compounds, 8, 52, 113, 137, 191, 205, 227, 232
tire levers, 7, 57, *58*
tires and inner tubes, 54–60
    flats and tube patching, 57–59
    folding tires, 60
    installation, 60

sidewalls, 40, 42, 44, 54, 59, 106
sizing, 40, 54
valves, 56–57
toe clips, 205–6
tools, 4–8
    axle-securing, 76
    bearing-extracting, 73
    bottom brackets, 194–96, 200
    crank-extracting, 6–7, 181–82
    derailleur hangers, 146–47
    headset, 18–19, 23–26 passim
    track lockrings, 136, *136*
    *See also* chain tools; chain whips; cutters; fourth hand tools; King Arthur tool; spanners; tire levers; wrenches
torque wrenches, 8, 99, 197
track cogs, 135–37 passim, *137*
track lockrings, 135–36, *137*
    tools, 136, *136*
truing stands, 3, *3*, 49, 50
twist shifters, 166–67

U-brakes, 121–22

V-brakes, 102, 105, 122–26
Vise-Grip pliers, 5, 80–81, 181, 234

wheel bearings. *See* hubs: bearings
wheels, 40–53
    composite, 53
    pie plates, 45
    rims, 40–41, 45
    rim strips and rim tape, 41–42
    truing, 3, 48–51
    wheel dish, 44, 50–51, 214–15
    *See also* hubs; spokes; tires and inner tubes
winter biking, 54
wrenches, 4–8 passim
    for bottom brackets, 194
    for caliper brakes, 110–11
    creative use of, 73
    "encouragement bars," 8
    for headset locknuts, 18
    *See also* pedal wrenches; spoke wrenches; torque wrenches

# INDEX OF NAMES

Baele, Sylvie, 57, 242, 243, 244
Bike Church, Santa Cruz, 246–47
Bike Kitchen, Vancouver, 16, 148, 224, 236, 244
Bike Saviours Bicycle Collective, Tempe, 57, 95, 195, 243–44
Bikes N' Roses, Chicago, 73, 236, 245
Bikes Together, Denver, 245–46

Chandler, Jody, 2–3, 211, 223, 241–45
Clonakilty Bike Circus, 55, 241
Community Bike Hub, Melbourne, Australia, 16, 147–48, 235, 244
Cooper, Jesse, 16, 148, 150, 224, 225, 236, 244
Costello, Tom, 243

Durham Bicycle Collective, 95–96, 242

Falini, Dave, 11, 225, 242, 243
Flat Bike Collective, Montreal, 243
Freeride Montpelier, 244

Garneau, Greg, 95–96, 242

Harris, Ryan, 163, 223, 243

Kelleher, Jack, 10, 55, 223, 241, 247
KickStand Community Bike Shop, Knoxville, 51
Kickstand Community Bike Shop, Vancouver, 244

Laudeman, Paul, 51, 241
Liman, Mack, 245
Limonez, Danni, 73, 236, 245

Mark, Ed, 225

Mason, Glen, 16, 147–48, 150, 223, 235, 243, 244
Muratore, Nicole, 57, 95, 195–96, 243–44

Newark Bike Project, Newark, DE, 242, 243

Recycle Bicycle, Harrisburg, PA, 66, 241, 245
Recyclistas Bike Shop, Victoria, BC, 163, 223, 243

Second Chance Bikes, North Charleston, SC, 57, 242
Somerford, Dave, 244

Velocipede Bike Project, Baltimore, 64
Vélocity Bicycle Cooperative, Alexandria, VA, 244, 245

WeCycle, Melbourne, Australia, 51, 242
West Town Bikes, Chicago, 52, 223, 245
Wheels for Winners, Madison, 95
White, Jeremy, 95
Willard, Ross, 65–67, 241, 242, 245, 246
Wilson, Alex, 52, 147, 223, 245

# ABOUT THE AUTHOR

**Sam Tracy** began scavenging behind Milwaukee bike shops in 1992, using a map torn from the phone book. Following a fortuitous encounter at the Uptowner bar, Wheel and Sprocket hired him on as a mechanic in 1993. After riding as a messenger through several Minneapolis winters, he moved to Arcata, California, to serve as managing editor of the *Auto-Free Times*. Returning home to Minnesota, Tracy found work at what was then Calhoun Cycle, fixing rental bikes and immersing himself in the experimental DIY frame-building culture for which the recumbent riders are known. From there he moved to San Francisco, wrenching and learning at the Freewheel before moving on to work with the homeless in Boston. Tracy and his wife, Kerri Spindler-Ranta, later served together with the Peace Corps in the Islamic Republic of Mauritania. They have since lived and biked in Riga, Latvia; Georgetown, Guyana; Washington, DC; Pretoria, South Africa; and Montevideo, Uruguay. Their journey in recent years is enlivened by the presence of their son, Atticus, now aged ten.

Tracy is the author of *How to Rock and Roll: A City Rider's Repair Manual*, *Roadside Bicycle Repair: A Pocket Manifesto*, and *Bicycle! A Repair & Maintenance Manifesto*.

## ABOUT PM PRESS

PM Press is an independent, radical publisher of books and media to educate, entertain, and inspire. Founded in 2007 by a small group of people with decades of publishing, media, and organizing experience, PM Press amplifies the voices of radical authors, artists, and activists. Our aim is to deliver bold political ideas and vital stories to people from all walks of life and arm the dreamers to demand the impossible. We have sold millions of copies of our books, most often one at a time, face to face. We're old enough to know what we're doing and young enough to know what's at stake. Join us to create a better world.

**PM Press**
PO Box 23912
Oakland, CA 94623
www.pmpress.org

**PM Press in Europe**
europe@pmpress.org
www.pmpress.org.uk

# FRIENDS OF PM PRESS

These are indisputably momentous times—the financial system is melting down globally and the Empire is stumbling. Now more than ever there is a vital need for radical ideas.

In the many years since its founding—and on a mere shoestring—PM Press has risen to the formidable challenge of publishing and distributing knowledge and entertainment for the struggles ahead. With hundreds of releases to date, we have published an impressive and stimulating array of literature, art, music, politics, and culture. Using every available medium, we've succeeded in connecting those hungry for ideas and information to those putting them into practice.

*Friends of PM* allows you to directly help impact, amplify, and revitalize the discourse and actions of radical writers, filmmakers, and artists. It provides us with a stable foundation from which we can build upon our early successes and provides a much-needed subsidy for the materials that can't necessarily pay their own way. You can help make that happen—and receive every new title automatically delivered to your door once a month—by joining as a Friend of PM Press. And, we'll throw in a free T-shirt when you sign up.

Here are your options:

- **$30 a month** Get all books and pamphlets plus a 50% discount on all webstore purchases

- **$40 a month** Get all PM Press releases (including CDs and DVDs) plus a 50% discount on all webstore purchases

- **$100 a month** Superstar—Everything plus PM merchandise, free downloads, and a 50% discount on all webstore purchases

For those who can't afford $30 or more a month, we have **Sustainer Rates** at $15, $10, and $5. Sustainers get a free PM Press T-shirt and a 50% discount on all purchases from our website.

Your Visa or Mastercard will be billed once a month, until you tell us to stop. Or until our efforts succeed in bringing the revolution around. Or the financial meltdown of Capital makes plastic redundant. Whichever comes first.

# Bicycle! A Repair & Maintenance Manifesto, 2nd Edition

Sam Tracy

**ISBN: 978-160-486-640-7**
**$24.95    256 pages**

There is nothing sacrosanct about bike repair. Its pursuit only requires the will to learn. At their finest hours bikes exist on a level above mere machines, and there's no reason why the joy should end when the ride is over.

Written by a longtime bicycle mechanic, *Bicycle!* covers everything you need to know to feed and care for your ride. This book cuts through the obtuse techno-speak and delivers maintenance clarity with a touch of humor and radicalism, while categorically denying mechanistry's supposed dreariness. *Bicycle!* is about encouraging society to learn for themselves how to make their bikes work, not because they have to, but because they want to.

With detailed descriptions of all maintenance tasks and repair situations, clearly illustrated with photographs and drawings, this guide will serve the need for a serious rider's manual. Professional bicycle workers—messengers, mechanics, pedicab drivers—as well as bicycle commuters have been waiting for this book. This second edition includes an abundance of helpful photos, an expanded index, and an updated resources section. Moreover, it benefits from insights gained through five years' worth of additional mechanic experience including low-cost and no-cost repair solutions the author developed while serving as a Peace Corps volunteer in Mauritania.

Some of the topics covered:
- Essential Tools
- Bike Components (Maintaining, Adjusting, Repairing)
- On-the-Road Repairs
- Build Your Own (Scavenging)
- Locks / Thief Deterrents
- Rust, the Elemental Bike Nemesis
- And much, much more!

# The Traffic Power Structure
Planka.nu

ISBN: 978-1-62963-153-0
$12.00   96 pages

The modern traffic system is ecologically unsustainable, emotionally stressful, and poses a physical threat to individuals and communities alike. Traffic is not only an ecological and social problem but also a political one. Modern traffic reproduces the rule of the state and capital and is closely linked to class society. It is a problem of power. At its core lies the notion of "automobility," a contradictory ideal of free movement closely linked to a tight web of regulations and control mechanisms. This is the main thesis of the manifesto *The Traffic Power Structure*, penned by the Sweden-based activist network Planka.nu.

Planka.nu was founded in 2001 to fight for free public transport. Thanks to creative direct action, witty public interventions, and thought-provoking statements, the network has become a leading voice in Scandinavian debates on traffic. In its manifesto, Planka.nu presents a critique of the automobile society, analyzes the connections between traffic, the environment, and class, and outlines its political vision. The topics explored along the way include Bruce Springsteen, high-speed trains, nuclear power, the security-industrial complex, happiness research, and volcano eruptions. Planka.nu rejects demands to travel ever-longer distances in order to satisfy our most basic needs while we lose all sense for proximity and community. *The Traffic Power Structure* argues for a different kind of traffic in a different kind of world.

The book has received several awards in Sweden and has been hailed by Swedish media as a "manifesto of striking analytical depth, based on profound knowledge and a will to agitation that demands our respect" (*Ny Tid*).

"The group's efficiency in evasion has created an enviable business model."
—Matt Flegenheimer, *New York Times*

"We could build a Berlin Wall around the metro stations, and they would still try to find ways to get around it."
—Jesper Pettersson, spokesperson for Stockholm's Public Transport Services

"Not a sentence without a message, not a word in the wrong place."
—Lars Wilderäng, Cornucopia

"Well written, well informed, and well conceived."
—Swedish Arts Council